BECOMING the
PEOPLE of GOD

Other Titles in the SEANET Series

Vol. 1

Sharing Jesus in the Buddhist World

Vol. 2

Sharing Jesus Holistically in the Buddhist World

Vol. 3

Sharing Jesus Effectively in the Buddhist World

Vol. 4

Communicating Christ in the Buddhist World

Vol. 5

Communicating Christ through Story and Song:
Orality in Buddhist Contexts

Vol. 6

Communicating Christ in Asian Cities:
Urban Issues in Buddhist Contexts

Vol. 7

Family and Faith in Asia: The Missional Impact of Social Networks

Vol. 8

Suffering: Christian Reflections on Buddhist Dukkha

Vol. 9

Complexities of Money and Missions in Asia

Vol. 10

Developing Indigenous Leaders: Lessons in Mission from Buddhist Asia

Volume 11 in the SEANET Series

BECOMING the PEOPLE of GOD

CREATING CHRIST-CENTERED COMMUNITIES IN BUDDHIST ASIA

PAUL H. DE NEUI, EDITOR

WILLIAM CAREY
LIBRARY

Becoming the People of God:
Creating Christ-centered Communities in Buddhist Asia

Published by William Carey Library
1605 E. Elizabeth St.
Pasadena, CA 91104 | www.missionbooks.org

Melissa Hicks, editor
Brad Koenig, copyeditor
Hugh Pindur, graphic design
Rose Lee-Norman, indexer

William Carey Library is a ministry of
Frontier Ventures
Pasadena, CA | www.frontierventures.org

Digital Ebook Release BP 2015
ISBN: 978-0-87808-860-7

Library of Congress Cataloging-in-Publication Data

Becoming a people of God : Christ-centered communities in Buddhist contexts / Paul H.
de Neui, editor.
        pages cm. -- (SEANET series ; Volume 11)
    Includes bibliographical references and index.
    ISBN 978-0-87808-042-7 -- ISBN 0-87808-042-2 1. Christianity and other religions--Buddhism.
2. Buddhism--Relations--Christianity. I. De Neui, Paul H., editor.
    BR128.B8B38 2015
    266.0088'2943--dc23
                                    2014036991

CONTENTS

Contributors vii

Introduction xiii

Part I: Becoming the People Who Reflect God's Kingdom through Worship

1. First Impressions of a Buddhist Visitor to an Evangelical Worship Service in Sri Lanka: A Liturgical Analysis 3
   G. P. V. SOMARATNA

2. Toward a New Breed of Churches in Japan 21
   MITSUO FUKUDA

3. Where Are Your Temples? Do Christianity and Buddhism Share a Temple Ethos? 31
   STEVE SPAULDING

Part II: Becoming the People Who Reflect God's Kingdom through Witness of Word and Deed

4. Context-sensitive Evangelism in the Thai Setting: Building Capacity to Share Good News 63
   ALAN R. JOHNSON

5. Apply Cultural Contexts to Generate Multiple Christ-centered Communities 93
   ALEXANDER G. SMITH

6. Communication Strategies for Christian Witness among the Lao 117
   STEPHEN BAILEY

Part III: Becoming the People Who Reflect God's Kingdom through Welcome

7. Creating Christian Funerary Culture:
   An Invitation to Japanese Churches 143
   KATSUHIKO SEINO

8. Changes in Thai Church: Moving towards a Relational Model 167
   UBOLWAN MEJUDHON

9. Appropriate Typologies for Thai Folk Buddhists 187
   PAUL H. DE NEUI

Index 217

Scripture Index 225

FIGURES

Figure 1: Contrast of temple ethos 42

Figure 2: The environment that facilitates effective evangelism..................... 72

Figure 3: The four "toolkits" for sharing the gospel..................................... 75

Figure 4: Lao worldview themes..129

Figure 5: Structure of characteristics of the Thai way of meekness 173

Figure 6: C1 to C6 spectrum adapted for context of popular Buddhism 209

Figure 7: Grid for viewing direction of C1 to C5 211

CONTRIBUTORS

Dr. Stephen Bailey was involved in relief and development work in Thailand and the Lao People's Democratic Republic for seventeen years with CAMA (Compassion and Mercy Associates) Services. From 2001 to 2011 he was associate professor of intercultural studies and director of the Alliance Graduate School of Missions at Alliance Theological Seminary in Nyack, New York. During that time he was also associate director of the International Fellowship of Alliance Professionals (2006-2009). Since 2002 he has served as a senior associate with the Institute for Global Engagement to promote religious freedom in Laos. His work on issues of religious freedom takes him back to Laos two or three times a year. Since 2011 Dr. Bailey has served as professor of intercultural studies at Simpson University where he teaches community development and intercultural studies. He has been married to Jacqui since 1983. They have four children and live in Palo Cedro, California.

Rev. Dr. Paul H. de Neui is an ordained minister with the Evangelical Covenant Church. He and his wife served as missionaries with several Thai church planting and community development organizations in northeast Thailand from 1987 to 2005. He completed his PhD in intercultural studies at Fuller Theological Seminary. Paul has been active with the missiology forum of SEANET for over ten years and has edited several SEANET volumes. Presently he is the professor of missiology and intercultural studies and the director of the Center for World Christian Studies at North Park Theological Seminary in Chicago, Illinois. In his classes he takes students to places around the world, including Thailand, at least once each year. He and his wife reside in Chicago and have four grown children.

Rev. Mitsuo Fukuda is the founder of the Rethinking Authentic Christianity Network, which has provided mission strategies and grassroot training systems for the body of Christ in Japan as well as in other Asian nations. He has also founded the Educational Policy Lab (NPO in Japanese) to help mayors, ministers, and officers of several local governments in Japan to implement Bible-based educational policies in their communities. His focus is on being a friend to community leaders and serving them through coaching and resourcing, in order to catalyze the development of communities where people respect justice, mercy, and faithfulness. After finishing the Graduate School of Theology at Kwansei Gakuin University, he researched contextualization and cultural anthropology at Fuller Theological Seminary as a Fulbright graduate student and received a doctorate degree in intercultural studies. His previous books include *Mentoring Like Barnabas*; *Upward, Outward, Inward: Passing on the Baton of Discipleship*; and *Developing a Contextualized Church as a Bridge to Christianity in Japan*.

Dr. Alan R. Johnson has served in Thailand since 1986 with the Assemblies of God. He received his PhD from the Oxford Centre for Mission Studies, doing an ethnographic study of a slum community in Bangkok later published by Regnum as *Leadership in a Slum: A Bangkok Case Study*. Johnson serves as the secretary of the Missions Commission of the World Assemblies of God Fellowship that seeks to foster Majority World sending. He is a member of the Assemblies of God World Missions (AGWM) Missiology Think Tank, serves on the global leadership team for the Asia Pacific Region of AGWM and served for one year as the Hogan Chair of World Missions at the Assemblies of God Theological Seminary (AGTS). He serves as an adjunct professor at AGTS in their doctoral program in intercultural studies. He wrote a monograph published by William Carey Library, *Apostolic Function in 21st Century Missions*. He and his wife have been married thirty-six years and have two grown children and five grandchildren.

Rev. Dr. Ubolwan Mejudhon grew up as a Thai Buddhist. Later she and her husband, Rev. Dr. Nanthachai Mejudhon, founded and co-pastor the Muang Thai church in Bangkok . She earned her doctorate in missiology from Asbury Theological Seminary. She co-directs the Cross-cultural

Training Center as well as ministries in other parts of Thailand. She and her husband reside in Bangkok and travel in ministry extensively throughout the country of Thailand and abroad.

Rev. Dr. Katsuhiko (Ken) Seino was born in Japan and brought up in a Buddhist family. He has received a master of divinity degree from Tokyo Christian Theological Seminary and a doctor of missiology degree from Fuller Theological Seminary. He served the church of Indonesia as a TEAM (The Evangelical Alliance Mission) missionary from 1976 to 1986. He returned to Japan and became a pastor in Tsuchiura in 1990 and continues to minister at the church there. He teaches missiology and Islam at Tokyo Christian University. Titles of his books include: *A Handbook for Japanese Missionaries; Islamization of Java; Implications for Missiology;* and *Developing a Christian Funeral Culture in Japan.*

Rev. Dr. Alexander G. Smith was born and raised in Australia until age twenty-one. In Canada he graduated from Prairie Bible College and later the International Institute of Christian Communication in Kenya, Africa. In the USA he earned his master of arts and doctor of missiology degrees at Fuller Theological Seminary and a master of divinity degree from George Fox Evangelical Seminary. Veteran missionary to Thailand, he founded the Thailand Church Growth Committee, and cofounded SEANET. He served as adjunct faculty at Multnomah University for eighteen years. Presently he is an advocate in the Buddhist World for OMF (Oversees Missionary Fellowship) International, under which he has worked for fifty years. He has published numerous books and articles on ministry in the Buddhist world, including *Siamese Gold.* His Asian pioneer church planting experiences deepened the conviction that multiplying contextualized local indigenous fellowships and training local lay pastors are priority strategies for mission. He resides with his American wife, Faith, in the USA. They have three adult sons and four grandchildren.

Dr. G. P. V. Somaratna is from Sri Lanka. He has a PhD in South Asian history from the University of London. He served as professor of modern history at the University of Colombo, Sri Lanka, and is now serving as senior research professor at Colombo Theological Seminary. He has published numerous articles and books on the history of Sri Lanka and the impact of Christianity upon Sri Lankan Buddhism. He is widely regarded as one of Sri Lanka's leading scholars on Ceylonese history. He and his wife reside in Colombo, Sri Lanka, and have two children and eight grandchildren.

Steve Spaulding was born in Japan and studied missions at Fuller School of Intercultural Studies from 1989 to 1991. He has had a career in mission, living with his family in Manila, Philippines as regional coordinator of the DAWN (Discipling a Whole Nation) movement in Southeast Asia. During that time he cofounded SEANET, the global network focused exclusively on the Buddhist world. Contacts through that network as well as his work within the DAWN movement have meant encounters and relationships with many throughout Asia. He is a resident missiologist with OC (One Challenge) International living in Colorado Springs with his wife, Marna. They have three grown children.

"In that day I will respond," declares the Lord—
"I will respond to the skies,
and they will respond to the earth;
and the earth will respond to the grain,
the new wine and the olive oil,
and they will respond to Jezreel.
I will plant her for myself in the land;
I will show my love to the one I called
'Not my loved one.'
I will say to those called 'Not my people,'
'You are my people';
and they will say, 'You are my God.'"

Hosea 2:21–23

INTRODUCTION

I will remain in the world no longer,
but they are still in the world,
and I am coming to you.
Holy Father, protect them by the power of your name,
the name you gave me,
so that they may be one as we are one.

John 17:11

Jesus prayed that his followers would be one. This petition expresses an obvious desired unity of purpose but also indicates something of the process required. Positionally, all believers are in Christ. But becoming one with each other as the people of God is a journey that includes all the challenges of bringing together the world's languages, ethnicities, forms and expressions. How well have we been doing? Throughout history Christ followers continually faced the challenges of becoming the people of God in reality and not in name only. This has always required a unifying Christ-centeredness to live out God's kingdom values and bear witness to personal and corporate transformation in and through a multitude of cultural manifestations. The challenge of becoming the people of God continues in our day, especially in places where the life-changing reality of following Jesus is being rediscovered and practiced in ways beyond traditional packaging. Christ followers are in the process of becoming what will one day culminate in a huge and startling celebratory gathering with representatives from every one of the people groups in God's beloved creation (Matt 8:11; Rev 7:9ff; 21:22–24).

In this volume SEANET (South, East, Southeast, and North Asia Network) is proud to present nine diverse perspectives under the theme, "Becoming the People of God: Creating Christ-centered Communities in Buddhist Asia." All nine come from actual present-day locations where the gospel of Jesus Christ has not been the historic dominant cultural norm. We are grateful for the diverse cultures of the Buddhist world that have stimulated multiple expressions of becoming Christ-centered communities living out the enriching and distinctly different dimensions of God's kingdom work on earth. We believe that within these articles are valuable lessons that speak to the global family of faith. In this volume we have categorized the articles under three aspects of the process of becoming the people of God: (1) becoming the people who reflect God's kingdom through worship (the posture where God becomes visible), (2) becoming the people who reflect God's kingdom through witness of word and deed (relationships that make responses possible), and (3) becoming the people who reflect God's kingdom through welcome (hospitality that extends grace to all as an invitation towards the source of life itself).

All contributors in this volume are practitioners who have a deep appreciation for the cultural heritage and important moral values found in Buddhist contexts. We are grateful to each author for his or her contribution in preparing for and presenting at the SEANET conference and then taking the time to reflect and rewrite those papers for even more clarity in the forms presented here. It has been my pleasure to work with each and every one of you. Special thanks to my very able assistant, Christopher M. Hoskins, for his dedicated help in corresponding with each author and prompting the best work possible from all of us, including myself. As always, the staff of William Carey Library have been extremely helpful in producing this volume (along with all previous SEANET volumes) and creating the helpful topical and scriptural indices (with help from Jenny Hoskins) at the end of this book. The creative art work on the cover by graphic artist Hugh Pindur is much appreciated. Many thanks to editor Melissa Hicks at WCL for keeping us all on track. Finally, thanks to Dwight Martin for help in local printing.

This volume is dedicated to all who have given, daily give, and will continue to give their lives to creating Christ-centered communities in Buddhist contexts around the world. The church grows upon the witness of these saints past, present, and future. Christ-centered communities seek to be more and more reflective of the kingdom and need ongoing guidance to do so. The words of hymn writer William Cowper express this desire:

> Dear dying Lamb, Thy precious blood shall never lose its power
> Till all the ransomed church of God be saved, to sin no more.
> ("There is a Fountain Filled with Blood" In Conyer's Collection
> of Psalms and Hymns, 1772)

In this volume you will find a wide range of topics and approaches that speak to what it means to become the global body of believers wherever God has placed you to serve. May the concepts presented here encourage your ministry as you move through the various stages of becoming a worshiping, witnessing, welcoming people participating in the transforming process of reflecting the kingdom of God.

For the sake of Christ and all his community,

Paul H. de Neui
September 2014

PART I

BECOMING THE PEOPLE WHO REFLECT GOD'S KINGDOM THROUGH WORSHIP

But you are a chosen people,
a royal priesthood, a holy nation,
God's special possession,
that you may declare the praises of him
who called you out of darkness into his wonderful light.
Once you were not a people,
but now you are the people of God;
once you had not received mercy,
but now you have received mercy.

1 Peter 2:9–10

CHAPTER 1

FIRST IMPRESSIONS OF A BUDDHIST VISITOR TO AN EVANGELICAL WORSHIP SERVICE IN SRI LANKA: A LITURGICAL ANALYSIS

G. P. V. Somaratna

Missionaries in their heyday complained that Sinhala-speaking Buddhists were the hardest people to convert, but during the recent past there has been a notable movement among this same group from Buddhism to Christianity (Beaty and Small 1926, 4). Buddhism has been the main moral and spiritual force in Sri Lanka for the last 2,200 years, having survived a prolonged period of nearly 450 years of persecution and discrimination directed at its adherents under Western colonial rule (Dharmadasa 1993, 88). Buddhist leaders expected to recover from colonial oppression in the postindependence era under a leadership democratically elected by the majority (Wickremeratne 2006, 192). However, they now have to face a serious challenge from a growing Christian evangelical movement under indigenous leadership. The Sinhala Buddhists who cross the boundary of Buddhism to embrace evangelical Christianity do so amidst social and cultural stigmatization.

An inquirer from a Buddhist background who makes his or her first visit to an evangelical church would notice several strange practices that he may not find in his Buddhist environment. His worldview thus far is determined by traditional Buddhism, which has been learned from childhood. The first thing such a person would do is a comparison of his familiar place of worship at the Buddhist temple in his village with the worship that he encounters in the evangelical church that he visits.

Buddhist Inquirer

Any Buddhist inquirers entering a place of Christian worship would be influenced by this worldview. However, they come to a Christian church because they have had some kind of tangible spiritual experience. They rarely come alone. They come either with a Christian friend or as a result of an invitation extended by a well-wisher to attend a worship service. They know that it is a different religion and are willing to experience a change. They may even have the desire to cross the boundary of Buddhism to enter Christianity. Some even have expressed disgruntlement with the Buddhist practices of their heritage.

They have not had any experience of Christian worship when they come to an evangelical church for the first time. Christian worship is totally new to them. Most of what they have heard as Buddhists is anti-Christian propaganda through the media regarding the use of unethical means such as financial, educational or medical practices that evangelical groups have used to induce Buddhists to change their religion. However, they know that they themselves have not come to the church as a result of any of the above means supposedly used by evangelical Christians. The power of Christ that they have experienced is motivation enough to even face any social ostracism.

Participant observation and in-depth interviewing have been the main methodologies used in this study. The study is based on selected areas in Sri Lanka. In our research we interviewed some new Christians from several villages in the southern and western provinces of Sri Lanka who were previously Buddhists. We tried to gather their first impression of their first experience of Sunday worship. For that purpose we had interviews with several new Christians in Colombo, Hanwella, Galle, Matara, Dewinuwara, Tangalla, Ambalantota, and Hambantota. Their responses to our questions have a remarkable similarity. Most of the churches we visited are churches of the Assemblies of God, Calvary group, Foursquare Gospel, and some independent churches. All of them have worship services with very similar format. Their places of worship lack any external symbols other than a cross placed above the Communion table. Their pastors are in plain clothes, and the worship service reminds a Buddhist of the patterns of a public musical show.

Newcomers have no previous knowledge about Christian practices of any kind. Nothing is known about the Christian liturgy used in traditional churches for worship. They have decided to experiment with a Christian worship service as a result of the request of a Christian who prayed for an answer to a problem they may have had. It may be because some problems in their life have been answered. It could be a healing of an acute ailment, a family relationship restored, a land dispute solved, occupational issues settled, and so on. Because of the tangible nature of the religious experience, they have decided to come to the church where there is regular congregational Sunday worship. They have already settled in their minds that this would be a place where relief from their mental distress would be reduced or eliminated.

Buddhist Worship

Buddhist public worship is conducted in a Buddhist temple. These can be found in any part of the country. Any Buddhist can perform their worship in any temple in the country irrespective of *nikaya* (sectarian) difference within the Buddhist order in Sri Lanka. Buddhist temples are not single units. They comprise the *dagoba*, (bo or bodhi tree), shrine room, preaching hall, *devale* (temple building for gods), and an altar for incense and other offerings. Usually there is no officiating priest or person to lead the people in worship. On special days such as full-moon days, there would be *pinkama* (meritorious act), accompanied by people observing *sil* (Buddhist teaching and meritorious rituals) at the temple. On this day food will be offered to the shrine of the Buddha accompanying the chanting of the Three Refuges and Five Precepts. There will also be a *bana* (preaching) on this day. The *bana* will be held at the preaching hall of the temple (Kariyawasam 1995, 5–24).

Buddhist Patterns of Worship

Buddhist worship is ritualistic. Therefore the worship is accompanied by offerings of increasing complexity which include food, drink, and clothing. Buddhist worship is generally performed in a public place such as a temple shrine room, in front of a *dagoba*, or at a *devale*. The worship of these objects is an important merit-acquiring act of devotional Buddhism in Sri Lanka.

The expression of respect and reverence is absolutely essential throughout the Buddhist worship in a public setting. The devotees respectfully clasp their hands in the gesture of worship in front of a religious symbol such as a statue of the Buddha or a *dagoba*, and recite certain familiar stanzas beginning with the *Namo tassa* (obeisance) formula. The term *sadhu* is used by Sinhala Buddhists for the purpose of reverential worshiping. It is somewhat similar to "amen" in the Christian usage.

Flowers take foremost importance by their ritualistic offering in worship. They are respectfully placed on the altar in front of a statue of the Buddha or a *dagoba* or any other place where such worship is performed. In addition to the flowers, other popular offerings of importance are those of lighted lamps, or burning joss sticks, camphor, and incense. The offering of food and drink is another feature of the formal procedure of worship. The religious act should be accompanied with hands clasped together in adoration in the gesture of worship. Stanzas and formulas in the Pali language are recited solemnly. Usually any act of Buddhist worship begins by repeating three times the formula of homage to the Buddha followed by the Refuge formula and the Five Precepts. The physical posture adopted by the devotees when performing these acts of worship is very significant because it expresses respect. Such expressions of public worship would usually be performed as general acts of merit acquisition. Religiously important days such as full-moon days or commemorative days of important dead personages are chosen for public worship, which is also known as *pinkama*.

The Buddhist worshiper, depending on his or her need, would go to a particular section of the temple or to some of the places of his selection. If there is a need for a propitiation of a god, they would go to the *devale* in the Buddhist temple premises. For blessing they would go to the *dagoba*; if it is an astrological prediction of a calamity, they would go to the bo tree to make a *bodhi-puja* (worship at the bo tree). Since the worship is merit-oriented, the merit-making act of the individual devotee needs no intervention of any priestly guide in a Buddhist temple.

It is only in the *devale* where the *kapuwa* (priest) would perform some rituals to appease or propitiate the deity for a fee.

Bana

Most of the Buddhist religious activities are individualistic in nature. Each individual seeks to worship at a time convenient to him or her. The preaching of doctrine in the form of a discourse undertaken in the preaching hall of a temple is an exception. It may be the closest parallel to an evangelical Sunday worship. The setting is in a separate building of the temple. However, it too is a merit-making activity. The devotees dressed in white enter the hall, leaving their shoes at the entrance or in a place arranged by the temple. They solemnly enter and sit on the floor, as there are no chairs in the preaching hall.

The Buddhist monk would come with a *dayaka* (lay devotee) to the hall and sit in a chair on an elevated platform. The *dayaka* would sit on the floor or on a lower elevation. In order to pave the way for the monk to preach, the lay devotee in waiting would chant the Three Refuges— the Buddha, *dharma*, and *sangha*. Then the monk would chant the Five Precepts and other stanzas before starting the sermon.

At the end of the sermon the monk would chant two or three stanzas transferring merit gained by listening to this *bana*. The merits are transferred to "gods" and departed loved ones. The devotees would then disperse, believing that they performed a meritorious act. There is no seeking of a personal deity or any ritualistic acts to perform to please such a deity.

Prejudices against Evangelicals

The following is what I have found are common prejudices found in the background of first-time Buddhist visitors to an evangelical worship centre:

> The use of unethical means such as financial, educational, medical, and the media by the Christian evangelical groups to induce Buddhists to change their religion has been viewed as a glaring abuse of the tolerance displayed by Buddhists

towards other religions, and a violation of fundamental freedoms enshrined in the National Constitution. The aggressive conduct of foreign missionaries in their attempt to spread Christianity and other Abrahamic religions, and undermine the traditional status of Buddhism in Sri Lanka, as has happened in South Korea in the last few decades, carries with it the seed for a potential religious conflict in the future. (Weeraratna 2012)

The extremist nationalist elements have directed violence against evangelical Christians in the very area we have made our study. They have, however, been much more reticent in taking similar action against the community cautiously referred to as "other Abrahamic religions," who are more numerous than the evangelical Christians, better organized, and more likely to defend themselves robustly.

Evangelical Worship

Evangelical Christian worship on a Sunday usually begins with a welcome. In some churches they bid a greeting like "good morning." Usually these services are led by a worship leader in the church chosen by the choir. They proceed to pray for various aspects of the worship service. They then go on to the first phase of the service. This is known as a period of praise and worship. The total period taken by the service is around one and half hours. The praise and worship may last from thirty minutes to one hour depending on the preference of the pastor in charge. In some churches each song is followed by impromptu praying; sometimes praying in tongues may be included. The prayer is noisy and lacks coordination. This part of worship by way of singing is given an important place in evangelical Christian practice. Bodily expressions of worship such as singing, swaying to and fro, clapping, and vocal praying may be observed. The practice of speaking in unknown tongues known as *glossolalia* also would be noticed. This is regarded as evidence of the presence of the Holy Spirit.

The words of the hymns, choruses, and songs are projected on a screen using an overhead or more recently, a powerpoint projector. There are some long-standing members who would know the Sinhala words to the songs by heart. The language used for all church activities is Sinhala. One would hear an English word or phrase occasionally interspersed. A choir with accompanying music is conspicuous. The sound of the bass and rhythm guitars is enhanced through electronic power amplifiers, while other instruments such as tambourines and regular acoustic guitars are also used. The most powerful sound is that made by a drum set.

The singing is interspaced by prayer, which is led by the worship leader and joined by the congregation. The prayers are impromptu and unstructured, and each individual could participate in any way they please. There would be a loud cacophony of voices and unstructured noises in this period. There would be bodily involvement during this period of worship. Some people would raise their hands above their heads, some would worship with hands clasped together above their heads. There would be others who would not do any of this but pray with eyes closed. The prayer session would at times be transformed into *glossolalia*. At some point in the Sunday worship a long session of corporate prayer would be introduced. It may extend from prayer for individual needs and moving up to perceived national needs.

After a period of a few minutes of prayer, the leader usually requests the congregation to participate in the singing of another song. This process may be repeated several times. The day's offering would be collected after the final song. One or more songs would be sung by the choir while the collection bags are passed around the congregation. Evangelical Christians are usually encouraged to donate a tenth or "tithe" of their income to the church.

The collection may be followed by public testimonies, which is also known as witnessing. This practice allows the believers to publicly give thanks to God and render religious meaning to a life event. As people remained seated, the leader would invite to the platform whoever was scheduled to deliver the day's sermon, usually the pastor. A Bible passage or two relevant to the sermon may be read before that. The preacher normally delivers the sermon standing. He looks at his notes that are on the pulpit in front of him. Before he starts the sermon, he prays to dedicate the sermon to God's honour. The sermon takes the form of a public lecture except for the Bible passages read or quoted. This is in contrast to the manner of a Buddhist priest, however, who liberally quotes Buddhist texts in the Pali language without any notes. At the end of the sermon they pronounce a blessing and disperse the crowd. At this juncture the children would be led away to Sunday school, which is held in some rooms of the church. The service ends with another period of prayer and benediction.

Strange

A regular visit to a sanctuary, like Christian worship on every Sunday, is anomalous for a normal Buddhist. Congregational worship may make them feel uncomfortable and surrounded by an unfamiliar crowd who are performing some strange rituals. Therefore evangelical worship services lack bridges for a Buddhist to feel comfortable. They do not find anything familiar to what they do in the temple. Yet the very difference seems to be the attraction as they seek something different from Buddhism, which they want to leave behind.

The place where Buddhists worship is a special building or a complex of buildings set aside for that purpose. When a devotee reaches the precincts of the temple, he will experience the distinctive smells, appearances, and sounds of the temple. These generate a feeling of holy serenity in the mind of the devotee. This may be because there is a clear demarcation between holy and profane in Buddhism. However, the evangelical churches do not generate any such awesome atmosphere because of the absence in them of any symbols of religious value. The first-time visitor from a Buddhist background would not believe that he is stepping into a place of worship.

Entrance to the Church

Those who come from a Buddhist background expect a building of religious significance. People who have seen a Catholic or Protestant church expect a religious building of certain architecture. Many have told us that they were disappointed to see a building like a house used as a church. It did not give any kind of religious appearance. When entering the church, they noticed that there was no necessity to remove shoes which they did in the Buddhist temple. The devotees in the building were not seated on the ground, but on chairs. One person said that they removed their shoes when they visited the gods depicted in statues and idols but were sad to see that the Christians do not remove their shoes, even when they enter the place where they worship the living God.

Place of Worship

The Buddhist who comes to the evangelical worship does not find a sanctuary. There is no central place to focus the worship such as a statue. The traditional Buddhist mind notes the absence of incense, flowers, and colours that they are familiar with in the temple. Everyone in the congregation is wearing clothes of various colours and not the traditional white they expect in the temple. People are seated in chairs wearing shoes. They could not see any mats or a floor made ready for people to sit. This erodes the sanctity of the sanctuary in the Buddhist mind.

While these seeming distractions put the newcomer in a state of bewilderment, his or her mind would be further confused by the way individual worshipers act in the church. Some are raising their hands, some are sitting with clasped hands, others have dropped their hands. The newcomer is confused as to what is the correct posture. The occasional outburst of speaking in tongues also confuses the visitor. Thist is because a similar kind of speaking in tongues is found in Buddhist *devales* where some devotees or priests would predict the future while in a state of trance.

Songs

The Buddhist person becomes confounded when it comes to singing. A Buddhist cannot understand why Christians use musical instruments and sing continuously for so long. In their mind this kind of fun making has no holiness attached to it. They gain the impression that this is a place where fun and frolic is made. It is totally alien to the Buddhist who considers music and singing as a worldly behaviour incompatible with Buddhism, as Buddhist precepts prohibit such activities.

No songs are sung in Buddhist places of worship. They only have chants. But they do not understand the meaning of the chants even though they recite them. Buddhists are of course familiar with music and song at the popular level but not as a part of worship of the Buddha or deities. There are certain type of songs sung only at exorcism ceremonies but these have their own tunes, and the musical instruments dedicated for them are different.

We received varying responses to the question about the use of music and song in evangelical worship. The average response of young people was that evangelical worship was like a musical program where loud music is played with a person or group singing in front of an audience. Another person said that it was like a wedding celebration in a hotel. The older ones said that the loud music hinders their spirit of worship. On the other hand, some have thought that this was the usual Christian way of seeking God. The average impression was that loud music with guitars and drums gives an appearance of a foreign element that the local culture could not merge with. Nevertheless, singing and soft music engendered a positive response from the newcomers. This was the first time that they were able to participate in corporate singing, even though they did not understand the meaning of some of the songs at the beginning. They also observed that the congregation was in a joyful mood while they were singing.

Embarrassment

For the Buddhist, worship is a solemn occasion. They do not even whisper during a preaching session. But in the middle of the evangelical church worship there was an announcement asking people to offer greetings of peace to one's neighbour. This practice is totally unfamiliar to Buddhists, who would not make familiar contact with strangers in that manner.

Another event that makes the first timer to the church uncomfortable was the welcoming announcement made from the pulpit. The newcomers were asked to stand in order to welcome them. Many of the respondents said that they did not get up, because they felt embarrassed to receive the attention of a crowd that was not known to them. The whole church would turn its attention to the one solitary individual. Even the people sitting in the front rows would turn back to look at the individual. It was uncomfortable to observe about two hundred people looking at one person. Very often they went privately to the evangelical services and prefer to remain incognito in this unfamiliar environment.

Distractions

There were a few practices that Buddhist visitors found it really difficult to approve of. One was the noise of the drums. One person said that she could not understand why a solemn worship like this had such noisy drumming, which in her mind was associated with the demon worship in Buddhism. Some churches are air-conditioned so as to prevent the release of the noise to the outside to prevent any opposition from the neighbours. In such buildings the drum is a further irritation. Others, however, said they did not find it difficult to accept drumming, since drumming of some sort usually preceded Buddhist ceremonies.

Welcome

The perceived attractions of the evangelical worship varied from individual to individual. All of them, however, were positive about the attention they receive individually rather than publicly. One couple told us that they were very encouraged by the two people who welcomed them at the entrance of the Tangalle church. Again, when the worship service was over, the old believers of the church spoke to them, and some even prayed with them. One poor farmer of Hambantota who came with his wife after losing all their personal assets said that he was astonished by the welcoming attitude of the believers in the church, even though their clothes were dirty and untidy. The impression of many of them was that they felt as if they were in a safe environment where affection was expressed amongst the believers. Members took a special interest in them if they knew that they were newcomers. Even after the worship was over, they noticed that believers usually waited and talked to each other. Members of some churches even shared a cup of tea together before they broke into groups for Bible study.

Worship in a Buddhist temple, on the other hand, does not have any such practices of welcome. Each person attends to his or her devotions and goes home. If they talk to anyone, it would be only to a person known to them. Buddhist temples are public places where people come to perform acts which produce merit for them. Fellowship is not a part of Buddhist worship.

There was a spirit of camaraderie about the way Christians treated newcomers. Our respondents said that neither the pastor nor the believers tried to convert them to Christianity but instead spoke to them gently and inquired about their lives. They noticed that the language used was different there from that used in Buddhist temples. Everyone was addressed by the Sinhala equivalent of elder brother, younger brother, younger sister, elder sister, and so on.

Preaching

Christian vocabulary was another area that made the newcomer confused and puzzled them. Words such as "sin," "dedication," and "offering," were used with different meaning than that of their Buddhist background. The newcomers found it hard to grasp the new Christian meanings. The expression that "man is a sinner" was offensive to them. The personal names associated with Christianity in Sinhalese are totally alien to them. Even proper names such as Peter (Peduru) and John (Yohan) that are found in the Sinhala Bible in current usage are different. Expressions like *talenta* (repentance), and such others are unfamiliar to Buddhists. Christian concepts such as heaven, hell, and salvation are beyond the understanding of the Buddhist mind.

To the Buddhist listener, Christian preaching lacks serenity. Buddhists will refer to the Buddha with the highest honorific terms in their sermons. Buddhist devotees will say "*sadhu*" in adoration whenever the name of the Buddha is mentioned. However, in the Christian sermons one may not find such respect given even to Christ. Often the pastor in his preaching would refer to Christ without any honorific whatsoever. The Buddhists were appalled by the way that Christians refer to Christ using an ordinary pronoun without the appropriate honorific form attached to it. Hearing the way these names were used during an evangelical service, a Buddhist visitor on his first encounter would make the assumption that the Christian God and the founder of the Christian religion must be much lower in status than the Buddha.

The traditional honorific terms and word forms used in the Sinhala language in referring to gods and the Buddha were absent in the evangelical Sinhala vocabulary when they referred to Christ and God during the service. The Buddhist visitors were unanimous in their feeling that inadequate respect was given in evangelical churches to religious persons.

A Buddhist monk preaches in the presence of a Buddha statue. He is seated on a chair covered with a white cloth. If he sits on the floor, he will see that the area is raised with cushions. A fan is in his hand. Some monks cover their mouth with the fan when preaching.

According to some respondents the attraction of the evangelical pastor was that he was like them. He was in ordinary clothes. The clothes did not give the appearance of a religious dignitary. He came to speak carrying a Bible. He placed the notes on the stand and delivered his speech. The difference from the Buddhist monks was that he prayed before he started and also ended with a prayer. One person said that it was known that the pastor had been a worse sinner than he is but is now a saintly man. Therefore he also could aspire to be a person like that.

The newcomers were unanimous in their judgment of the sermon. Their view was that they could not understand anything of the preacher's quotations from the Bible. The Christian doctrinal expressions, names, and biblical books were not familiar to them. They found the preaching uninteresting and some fell asleep during the sermon. However, they accepted with concurrence the things they heard about ordinary living. The words of exclamation often uttered in evangelical worship services such as "Hallelujah!," "Amen!," and "Hosanna!" were unintelligible to them and at times irritating.

Collection

The collection of funds at the worship service was confusing to some. However, some newcomers believed that it was the tradition of the new place and therefore did not think much about it. Another person said that they were accustomed to giving money to temple collections and therefore did not feel anything strange about it, even though the Buddhist *bana* sessions have no such collection bag sent around. A young person said that they enjoyed putting money into collection boxes in temples therefore they did not feel anything strange about it.

However, two respondents said that when a Buddhist temple asks for money for various things they will publicize the names of the givers. The collection in the temple is taken from the devotees, but no help would come to the laity from the temple, as the *sanghika* items (personal items used by Buddhist monks) are prohibited for lay usage. The visitors were even happy to give one-tenth of their income to the church since they could clearly see where the money was going in the evangelical church setting.

Benediction

Christian preaching ended with a benediction. The parallel in Buddhist sermons is two or three stanzas that the preacher chants at the end, transferring merit to gods and dead relatives. The Christian benediction is in Sinhala, while the monks chant in Pali. However, even though the Christian benediction formula is in the local language it is not, however, intelligible to a Buddhist newcomer. Father, Son, and Holy Spirit are not in their vocabulary, and therefore the blessing does not resonate with any meaning in them or to them.

Buddhist devotees bow and worship the monks before they leave the temple precincts. Some newcomers to the church also thought that they had to go and worship the pastor after the sermon was over. But they did not see anyone doing this. When they went to the pastor, he spoke to them kindly and inquired about their well-being. That pleased them and they realized that the pastor was a different kind of minister.

Positive Attitude

The above-mentioned irritations in an evangelical worship service may remain for some time, even after several visits to the church. But Buddhist newcomers have other reasons to attend regular evangelical worship services even amidst this kind of unease. The predominant reason that many of them decided to attend evangelical Christian worship was the result of a strong tangible and very personal experience. Some came alone; however, many came with at least a part of their family because of the power of the change that had occurred in their lives. It may have been healing of a sickness that the doctors found impossible to treat, or a character change that the family members saw. Something was evident and the family wanted to know more.

Conclusion

Sri Lanka is a multiethnic and multicultural society. Therefore everyone has had to deal with people of religions other than their own on an everyday basis. They are able to accept the differences because they know that other religions are different from theirs. For that reason, when they come to church for the first time, they expect something new. The attitude and reactions of individuals may vary. However, in our research we found that there is a consensus with regard to some factors. There was almost unanimity about the welcome, acceptance, and the fellowship which they found in the church community as well as the pastor. There were some irritants that the newcomers encountered. These irritants became less pronounced as time went on and the Buddhists continued attending the worship services continuously.

Nevertheless, the responses from this research point to certain areas that the church should take into consideration in order to nurture a flock that belongs to the first generation of Christians who come from a Buddhist background. Among these are the use of Christian language and vocabulary known only to Christians, the absence of honorific terms when addressing the Lord Jesus Christ, and countercultural behaviours such as showing scant respect for the holy and serene. Shaming newcomers by asking them to stand up, using loud musical instruments like drums, and practicing chaotic prayer habits all may need to be addressed by the church that is working in Buddhist contexts for Buddhist people.

This had been the first experience of Christian worship for all of them. They were not aware of any other form of Christian worship and therefore had not been exposed to any other kind of Christian liturgy. Consequently, they cannot make any comparison of Christian worship styles other than the outward appearance of what they saw and experienced in the church buildings. What they know is only Buddhist worship styles. If there were any comparison, they would be with Buddhist practices.

For a Sinhala Buddhist in Sri Lanka, converting to Christianity is to accommodate a much maligned identity that places one in a position of exteriority when understood from the perspective of the hegemonic nature of Sinhala Buddhist nationalism (Fernando 2011, 160). Several nationalist political parties have criticized evangelical

Christians of engaging in "unethical" practices of proselytization, and representing an American form of modernity that is irreconcilable with local cultural forms. In spite of this, most of these newcomers were willing to risk the barriers of social and religious opposition to visit so-called "fundamentalist churches," because they did not find love and care in their own environment. They had lost hope within their own social and religious system.

In order to look forward to the future well-being of the church, some facts may require our attention. These newcomers found certain Christian practices very attractive. The first among them was the affectionate acceptance of newcomers to evangelical churches. They experienced this through the greetings they received at the entrance of the church, the few words that the ushers spoke and by being guided to their seats. All of these made them feel accepted. When the pastor or an elder came to speak to them before the service, it was much appreciated. When compare with their Buddhist background, monks never come to them when they are in the temple to worship. Buddhist devotees also have nothing to do with other Buddhist devotees. Each minds his or her own business without any consideration of others.

As newcomers, Buddhists may feel unsure of how they will be received by others in the church. They may fear being alienated in their dealings with the older members of the church. The acceptance and love that they find in evangelical churches is a very strong factor that gives confidence to the newcomer. This acceptance surpasses all sorts of barriers and weaknesses that the first timer may face. Christian love and brotherly acceptance of the newcomer overcomes all the social barriers that are present in Sri Lankan society. The love that is found in the evangelical Christian community is the most important factor of a healthy church from time immemorial. Jesus' statement is "By this everyone will know that you are my disciples, if you love one another" (John 13:35). It has to be recognized that this is the greatest strength that the evangelical Christian church has. It has to be guarded, nurtured, and encouraged.

References

Beaty, A. S., and W. J. T. Small. 1926. *Survey of missionary work in Ceylon: Chiefly relating to societies affiliated to the Christian Council.* Colombo, Sri Lanka: Christian Literature Society.

Dharmadasa, K. N. O. 1993. *Language, religion and ethnic assertiveness: The growth of Sinhalese nationalism in Sri Lanka.* Ann Arbor: University of Michigan Press.

Fernando, W. N. O. 2011. The effects of evangelical Christianity on state formation in Sri Lanka. PhD diss., University of California Santa Barbara.

Kariyawasam, A. G. S. 1995. *Buddhist ceremonies and rituals of Sri Lanka.* Colombo, Sri Lanka: Wheel Publications.

Lumsdaine, David Halloran, ed. 2009. *Evangelical Christianity and democracy in Asia.* New York: Oxford University Press.

Uyangoda, Jayadeva. 2007. *Religion in context: Buddhism and socio-political change in Sri Lanka.* Colombo, Sri Lanka: Social Scientists Association of Sri Lanka.

Weeraratna, Senaka. 2012. Manipulative Christian conversions in Sri Lanka: Some perspectives. Lankaweb, November 17, 2012, http://www.lankaweb. com/news/items/2012/11/17/manipulative-christian-conversions-in-sri-lanka-some-perspectives/ (accessed December 11, 2013; site dicontinued).

Wickremeratne, Swarna. 2006. *Buddha in Sri Lanka: Remembered yesterdays.* Albany: State University of New York Press.

CHAPTER 2

TOWARD A NEW BREED OF CHURCHES IN JAPAN

Mitsuo Fukuda

In an attempt to help catalyze house church multiplication in Japan by providing resources and networking for house church planters, I founded the RAC Network. Though the acronym remained the same, the name of the network was changed in April 2002, from the "Research Association for Contextualization" to the "Rethinking Authentic Christianity Network," in order to reflect a new focus. Prior to 2002, our main activities had been publishing missiological periodicals, and our vision was to see a contextualized Japanese Christianity.

The major reason why we changed direction stemmed from a strong desire to see New Testament Christianity actualized in Japan. It was discouraging and exhausting to see such little fruit come out of our publications, lectures, and conferences. We realized that churches where direct access to God is encouraged and which have a flat and personal relationship structure, rather than a hierarchical structure, most contextually reflected the lives of people.

I will try to describe how we changed our focus from just doing research to actually being "in the field" coaching house church planters.

Contextualization and Emerging "Japanese Christianity"

When I was baptized about thirty-seven years ago, I asked some longtime believers what percentage of the Japanese population were Christian.

Their answer was that there was less than 1 percent. Today. I have to say that the real rate is far below 1 percent. Itami City, where I live, has a population of 200,000 with eight churches, including a Catholic church. Only five hundred people participate in a Sunday worship service at least a couple of times a month—a rate of only 0.25 percent. Unfortunately this seems to be the average for all of Japan.

In the late 1980s I came to realize that one of the major reasons for this stagnation was a lack of contextualization. The Apostle Paul said,

> Though I am free and belong to no one, I have made myself a slave to everyone, to win as many as possible. To the Jews I became like a Jew, to win the Jews. To those under the law I became like one under the law (though I myself am not under the law), so as to win those under the law. To those not having the law I became like one not having the law (though I am not free from God's law but am under Christ's law), so as to win those not having the law. (1 Cor 9:19–21)

My evaluation is that Japanese churches have largely failed to become Japanese in order to win the Japanese.

Yasuo Furuya, a Japanese theologian, wrote that the "head" of the Japanese church is a German-established church equipped by profound theology, but without evangelism or contribution to the church fund. The "hands and legs" are that of American denominationalism, a highly democratic system; but the "heart" is full of Japanese codependency (1995, 38). The Japanese church is like a ghetto for the intellectual elite who enjoy theological discussions and a clubby atmosphere, but are not earnest in communicating God's love to their neighbors.

Throughout Japanese church history, church forms have continually been imported from Europe, from the US and Canada, and recently from Korea and other countries as well. Each has been uncritically adopted, and then abandoned on hearing the latest success stories from other countries. For example, the cell church strategies of a particular megachurch in Korea have been imitated by many churches in various denominations in Japan. Numerous copies of manuals on how to form regional small groups have been published. However, few churches have been successful, and no church has become like the church in Korea.

This "copy machine syndrome" has brought continual disaster to the Japanese churches. Six sure ways to destroy a church are: (1) imitate the ways of a successful pastor, (2) use his method of evangelism and pastoral ministry, (3) teach the other pastor's experience as a principle or dogma, (4) announce that this is the only way, (5) communicate that other ways are sinful, and (6) oppose those who don't employ the "correct" way.

As Harvie Conn described, Christianity in Japan (as well as in other Asian countries) has largely been a "potted plant" (1984, 246). It was transported to Japan without really being transplanted. Therefore, my concern used to be for the transplantation or "critical contextualization" (Hiebert 1984, 75–94) of employing Japanese cultural forms in Christian communication. I tried to find the essence of Christianity in the Western churches and then leave behind the Western cultural soil as much as possible, adopting only this essence and dressing it with Japanese cultural forms (Fukuda 2012).

However, I have recently started to think about a fresh incarnation. If we could allow Christianity to emerge in Japanese soil without even considering its counterparts in foreign Christianity, that might be better. Both transportation and transplantation are based on the idea of the translation of a model whose starting point is, in the first place, a foreign idea, and which must then be interpreted and then introduced into the native soil. But a fresh incarnation emerges in the soil of a culture where the seed of God's words is sprouting.

The seed has already been planted in Japan. We have millions of translated Bibles and at least 200,000 committed witnesses, as well as churches, mission schools, Christian hospitals, and church-related publications. Our focus has to be on how to allow the Spirit of God to grow the seed. In my opinion, the house church is the ideal setting where God incarnates his heart in his church.

The House Church

As Banks stated, "Not until the third century do we have evidence of special buildings being constructed for Christian gatherings" (1994, 41). Church historians estimate that the number of members of New Testament house churches rarely reached more than fifteen or twenty people. This is why Simson suggests that there is a "20-person barrier" to overcome. He explains, "In many cultures 20 is a maximum number where people still feel "family," organic and informal, without the need to get formal or organized" (2001, 17).

The average size of the Sunday worship attendance in Japan is thirty-six people (Church Information Service 2012). Many Japanese Christians think that their churches are too small, and look to megachurches overseas as models. But our model—as well as more important principles—should be drawn from the New Testament. In reality, the problem of most churches in Japan is not that they are too small, but that they are already too big. As a result, Japanese churches have lost their attractiveness. They are not spontaneous or lively but, like a boring classroom, they are mostly irrelevant to the reality of peoples' lives (see Yamamori 1974). If the church is small enough to maintain the dynamic of a family of God whose headship is Christ, the Holy Spirit will lead the members to appropriately apply the essence of Christian truth for the cultural environment of each individual house church. There should be no need to introduce structures from other places, nor any need for a central administrative authority to homogenize the diversity of the churches (see Allen 1962, 131).

Dean S. Gilliland believes that this contextual aspect is part of the reason Paul's churches survived under immense pressure, growing in each place and multiplying among the unevangelized. Gilliland states that "Christianity was vibrant and alive because each local church found its own expression of the Christian life while at the same time it was joined in faith and truth to all other congregations that were also under Christ's lordship" (1983, 209). It is easy to imagine that in these scattered small churches, people would have shared similar lives, related naturally with each other, and met the special needs emerging from a common socio-cultural context.

A house church seems to have several advantages in terms of contextualization. One advantage is that while the context of the traditional church exists in the relatively artificial environment of the so-called three "sacred p's"—sacred programs run by sacred people in a sacred place—the house church emerges from and is centered in the context of daily life. The second advantage is that it is small enough to be flexible to adapt to its local culture. The third advantage is that it has a flat leadership structure, where various cultural forms can be employed easily through open discussion. The expansion of the house church movement would likely reveal various contextualized church forms in Japan.Examples of the Emergence of "Japanese Christianity" We are finding that simple structures—such as participatory Bible studies where the Bible itself is the teacher, and everyone in the group is involved in the teaching/learning process, as well as the application of what is being learned to daily life—are effective ways to touch the hearts of Japanese people (see Dale and Dale 2002, 111–13). For example, one day seven young people gathered in my house and joined a participatory Bible study. I was not there to teach, but just to observe. They chose a passage from Romans 6. I thought that it would be too difficult of a section for them as it included the concepts of baptism, dying and being resurrected with Christ. Several verses were read and a college student, who was functioning as a facilitator, asked what the "new man" and "old man" meant.

After some quiet time, one young man remembered a fight that he and two of his friends had had that afternoon. They were also there with him at the Bible study that night. After the quarrel, one had angrily said to the others, "Leave me alone. Stay away from me!" Sometime later, both of them reconciled and were able to say each other, "Let's be good friends from now on."

The young man applied his experience to interpret the Bible verses and explained. "The 'old man' is like a person who says to Jesus, 'Stay away from me!' and the 'new man' is like a person who says to Jesus, 'Let's be good friends from now on.'" When the other young people heard his explanation, all of them understood the Bible verses and connected the meaning with their own spiritual journey. What an amazing interpretation! If I had explained those verses, I could have quoted profound theological statements about all of those subjects, but I wouldn't have impacted their lives in that way.

Let the Bible itself teach people! The young man was used by God as an interpreter and mediator of God's truth using his own thoughts and terminology. Today in Japan we do not need the interpretation of a famous Bible scholar from the West, but a divine intervention of the Holy Spirit moving in people's hearts and minds. "God chose the foolish things of the world to shame the wise" (1 Cor 1:27).

The heroine of another story is an older lady. She had been coming to a house church meeting for a long time; however, my evaluation at that time was that she did not really want to have a life-changing experience. She continually grumbled during our meetings: "I could not do that even if Jesus told me to do that" or "I don't believe in the ideas of the Bible, because in my real miserable situation I could not pursue such an ideal." Her negative statements sometimes seemed to have a serious impact on newcomers.

Several months after we started using a participatory Bible study in the meeting, she made a comment on the Scripture verses. "Jesus said. 'For judgment I have come into this world, so that the blind will see and those who see will become blind'" (John 9:39). She said, "This passage describes my situation. I was blind and I was a sinner. Now I understand that I could not see the truth anymore, even though I insisted that I could see. My sin was that I claimed I could see." When my wife and I heard her comment, we wept. It was not the fruit of a good sermon, but the work of the Holy Spirit in a small interactive setting that helped her to realize her sin.

The effectiveness of good preaching is often limited by the giftedness of a teacher. When a preacher is speaking and everyone is listening, even if the preaching itself is impressive, the listeners become a passive audience who want to be entertained more. Only a gifted preacher can continually satisfy an audience with new knowledge and breathtaking illustrations. Maybe he will establish a huge cathedral and a large following, but when he leaves, the people will most likely be scattered like sheep without a shepherd. To ensure the contextuality of a church, it is necessary to allow people direct access to God through Jesus Christ. No one should be between God and his people except one mediator, the man Christ (1 Tim 2:5). Ordinary people can hear God's voice and do the extraordinary work of God without the hierarchical administrative system of human leadership. God will give contextualized answers to the questions that God's people are asking from within their real-life settings.

One more example of the emergence of "Japanese Christianity" is a new way of evangelism that we are seeing in Japan. One of the "hot" targets for evangelism in Japan is nurses (Fukuda 2004). There are three interesting characteristics of this group: (1) They want to be healed. The work of a nurse is often like being a slave to the sick. They are surrounded by people needing medical care. Due to the stress of their hard work, they are tired and need to be healed. (2) Many nurses are involved in the New Age movement. They know the limitations of medical science. Some of them care for those who are dying and/or suffer from hopeless conditions. They tend to search in the spiritual world for answers to questions about man's finite existence. Although it is extremely expensive to participate in New Age exercises and various programs, their relatively high incomes allow them to afford it. (3) They give serious thought to the well-being of life. They are scientific people and are good at analyzing their psychological problems. But they have not been able to find the answers to the questions that are pressing in their lives. They are seriously seeking hope, purpose, happiness, and acceptance.

One of my mentees is a nurse. After finishing the church planters' training, she began with friendship evangelism and led a nursing school faculty member who was a devout New Age practitioner to Christ (see Fukuda 2010). The process of her conversion was very different from what we see traditionally. Because the nursing school faculty member was familiar with visualization from New Age practice, my mentee led her to visualize her past experiences. She saw herself and her ex-boyfriend in her imagination. Although he had once made her mad and had wounded her, strangely enough, she saw herself hugging him, and they were weeping together. She did not understand why she did such a thing. After a while, she understood the whole picture. Jesus approached them and then hugged both of them with his warm hands.

When this lady saw Jesus in her imagination, he was bathed in tender light and she understood supernaturally that he would never leave her or abandon her. For her, conversion and healing came at the same time. The experience was so real that she cannot stop testifying about it to her friends. It started a chain reaction. Just three days after her baptism, she shared her experience with a friend who had once been a partner in reading tarots. She led her friend to experience Jesus, and the same thing happened in her friend's life. They began meeting weekly for prayer and accountability, and after three months they started a church in one of their homes where they used to read tarots. They have experienced God directly and are bold enough to share their experiences with other nurses. And then in quick succession, three students and one single mother who is a friend of the second faculty member accepted Christ.

This new type of evangelism for nurses was not developed by clergy or missiologists. It did not happen in a big conference room or in a fancy cathedral with stained glass. It emerged in a family-like small group of Christians who had a passion for communicating Christ's love to their friends.

Conclusion

How can we release the biotic growing potential that God has given us? Some spiritualistic thinkers insist that we should throw away all institutional structures. However, for the healthy multiplication of churches, some simple, reproducible structures such as participatory Bible studies and other house church strategies are needed. These structures should not be complicated and administrative, but simple, organic, family-like, relational, catalytic, and spontaneous, where ordinary people have direct access to God.

In these structures the most contextualized forms of Christianity can be developed. Now these kind of cutting-edge experiments are being conducted, and hopefully, in the near future, a new breed of churches will emerge in the real-life settings of life in Japan.

References

Allen, Roland. 1962. *Missionary methods: St. Paul's or ours?* Grand Rapids: Eerdmans.

Banks, Robert. 1994. *Paul's idea of community.* Peabody, MA: Hendrickson.

Church Information Service. 2012. *The Protestant church in Japan.* Niiza, Japan: Church Information Service.

Conn, Harvie M. 1984. *Eternal word and changing word.* Grand Rapids: Zondervan.

Dale, Tony, and Felicity Dale. 2002. *Simply church.* Austin, TX: Karis.

Fukuda, Mitsuo. 2004. A house church among Japanese nurses. In *The realities of the changing expressions of the church*, ed. David Claydon, 27–28. Lausanne Occasional Paper no. 43.

———. 2010. *Upward, outward, inward.* Gloucester, UK: Wide Margin.

———. 2012. *Developing a contextualized church as a bridge to Christianity in Japan.* Gloucester, UK: Wide Margin, 2012. Published in Japanese in 1993.

Furuya, Yasuo. 1995. Nippon Dendouron (*Perspectives on evangelism in Japan*). Tokyo: Kyobukan.

Gilliland, Dean S. 1983. *Pauline theology and mission practice.* Jos, Nigeria: Albishir.

Hiebert, Paul G. 1994. Critical contextualization. In *Anthropological reflections on missiological issues,* 75–92. Grand Rapids: Baker Academic.

Simson, Wolfgang. 2001. *Houses that change the world: The return of the house church.* Waynesboro, GA: OM Publishing.

Yamamori, Tetsunao. 1974. *Church growth in Japan.* Pasadena: William Carey Library.

CHAPTER 3

WHERE ARE YOUR TEMPLES? DO CHRISTIANITY AND BUDDHISM SHARE A TEMPLE ETHOS?

Steve Spaulding

Sitting across the table in a dingy Indochinese hotel dining room, a look of concern comes over the face of a prominent local church leader. Non-Christian religious leaders question his church's viability by asking, "Where are your temples?" Where is the edifice that reflects your spiritual rootedness, place and authority within the society, membership, professional class, territory, financial strength, religious rites, and public worship?

This question, personal and missiological, arises from several quarters: the interreligious context (here, Buddhist), the Christian missionary community, the perspective of inquirers and young followers of Christ, and eventually the leadership of Christian churches. This question involves a whole array of social and religious expectations on the part of peoples raised within a Buddhist *cultus* of temple, complete with rites, sacrifice, professional caretakers, cruciality of space, the housing of deities and holy artifacts, as well as distinctions in religious, gender, age, and other roles. From the Buddhist perspective, why would a religion intent on mass conversion, church planting, and impacting an entire country not have large, visible edifices to stake its claim in the territory?

Christian leaders have put this question squarely to the indigenous church of nations in the Buddhist world with reference to the apparent indispensability of a temple ethos within Buddhist cultures. Honest inquirers both within and outside the church ask, what is the viability of a religious alternative that does not have resources sufficient to erect its own alternative sanctuary? Is there a dynamic equivalent to the system in which they exist, sometimes at great cost or already ample discontinuity?

What are some functions and meaning of "temple" in Buddhism and in Christianity? The most fascinating feature of this question is the pregnant silence one finds in the literature on the subject. Part of the silence on temple within Buddhist literature is due to a realization that the visible structure does not well represent the heart of the religion and has in most cases become a prime perpetuator of religious institutional power. Rarely indeed will one find mention of temple in Christian theological works either, including works on ecclesiology. This also can be somewhat of a smokescreen for other governing metaphors in the communities both within and outside the church. The silence here refers to the distance between the clergy's and the faithfuls' acceptance of and high dependence upon the visible edifice and the accompanying paucity of sanction for the same from within the creeds, doctrines, and religious apologetic.

Temple Ethos and the Functions of Temple

Given the paucity of a proper apologetic for temple within most of the traditions in either religion, what then is a temple ethos? What are the legitimate functions of temple in these major faiths, given their prominence in the larger religious landscape? By "ethos" we mean a temple world or the aggregate of functions that religious temples, their structures, symbols, artifacts, professionals and frequenters fulfill.

The Spiritual

In most temple contexts, "power-protection" is intimately associated with temple function, both in terms of establishing or maintaining sacred space, rites of protection against malevolent powers or vindictive deities, rituals of blessing, and celebration of festivals of gratitude for such power-protection or other provision. The temple is also a pointer to the divine, whether in a pantheistic, animistic, monistic, or monotheistic context. Correspondingly, temple represents encounter with the divine or transcendent. God means to meet with his people—in a particular place and time. Temple usually expresses the nexus of this intention. Temple is both symbolically and concretely the center of worship. This speaks directly to the inherent inclination towards idolatry within any temple ethos, for the closer one gets to the physical center of worship, the greater the temptation to worship the pointers to the divine rather than the true object to which the signs, symbols, and structures point (see Nicalo Tannenbaum's anthropological study of the Sham of rural north Thailand, 1995).

The Religious

Temple is the centerpiece of a religious society's rites and rituals, whether of birth, marriage, death, or a host of other critical festivals, celebrations that tie the temporal to the eternal, the immanent to the transcendent, and the menial to the meaningful. Temple is the grand intermediary between the *laos* (masses) and the holy, both in terms of place and people. For all temple institutions have a temple mount or sanctified ground and a temple class or religious professionals who are set apart for holy practices to which the masses are not granted access. This is a *sine qua non*, it seems, of most established religion. Temple is often the fountainhead of religious instruction, from which emanates the conserving elements of religious belief, the reinforcing of primary tenets. Temple represents institutionalization of the religion. In this sense, by its grandeur and prominence it speaks to the permanence and stability of the religion. Its attendant professional class of priests, monks, and clergy manifests its durability, the assurance of staying power over the generations. Temple generally elicits a sacrificial system, whether propitiatory/soteriological or simply pragmatic and self-perpetuating, extracting resources from the populace to maintain its physical plant and operations. Lastly, temple is a house for the god and therefore a domestication of deity; put crudely, a manageable and convenient holy place to set perimeters about our creator, protector, provider, judge, and savior.

The Sociocultural

Temple has as much a social meaning and function as a spiritual or religious one. It is a community center, often used for more than strictly religious functions, yet making sacred the secular by virtue of its primary associations with the transcendent. As such, temple represents social continuity, permanence, stability. Destroy the temple and you have often cut the lifeline of the community's very identity and survival. Even the poorest rural communities in temple societies have scrounged up the resources to erect their own religious edifice, as much for their own social cohesion and identity as out of religious obligation to local or transcendent deities. As David Gellner points out, temple is also a center of learning, specifically moral instruction and this especially for the socialization of the society's younger generation (Gellner 2001). Temples generally reflect local art, architecture, and hence culture. The most ready expression of local cultural art forms can be found in the temple architecture and artifacts within the compound.

The Anthropological

From a social-relations standpoint, the temple is itself a statement of position, place, prestige, and hierarchy, and distinguishing of every member of the society by strata in relation to the holy, whether by age, gender, disability/deformity, ethnicity, or vocation. The physical layout of the entire temple vicinity and internal structure distinguishes one group from another in general access to or restriction from the holy. The power of place is intuitive in any temple structure.

The Political

The imposing presence of a highly visible religious structure says something about the political establishment of any society. State sanction must be present for temple to function openly and appropriately. Where a society has politically agreed to pluralistic expressions of religion, multiple temple systems can vie for or appeal to niche populations. But in most cases, the society's political establishment has tended to favor the prevailing and historic religious tradition, often in symbiotic fashion. Separation of church and state is not the historic pattern, and even where this has been established, there is rarely a long sustaining of such an ideal. There is in the history of religion within nation-states a nexus between nationalism and national religion that has fueled both trenchant resistance to any religious competitors as well as some of the severest nationalistic conflicts. As such, temple often embodies a negative extension of the domination system of the political establishment. This is also reflective of the unseen domination system of demonic powers, which will use religious hierarchies to oppress people.

The Economic

The property and industry associated with elaborate temple structures has been wittingly or otherwise erected and supported by the poorest of peoples throughout history. Karl Marx was incensed with the manner in which religion, from his perspective, was rightly caricatured as the one institution that by default never gave back, a kind of economic black hole, and the temple at its center presented the greatest expenditures of energy and expense. These structures are then maintained through equally elaborate systems of temple collections, ritual ceremony costs, and especially the support of its professional clergy/priesthood.

Attention is not given here to gross social and sexual abuses of temple systems, which have indeed occurred within every temple milieu over time, and which might rightly be considered as part and parcel of the long-term implications of temple institutionalization within religiously corruptible systems. Within this consideration is also the presence of the demonic in a particularly religious garb—a religious spirit that is clearly part of the domination system that strips dignity and destroys humanity through the use of religious symbolism, strictures, and open oppression.

To conclude, there is wide diversity in the function of temples across the religious spectrum, but these functions fall largely within the social, religious, and anthropological or cultural spheres. The following sections will deal with whether Buddhism and Christianity have a temple ethos and what the answers will mean for missiology. While temples function at these various levels in most religious contexts, can common ground be found between Buddhist understandings, expectations, and assumptions and the temple understanding of contemporary Christian church and mission?

Is There a Buddhist Temple Ethos?

In the typical encyclopedia of religions, the index entry for Buddhist temple contains far more occurrences of illustrations/photographs than actual textual references. It seems the institution is appreciated for its aesthetics far more than defended for its religious function. What was the founder's position and conditioning in this regard? Much of the history and pilgrimage of the Gautama Buddha has mythical qualities and is anecdotal, but it is common knowledge that a significant part of Siddhartha's maturation was in juxtaposition to the sixth-century-BCE Indian animisms and pantheon. The shrines, temples, and millions of attendant gods of his Hindu homeland were in large part the cause of the Buddha's early launch into an atheistic philosophy of high ethics and contemplative detachment. He established the community—the *sangha*—of followers very late in life and seems to have given little thought or preparation to the inevitable institutionalization of a religion.

From the Theravada core and reflected in most other Buddhist traditions, temples provide the most consistent visible connection for the *sangha*—community of those entered upon the Middle Way of merit making toward enlightenment—in their practice of contact with holy things (other holy things including *sutras* (chanted texts), *stupas* (monuments), Buddhist statues, ancestors, deities, and spirits) (Earhart 1993, 924). The scholarly portrayal of Buddhism in most streams/ traditions is largely unapologetic for the encrustations of local animisms that normally accrue to the temple system. While technically Buddha is not a god, there is worship of the Buddha and often a wide array of local deities and spirits supported within most temple systems. For example, in references to both Chinese and Japanese systems, temples are by definition the residence of god(s) or Buddhist divinities, represented by statues and revered through scripture recitations, offerings, and rituals (ibid 1071, 1185). The temple in Buddhist religious life is connected with the almost-omnipresent monastic orders. In this case, it is the representative, material setting apart the holy from the unholy, the residence and retreat for those on the path toward enlightenment, and especially the locus of the teaching of the Buddhist way, for the monk is not only a meditative pilgrim but also connected to the laity through the function of teaching, and the temple is the primary location for this activity.

The placement or location of the temple within the village has always been strategic, balancing the taboos of power and place with the central role the temple has in civic life, standing apart from the clustered houses, yet the hub of village life (Earhart 1993, 927). Temples have for centuries been the favored place for religious functions as well as generic community gatherings.

Of course the ritual life of the Buddhist community is attended by the temple and most crucial celebrations and commemorations: annual festivals and entreaties, holy days, rites of passage like ordination, and preeminently those rites surrounding death, are all attached to temple proceedings and location. At the popular level, one veteran missionary, based on decades of work in Southeast Asia, affirmed that for many Buddhists the two primary means of making merit are: (1) going to temple, and (2) building temples, since this is so money intensive and therefore exacting such sacrifice, and then so impressive that the hope is some merit for the life to come has been achieved. This is reminiscent of popular-level Roman Catholic Church behavior before the Reformation and throughout many corners of the more conservative RCC world even today. Merit making as centered on a temple ethos seems frighteningly close to the aberrations we point to within the Christendom model of church: facility intensive and eliciting all the wrong motivations and activities for favor with God.

Another latent function of temples, not apparent in the standard presentation of the religion but introduced indirectly in the discussion of its missionary nature (and hence, the outer borders of the religion's demographic centers), is the visible, territorial placement of temples as representative of Buddhism's expansion. The Burmese have proudly maintained that Myanmar is "the Land of a Million Pagodas"—clearly a statement of Buddhism's omnipresence in the culture and the value placed on physical reminders of this almost-imperial territoriality. When dealing with Buddhism's expansion into the West and other traditionally non-Buddhist arenas, the numbers of temples are prominent as indicators of relative acceptance of, or resistance to, the new religion, similar to the notion of receptivity to Christianity by the presence and number of visible church buildings (i.e., South Korea). Max Weber in his study of religions distinguished between emissary, promissory, and commissary missionary activities, based on the degree of pressure with which the obligation to convert others is felt within the religion (Weber 1951). Buddhism would fit within the emissary category, where Christianity would fit the promissory, and Islam the commissary. As an emissary missionary religion, Buddhism highlights the establishing of a presence and minimizing differences between one's own religion and the religion one encounters while retaining commitment to the tradition. It could be debated whether in fact, due to this more pliable nature, Buddhism "assumed a national form to a far greater extent than missionary religions of the promissory or commissary types" (Sharma 1993, 129). And the argument might work the other direction when East Asia's nationalized Buddhist traditions capitulated to the advance of communism in the twentieth century. But of these three world religions, it seems that history bears out that Buddhism is the most accommodating.

From a survey of the role of temples in different contexts such as Nepal, Thailand, and Japan, different Buddhist societies and subcultures have developed differing models of use for temples, so that generalizations can be problematic. Yet as cited in the list of overall functions, there is a broad commonality among these very different contexts in: domestication of the religion, a centralizing and stabilizing social force or center, an association with the professional religious class and duties of the community to support the religious cults, a strong sense of power-protection and spiritual space or territory, the primary locus of communal rites and rituals, and a house or shrine for the local deity (or deities).

There is an almost-universal temple/monastery presence within Buddhism, yet the religious literature does not give it pride of place or even a solid apologetic. It seems to have become a sociological necessity in bolstering the institutional Buddhism and the staying power of the religious system accruing to it.

Is There a Christian Temple Ethos?

Merriam Webster defines "church" as, first, a building, especially for Christian public worship. What exactly are we saying if we seek an answer to the question, "Is Christianity a temple religion?" Posing the question this way is, in a sense, unfair, since religion and even Christianity is being inserted as part of the equation. This is intentional, of course, as temple has emerged as a fundamentally institutionalizing force across religions. Most pietistic followers of Christ recoil from the notion that Christianity is even a religion. Andrew Walls draws a word picture of the two competing tendencies within Christianity—one toward domestication and rootedness and the other a more pilgrim or missionary impulse (Walls 1996, 51–54). Others such as Ralph Winter and Art Glasser, both of whom taught at Fuller's School of World Mission, made a similar distinction between the modality (the local/congregational) versus sodality (the more missional/outward-moving) structures in Christendom.

In answer to the question of a Christian temple ethos, we proceed from three points: (1) Biblically, we can find evidence against a physical temple continuity in the NT (see Fig. 1). (2) Theologically, there is both strong NT support for a temple reality in the essence of the church and scant support for the "temple" as it is attached to "church" in the popular mind. (3) Practically, in the general population there is wide acceptance of a temple ethos attached to the physical structure and activities of the institutional church.

Ironically or sensibly, both Buddhist and Christian religious histories hold up the founder as iconoclast, introducing into their heavily institutionalized and religiously corrupt environs radical new communities, recognizable not by an alternative institution but by a lifestyle and vital community, a fellowship or followership to the founder. Over time the community, gaining acceptability through a fiery trial of persecution, establishing moral credibility and numerical growth, ultimately became an institutionally sanctioned center of the originally antagonistic society, domesticating its radicalness in structures that increasingly drew separation between the holy and the unholy. This happened until the faithful associated the religious experience with the physical symbol, revisiting the very institutional nominality from which the founders recoiled. In this sense Christianity and Buddhism do, negatively, share a certain temple ethos.

The simple chart below portrays the proximity in the histories of critical elements to the emergence and sustaining of a temple ethos in both religious traditions.

Other parallels and contrasts can be drawn between the common understandings and functions of temples in various Buddhist traditions and those within Christian "church" counterparts. Within each religion, there is vast disparity among different traditions/denominations on the meaning of the temple. For the proper roots of Christian self-understanding of temple, we turn to a biblical—Old and New Testament (OT/NT)—survey.

"Temple" Posture	Buddhism	Christianity
Theological underpinnings	Ambiguity or silence	Ambiguity or silence
Founder	Rejection/ discontinuity	Replacement/ continuity ...discontinuity
New order	Creation of new community: sangha	Creation of new community: church
Popular culture and clergy	Necessity by accommodation	Necessity with tacit theological embrace

Figure 1: Contrast of temple ethos

A Biblical Survey of Temple

This overview of the biblical material on the topic will emphasize the establishment of temple in relation to its roots in the tabernacle system, Christ's treatment of the temple, Stephen's trial, the Apostle Paul's ecclesiology, other dominant NT motifs drawing upon temple language and symbolism, and overarching conclusions.

Old Testament Tabernacle and Temple Systems

How did the temple *cultus* come into being for the Israelite people? The temple has all its roots in the tabernacle system associated with the Exodus and the large worshiping community of Israel en route to the Promised Land. The entire episode on Mt. Sinai originates from the initiative of a sovereign YHWH, intent on saving a people for himself, so that all the nations under heaven might come to know him. Only after the tabernacle had been in use traversing the wilderness with the pilgrim people and entering the land, do kings, themselves symbolic of a move against the original intent of their rightful King (1 Sam 8:6–8), seek a permanent resting place for their deity, coterminous with their own need for kingly palaces (see 2 Sam 7:4–11). In this second passage there is ironic juxtaposition between God's own understanding of a distinction between the temple (a "house") and the tent (tabernacle) as well as between his resistance of domestication and his intent to bring his people to a place of peaceful rest and residence. God is not only clear in his response that there is, and never has been, a need to house him; he also turns the discussion back to the people and their king, whom he has moved, both out of Egypt as well as from pasture to throne room. God views Israel's need to house him as a mere reflection of their own need for stability and rootedness. While he calls his people into a Sabbath rest, there is little indication that God desires the people to settle permanently in one place. This contradicts God's grander purposes for the nations, and might render the people complacent or, in the end, superciliously religious.

At the dedication of Solomon's temple there appears to be an odd understanding that this mighty and costly project is really a practice in some futility since, in the prayer of dedication, Solomon acknowledges the impossibility of a human creation housing its Creator (see 2 Chr 2:6; 6:18). The OT ends with Malachi's prophetic words: "'My name will be great among the nations, from where the sun rises to where it sets. In every place incense and pure offerings will be brought to me, because my name will be great among the nations,' says the LORD Almighty" (Mal 1:11). This contrasts dramatically with God's reserved right to uproot and "make . . . a byword . . . among all peoples" the very temple that was to house his name at the dedication of Solomon, if the people rejected his kingship and squandered their vocation as a light to the nations (2 Chr 7:20). But the censorship of Israel's missed calling is clear; the functions of the temple will in the end be uprooted and flung to the very ends of the earth—somewhere in Malachi's future—so that God's missionary impulse, his original sanction for the Jerusalem temple, will be satisfied.

Christ's Treatment of and Relationship to the Temple

The synagogue, introduced into the life of the people of God by necessity between the two testaments during their exile from the Holy Land, needs brief mention here. Synagogue is a kind of halfway house or an extension of some of the temple functions within an exilic era people of God. It carries a vestige of the "holy place" (with holy men, literature, times, practices) for those who are separated from the original. It houses the word of God without the Ark of the Covenant. Its primary function is social and instructional; the place of reading, revering, and listening to exposition of the Torah as the community of God in a non-temple construct. It could not be seen in the numinous or celebrative and redemptive functions of the temple system, especially in regard to the sacrificial system. It was the primary form of meeting place which Jesus, entering ministry during the Roman occupation and traversing the countryside (while coming up to the temple on specially holy days), exploited in his ministry years for teaching and confronting the religious practice, ethic, and teaching of the Jews in his time. It was also the locus of Paul's missionary advance, as one obligated to "first to the Jew" (Rom 1:16), but also became at times the center of his general teaching/ discipling ministry. Although it is also clear that Paul did not make any connection between the establishing of the church(es) in his missionary journeys and the synagogue of the Jewish diaspora. It might be seen, explicitly or more often implicitly, as a sort of model of congregational church life in practice (structure and functions), whereas temple is viewed often as the archetypal model of church in its spiritual life.

How did the coming of Messiah bear on temple in the Judeo-Christian continuum? What was Christ's interaction with the Jewish temple of his time, and what was his particular vocation when it comes to any subsequent dealings with temple? As an ecumenical evangelical, Wright is a first-class historian of Jewish first-century expectations and the political and religious milieu into which Christ emerged announcing the reign of God. He convincingly portrays Christ's vocation as largely centered on the controversies of the Torah and the temple and his intent to both fulfill and replace the entire temple system with himself. Jesus' encounter with the woman at the well is deep with symbolism pertaining to his mission and calling. His radical approach to women, Samaritans, and the immoral is all captured in this one brief conversation. Yet the passage unveils in parallel fashion his regard for the temple as a cosmic expression of God's communion with humanity and how his vocation was to eclipse the entire institution. The woman's apparently diversionary side trail into discussion of places of worship allowed Jesus an excursus on his messiahship in the context of temple and worship. For her, the popular Jewish myth held that worship was a matter of place and event; for Jesus, it was soon to be, indeed already present, a matter much more of spirit and truth.

The temple was of course, in this period, the heart and center of Judaism, the vital symbol around which everything else circled. It was the center of Israel's national and political life: the chief priests who were in charge of it were also, in company with the shaky Herodian dynasty and under Roman supervision, in charge of the whole nation. Furthermore, the temple carried all kinds of royal overtones (Wright 1999, 62–63).

> Though Jesus' action in the Temple must naturally be seen within this wider context of disaffection, it goes way beyond it into a different dimension. His attitude to the Temple was not "this institution needs reforming," nor "the wrong people are running this place," nor yet "piety can function elsewhere too." His deepest belief regarding the Temple was eschatological: the time had come for God to judge the entire institution. It had come to symbolize the injustice that characterized the society on the inside and the outside, the rejection of the vocation to be the light of the world, the city set on a hill that would draw to itself all the peoples of the world . . . During his Galilean ministry, Jesus acted and spoke as if he was in some sense called to do and be what the Temple was and did. His offer of forgiveness, with no prior condition of Temple-worship or sacrifice, was the equivalent of someone in our world offering

as a private individual to issue someone else a passport or a driver's license . . . [The destroyed temple] would be followed by the establishment of the messianic community focused on Jesus himself that would replace the Temple once and for all . . . And all this judgment-with-finality was directly in line with the tradition of the prophets, especially Jeremiah. When we allow these positive symbols to generate a larger picture of Jesus' intentions, we find once again that the focal point of it all is the Temple" (ibid, 64–66, 70).

Jesus' temple action, the casting out of the money changers and their trade in religion, was much more than angry reaction to religious oppression or misuse of the house of prayer, though these were utterly pertinent. It was also highly symbolic of all Jesus had come to do by way of judgment and issuing in God's new messianic order through his people. Jesus touched the very nerve of Jewish religious self-identity through his temple actions and citations, touching off a furor that culminated in his raucous trials and crucifixion. According to Walter Wink's summary of Jesus' temple action,

Jesus' death . . . exposed and annulled the whole system of sacrificial victimage, and thus terminated Temple slaughter—in short, sacred violence . . . His action was understood symbolically. It was not a "cleansing" or reform of the Temple, to restore it to pure sacrifices or to eliminate business activity from the Temple precincts . . . Jesus abolishes the pollution system maintained by the Temple through its inherent separation of the sacred and the secular. This separation worked greatly to the financial advantage of the priestly ruling elite (Mark 11:17b) . . . The violence that countless animal sacrifices were supposed to quench was never satisfied . . . The church understood his act [Jesus' crucifixion] as a sacrifice to end all sacrifices that exposed the scapegoating mechanism for all the world to see (Wink 1992, 125–6).

Consider then this connecting thread from the early days of his ministry to the early years of the NT church: Jesus' claim to lordship over the Sabbath and superiority over the temple in the context of

God's desire for "mercy, not sacrifice" (Matt 12:7). Jesus' denunciation of routine temple business, and his violent temple clearing (Matt 21; Mark 11; Luke 19; John 2). Jesus' minimizing the temple's glory and declaration of divine judgment (Mark 13:2; Luke 21:5–6). Jesus' bold claim to replace the judged temple system with a temple of his own making (John 2:19). Jesus' rebuke of the domestication and robbery of God over against the temple's original purpose of international prayer and blessing (Mark 11:17). The trial of Jesus in which various claims were made to his intention to destroy the temple (Matt 26:61; Mark 14:58). The mockery at the scene of the crucifixion by various ones about Jesus' claim to destroy the temple and in three days restore it (Matt 27:40). The tearing of the temple curtain at the moment of Jesus' death, the symbolic destruction or making redundant of the holy of holies through the once-for-all shed blood of the eternal covenant (Matt 27:51). The trouble that Stephen and Paul got into with Jewish authorities over temple actions or statements of judgment (Acts 6:13–14; 21:28; 24:6).

Stephen's Defense and Martyrdom

Stephen's sermon, taken in context, is a simple defense before the Sanhedrin of his personal stance on the issue of the temple. He had been lumped together with Jesus as one who spoke against "this holy place." The circuitous reiteration of Israel's history, with which his hearers were at least as familiar as anyone else in Israel, almost constitutes a death wish on his part for its studied departure from the cherished temple myth of the Sanhedrin and popular Jewish religious imagination. Of course, having a Greek name might not have helped his situation, but Stephen perfunctorily aligned himself with his new Messiah and rendered the temple obsolete, not on some personal bias but rather on the very history of this chosen people's God.

Among the recurring themes of Stephen's sermon are the appearances and visitations of God and the inability of God's people to grasp their intent. All the examples given have a direct bearing on the answer Stephen was to give regarding his stance on the temple. Foreigners are everywhere throughout the chapter. God is meeting his people en route, emphasizing the pilgrim nature of this faith. There is very little in the sermon about the beloved temple itself, which is the focal point of his defense. Stephen seems intentionally to be drawing attention to the nations other than Israel, the divine encounters other than in the temple, the lands beyond the Promised Land. Why? Because God is not the God of Israel only but of the nations; his sovereign designs lie anywhere people will truly and spiritually worship him. The temple—read election—was not the end but the means to a far grander end, God's glory and worship among all peoples. Is it ironic that immediately after Stephen's high-profile martyrdom, over the redefinition of the place of the holy away from the inviolate temple *cultus* within Jerusalem, the community of Christians emptied out into the surrounding countryside under the weight of a fresh outburst of persecution and irreversibly altered the demographics of the faith into an international dispersion and mission?

In his excellent commentary, *The Message of Acts*, John Stott notes that "Stephen is seen by some as showing a bias towards the tabernacle [versus the latter temple] because it was mobile. But he expresses neither a preference for the tabernacle nor a distaste for the temple. For both were constructed in accordance with God's will" (Stott 1990, 138). Stephen's sermon allows, contra Stott, for a clear distinction between what God instituted in the impermanent or mobile tabernacle ethos, and the intent of finding a dwelling place or house for the divine in that of the temple.

Three observations need to be made in this regard. First, while Stephen does not seem to favor one form over the other, he clearly rehearses the divine dictates regarding the building of the original tabernacle as well as its mobile status, within the context of a message dominated by the superiority of a God who is ever-present among his people, especially regardless of their location in relation to the holy as a religious grounding.

Secondly, the claim that both the temple and the tabernacle were constructed in accordance with God's will is not, at least evenly, supported. The construction of the tabernacle is unequivocally, start to finish, a divinely initiated program (Ex 25–27). The temple, conversely, is recorded as the brainchild of King David, who doubtless sincerely desired a better house for God than the by-then old and well-worn temporary structure resident at Shiloh. The erection of a "more substantial and permanent" (ibid.) dwelling place for God can be tied directly to the monarchy, which itself had been resisted by God as an acquiescence to pagan nationalisms and a subversion of his own kingship (Deut 17:14–20; 1 Sam 8:5–9). The temple did indeed become a structure in which God was willing to continue to "put his name" (2 Kings 21:4,7; 2 Chr 33:7) or even to dwell, in a manner of speaking, yet the caveat always remained that this was a far cry from the uniqueness of a deity who is Creator of all and whose dwelling is always first and foremost within and among people.

Lastly, Stephen never actually mentions the temple. He has been asked to defend the accusation as to whether he, apparently like Christ, has spoken "against this holy place" (Acts 6:13). But he instead goes into a lengthy excursus on the divine source of the tabernacle, only alluding to the later temple founding as a substandard ("the Most High does not live in houses made by human hands," 7:48) and decidedly human attempt to find a "dwelling place" (7:47) for him whose hands have made all these things.

Early Church Ecclesiology and Pastoral NT Temple Theology

In a discussion on the cessation of OT sacrifices, Walter Wink delivers another blow to the temple system:

> Paul is, in very short order, speaking of the body of Christ as a new temple of which believers are individually members. But if our own personal or corporate bodies can be thought of as temples of the Holy Spirit (1 Cor 6:19–20), or if we can present our bodies as living sacrifices to God (Rom 12:1), what further use is the Temple? If Jesus has died, once for all, to free us from sin, then the Temple is superfluous, superceded. Jesus' death is the end of ritual sacrifice. When he dies, the curtain before the Holy of Holies is torn from top to bottom (Mark 15:38), a symbolic statement of the exhaustion of the Temple's holy powers. Spiritual sacrifice has taken the place of animal slaughter (1 Pet 2:5). God desires mercy, not sacrifice (Matt 9:13;12:7; Hos 6:6). (Wink 1992, 124).

Paul indeed tied his doctrine of the church to the historic temple of the people of God. But this he did very much in the vein of Christ's and Stephen's precedents. There is a simple path one can take in the discovery of Paul's emergent ecclesiology, and that is his conversion. This first personal interchange between a heavenly Christ and the persecutor of the same, earthly Christ, is the most basic building block for an ecclesiology that speaks of the church as, first, the body of Christ. Paul physically persecuted and imprisoned real bodies, and was taught at his conversion that this was in fact the body of Christ. This was an incarnational ecclesiology, filled with metaphors of a flesh-and-blood, dynamic, and immanent nature. But, secondly, it was the temple of God as a radical, new spiritual entity (i.e., people). This presented a whole new understanding of edifice, which is again dynamic, living, mobile, universal, and local; a building in process under the sovereign hand of God himself, not remotely of any human construction and built solely upon the foundation of Christ.

When we approach the great treatment of the Jewish faith in the context of the NT (Hebrews), we're faced with further discontinuity. There is no mention of the temple in the entire book, much of which is devoted directly to temple functions and their interpretation into the new covenant community. Interestingly, seven out of ten NT usages of the world "tabernacle" are to be found in Hebrews (mostly in Heb 8–9). Five of the six NT usages of "sanctuary" are in Hebrews (6–9). Sixteen out of thirty instances of "covenant" and twenty-seven of seventy-one NT instances of "priest" are also in the book.

The entire discussion of Jesus' high priestly role after the order of Melchizedek is a lengthy excursus on the circumventing of the temple establishment to show the extent of the blessings of the pre-and post-temple priesthood of Christ. Where Jews would have been inclined to associate priesthood with the localized temple system, the writer of Hebrews painstakingly separates these two, in order to grant a better covenant for a much larger constituency, those who could not celebrate the Jerusalem faith and fulfill its sacrificial requirements.

When the familiar temple practices are visited in Hebrews, they are cast further backward into the pre-temple, tabernacle *cultus*. And the purpose of the discussion seems to point to the sanctifying of those very things, places, and people that have no access to the holy place. Sacrifices of the fixed temple are replaced by the sacrifice of praising lips and selfless sharing with others. The enduring city of Jerusalem and the stability of its temple court are unsure, replaced by the hope of an eternal city yet to come, and the scandal of Christ's scapegoat sacrifice is to be embraced by all those who go with him outside the gate—for true sanctification. Note especially Hebrews 13:10–16.

The Apocalypse and Temple-Tabernacle Revisitations

There is a fascinating capsule on the whole distinction between tabernacle and temple, in the final episode of John's revelation, in which God's new, or rather renewed, creative order is being introduced. "And I heard a loud voice from the throne saying, 'Look! God's dwelling place [tabernacle] is now among the people, and he will dwell with them. They will be his people, and God himself will be with them and be their God'" (Rev 21:3).

After a lengthy and glorious description of the new Jerusalem, coming down out of heaven from God (Rev. 21:2), John makes the point that "I did not see a *temple* in the city, because the Lord God Almighty and the Lamb are its temple. The city does not need the sun or the moon to shine on it, for the glory of God gives it light, and the Lamb is its lamp" (Rev 21:22–23; emphasis added).

While the *skene* of God, his mobile dwelling, is come in among men, eternally, the *naos* of God, his shrine or temple, is not to be seen, since God Almighty and the Lamb are its permanent structure and establishment. Walter Wink elucidates:

> In the New Jerusalem, according to Revelation 21 and 22, there will be no temple, no altar, no sacrifice (21:22), even though the imagery of those chapters draws directly from Isaiah 60, where the wealth of the nations flows to Jerusalem specifically to beautify the sanctuary. The offering of sacrifice was a universal rite in the religions of the ancient world—so much so that the church's refusal to perform sacrifices brought down upon it the curious charge of "atheism." (Wink 1992, 125)

Read this story now with early Christian eyes, and what do we find? That the temple, for all its importance and centrality within Judaism, was after all a signpost to the reality, and the reality was the resurrected son of David, who was the Son of God. God, in other words, is not ultimately to dwell in a human-built temple, a timber-and-stone house.

God will indeed dwell with his people, allowing his glory and mystery to tabernacle in their midst, but the only appropriate way for him to do this will not be through a building but through believing human beings, redeemed *imago Dei*.

Jesus—and then, very quickly, Jesus' people—were now the true temple, and the actual building in Jerusalem was thereby redundant, and, incidentally, destroyed. We must remind ourselves, crucially, that the temple was, after all, the central incarnational symbol of Judaism. The temple was the place where heaven and earth actually interlocked, where the living God had promised to be present with his people.

Jesus, at the very center of his vocation, believed himself called to do and be in relation to Israel what, in Scripture and Jewish belief, the temple was and did. He, rather than the temple, was the place where, and the means by which, the living God was present with Israel (Wright 1999, 110–11).

Is Christianity a Temple Religion?

The original question that troubled my pastor friend, "Where are your temples?" challenges Christians as well. If we answer this question in the negative, what exactly are we saying? In fact, we can answer strongly in the affirmative: that there is a temple remaining for the people of God upon which the entire negative assertion is predicated. 1 Corinthians 3:17 promises God's judgment on anyone—in this age—who destroys God's temple! Yet in this rendering the temple has moved from Jerusalem to Corinth, from edifice to populace, from ritual to *koinonia*—in Paul's message.

In the negative, we cite the following by way of an overwhelming NT transition. The temple belongs to Jesus as God's Messiah: "My house will be called a house of prayer for all nations" (Mark 11:17), "my father's business" (Luke 2:49 KJV), "my father's house" (Luke 2:49; John 2:16). Jesus is "greater than the temple" from the outset (Matt 12:6). Jesus is the temple: his body in particular is the new temple, as he stated in code before his questioning disciples and critics (John 2:18-22). By way of extrapolation, when Paul maintains for the Colossians that in Christ all the fullness of the Godhead dwells in bodily form (Col 1:19; 2:9), he's paralleling John's statements of incarnation (John 1:14)—the Word, equal to God, becoming flesh and tabernacling among us. And in John 10:30 and 14:9, Jesus declared: "I and the Father are one;" "Anyone who has seen me has seen the Father." Jesus declared with some finality God's judgment on the physical temple (Mark 13:2). "Your house is left to you desolate" (Matt 23:38). Jesus' victory over the forces of darkness at the moment of his death was accompanied by the great sign of the cessation of the temple barrier in terms of access to God, the rending of the temple curtain, the great separation of the people from the Most Holy Place and the great clergy-laity divide of high priest and the common faithful (Matt 27:51; Mark 15:38; Luke 23:45).

Jesus' body is his church: (1) he identifies fully (and twice) with his incarnation in earth post-Pentecost in Saul's radical and unforgettable conversion experience (Acts 9); and (2) Paul later with groups like the Corinthians—for all of their carnality and internal conflicts—was bold to declare them "now" the body of Christ and, almost in the same breath, remind them they are the temple of the Holy Spirit (1 Cor 12). The church is the temple of God in this age. First, in 1 Corinthians 3:16–17 the Corinthians (plural) are warned of God's judgment on those who destroy the temple, which is now to be understood as the church ("you")—don't destroy God's temple, the church! Paul's entire context here is the history of his own church planting, apostolic ministry, as a master builder of the church of God in Corinth and Asia, building the church on the foundation stone, Christ. Corinth was a pagan temple paradise, much like Athens, with its myriad gods, shrines, etc., and much like modern Asia's tenacious temple cultures. Second, in 1 Corinthians 6:19 the believers are reminded that their personal bodies are the "temples of the Holy Spirit, who is in you." In 2 Corinthians 6:16, Paul again states emphatically, "We are the temple of the living God." Lastly, in Ephesians 2:21, Paul's treatise on the church in this seminal epistle again sees the church as dynamic, in process, and rising into or becoming a "holy temple in the Lord."

Our edifice complex cannot find NT sanction, but rather seems to demonstrate a reversion to a subset of OT pre-messianic understandings. Our terminology has been misleading: "sanctuary," strictly derived from the temple system; "altar," reflecting OT altar attachments; "Lord's table," erecting a physical locus for what was to be a memorializing of Jesus' death at every meal shared by disciples; "going to church," a come-to structure, a local place associated with meetings together and with God (through corporate worship); "Bethel temple," naming our buildings instead of ourselves as the locus of meeting with God through a priest; "cathedral," deriving in the Latin from "chair" or the bishop's official throne; "going into a time of worship," completely alien to NT (or even OT) parlance or commitments (Rom 12:1–2; John 4). The use of this terminology is not merely cosmetic or semantic idiosyncrasy; it moves the general understanding of the meeting of God with his people and his "re"presentation on earth away from human flesh and back into physical edifices, which can never house the presence of God. It is a completely inadequate attempt at something God has made ample provision for, in the incarnation of his Son through his body the church. So it empowers inanimate objects with divine function while stripping the body of its proper and divine role in the earth. This has to be damaging to both body life and to witness, for the world has grown at least as accustomed as the church to thinking of church as primarily visible human institution and structures as opposed to an incendiary, organic, and mobile fellowship. Of course practically the costs to an edifice-dependent temple Christendom and therefore to mission have been almost immeasurable when taken together.

Philosophically, though, this thesis does not throw down the gauntlet before all traditional, visible church structures. That will at least have to wait for further insight and much more careful study of both Scripture and church history. After all, we're never able to overgeneralize on a religious system that has survived more than two millennia. We are, rather, after the heart of a question that might take the church out of its captivity to a Euro-American Christendom and into a renewed opportunity to actually touch all of humanity, not simply a "little raft" of an elect enclosed within four walls.

There is also the issue of worship and the consideration of cultural predispositions to worship in place. Encounter is a fundamental assumption of any true worship. Historically people look religiously to the numinous within specific time and specific space. This would surely be explanation for the propensity among Christians to rename their crude or grand physical structures after the pattern provided by God to his OT people. And there is genuine room for that propensity within the framework we're dealing with here. The catch has been what sort of structure and limitations attend to the choices we have traditionally made in erecting local edifices to temple our experience.

The first question in a comparative religious study between the Christian and Buddhist contexts might be, given the fundamental tenets of Buddhism, what/whom exactly do Buddhists worship? The function of temple for Buddhists may be much more sociological than purely religious when filtered through the actual teachings and practices of the *sangha*. A theological consideration here is the profane/sacred dualism from which we are all seeking to recover in a postmodern renaissance. A theology of the kingdom, of common grace, and of living all of life *coram deo*—before the face of God—tends us away from isolated or demarcated experiences of the holy, either in time or in space, and rather toward the routinization of the holy within the profane; the sanctifying of all of creation to the King to whom it all rightfully belongs through both creation and redemption. Salt and light speak to this interpenetration of the holy within/among, even overwhelming, the common.

Paul's treatment of the early church as the clear replacement of the Jerusalem temple (right around the time of its physical destruction in fulfillment of Jesus' words) seems to relate directly to this routinization or habituation of the holy. God has established this new society as his "holy nation," sanctified through the blood of Christ, to declare the praises of him (1 Pet 2:9)—indeed wherever they find themselves, and, in this vein, as the true, contemporary temple of God, radically decentralizing the meeting or the "holy place" into a countless number literally filling the earth. It may be reminiscent of Joshua's conquering of the land of Canaan, since God had promised that anywhere he placed his feet would be his in God's name (Josh 1:3).

Jesus' treatment of the issue of the proper nature of worship with the woman at the well anticipates the same: a time is coming—and is now—when people will worship neither in this mountain nor in Jerusalem, but in spirit and in truth. This is a discussion of the matter of location of worship, and Jesus both universalizes and trivializes location by his response. God is after true worshipers for whom location is utterly irrelevant on the one hand and properly/potentially universal on the other. This would be good news to a despised Samaritan, and indeed to all those outside the prickly, rather formidable system of hurdles for acceptability within the Jerusalem establishment. When Jesus was in

Jerusalem on his final Passover pilgrimage—to become the Passover—certain Greeks came to his disciples with an innocent enough request: "We would like to see Jesus" (John 12:21). To which Jesus, as though suddenly galvanized, responds: "The hour has come for the Son of Man to be glorified" (v. 23). All the other hours were misplaced, but this is the hour. Why? Because with these Greeks coming into Jerusalem and seeking an audience with the true temple of God, we now have an embarking upon the great globalization of the faith. All must be drawn to the Son; he must be lifted up—now. The experience of God is simply too limiting if confined to Jerusalem; there are only so many Greeks (read *goyim* or outsiders) who can be expected to make the pilgrimage (this is not a pilgrimage faith). We must make this quest for a sight of Jesus universally answerable. He is to be humanity's perennial (read time) and universal (read apostolic/catholic/place) Passover.

If the church is the re-incarnation of Jesus, which we may robustly maintain in our ecclesiology, then if it is anything, it is accessible. When the Word became flesh, it did not temple among us but tabernacled among us. The difference is simple: the tabernacle was the mobile vehicle of the practiced presence of God, moving with the cloud and fire of God's designs beyond the horizons of the people's imagination and settledness. "We have seen" (John 1:14), or as John says in his epistle, "we were witnesses" (1 John 1:1) with all of our senses of, this perfect self-disclosure of God. But now, as John so clearly reminds us, we are the primary remaining self-disclosure of God in the world—indeed, in the whole world (contra Christ's limitation to Palestine)—1 John 4:12. In fact, 1 John is the "as he is" book in Scripture. In this world, we are "as he is" (1 John 4:17 KJV). For all humanity to have an experience of the God we worship, the "temple" of his body must be made available everywhere and at all times. This is the rationale for saturation church planting. Worship is the root and fruit of mission, occurring within the temple of God, Christ's body, lived in and energized by his Spirit.

The more appropriate question here might be, "Is Christianity a religion?" Religious categories seem to require a temple ethos, as part of the institutionalization of any movement or sect—which Christianity does share with all other religious movements. The early church was a sect by all religious-anthropological indicators—and by popular opinion. Can we avoid the development of a temple ethos within religious movements as part of the inevitability of institutionalization? History would indicate that we cannot adequately resist institutionalization within maturing Christward movements. But this is where our theological understandings of "temple" need to impinge upon our understandings of movement and maturation; there is growing widespread reaction to the degree of ossification and institutionalism within Christian denominations and movements. These tendencies might be summarized in two dominant dynamics common to much religious history: (1) The separation of the laity from professional religious class in the supposed interests of "leadership" and continuity—an often unwitting separation of unholy from holy people. (2) The mammoth investment in and maintenance of a physical edifice as the visible center for worship—hence, a separation of the unholy from holy space—and religious symbolism within the larger community. Both of these tendencies are most clearly manifest in "the temple compound" of any religion, a perennial reminder to the people of faith of, among other things, a fundamental separation, distinction, and taboo of both place and people—to which only a few are granted full access.

If the Old and New Testaments can be distinguished by anything at all, it seems here would lie the boldest contrasts: (1) That, in Christ, the *laos* (laity) are all granted unmitigated access to holiness, to priesthood (1 Pet 2:9), to God's throne room—or "the Most Holy Place" (Heb 10:19–22); that no one individual is any longer to be elevated to "father" or "rabbi" (Matt 23:9–10; Phillips); and that leadership in the new order is granted under a titleless, character-defined criterion and universally-gifted community (1 Cor 12–14; 1 Tim 3:1). To cite Snyder's vantage point: if we take the NT on its own terms, however, and analyze its own vocabulary of ministry, we find a "resounding negation" of the assumptions underlying the professional religionist view (Snyder 1977, 84). (2) That, in Christ, the place of the holy is wherever the people gather (boldly!) in his name (Matt 18:20; Heb 10:19); that the mission of this people is to move out into the profane and sanctify it; and that forgiveness of sins and discipline of sinners (Matt 6:14–15;18:18), the sanctifying of one another (1 Cor 7:14), a pleasing sacrificial system (Rom 12:1; Heb 13:15–16; 1 Pet 2:5), prayers and intercession, appropriate worship (Rom 12:1), gifts and offerings (2 Cor 8:19; Phil 2:17) may, indeed must, be done in the context of the community of the King—not in some permanently specified or erected edifice or compound and not sanctioned by the office of professional clergy or an elevated priesthood.

Conclusion

Returning to the original question—"Where are your temples?"—in the religious expectations of Buddhists and Christians for whom the physical presence of a temple is equivalent to the center of the worshiping or religious community, we might propose the following conclusions. The question is sincere, real, and felt on both sides. From the perspective of religious sociology, it is also clear that a community of faith seeks and requires symbols and rituals that lend themselves to a temple ethos or presence. From the vantage point of power, politics, and religion, it is a fact of religious life that where the host society holds to one preeminent religious scheme, introductions of alternative missionary faiths meet with official and popular rejection or outright persecution. The host religion in most larger societies is somehow tied to state sanctions or holds a symbiotic relationship with powerful societal implications. Some Christian leaders have desired a temple ethos as a kind of territorial or symbolic "taking the land" or establishment of a critical mass for both popular appeal, visible and political clout, for the advance of religious freedom, and ultimately a voice in national life.

From the OT there is a mixed record on the Jewish temple, at least when it is compared with the introduction of the original tabernacle. The initiator, the induction, the physical makeup, the systems of maintenance, and "location" were among some of the clear contrasts, but the greatest would have to be the corruption of the latter over time and God's mounting judgment upon it. From the NT there is ample evidence within Christ's teaching, prophecy, temple action, and crucifixion, as well as Stephen's unmistakable treatise and Paul's (and Hebrews') elaborate ecclesiology of the complete replacement of the temple system and ethos in favor of first Christ himself and later the church as the new Israel and Jesus' body incarnate, achieving what the temple simply could not, in both universally accessible worshiping presence and universal priesthood.

From the history of the church we have both a witness to the power of institutional faith and gross departures from the very costly NT replacement of the whole temple system with the body of Christ. Note particularly the widespread association of church with edifice and all that this has cost the church in resource expenditure, misplaced identity, and especially the layered attachments of the holy with an underutilized and often inaccessible physical structure. I heard recently that a house church movement in China, by contrast, has issued inflammatory language to demonstrate its aversion to the Western church's love affair with church-as-building: "For every dollar spent on church buildings, a soul goes to hell." The vocabulary built up around the church buildings has more often than not paralleled the OT temple model, taking captive critical functions of the NT church life back to inanimate and pre-Calvary symbolism.

From the perspective of contextualization in mission, it seems on the face of it that church buildings and other edifices serving the Christian community would present a kind of dynamic equivalence or temple-centered worshiping communities for Buddhist-background believers. This illustrates the quandary in which much contemporary missiology has found itself, seeking culturally sensitive expressions of NT faith in other religious contexts. John Davis deals with this quandary in the final chapter of *Poles Apart* (Davis 1993, Chapter 10). The leadership of the church in many non-Western contexts has often, in the supposed interests of church growth and dynamism, accommodated its style to the prevailing leadership of the culture, only to reveal its mirroring that sort of leadership that Christ castigated as monolithically "Gentile" and to be rejected by the new community of the King. As Snyder reminds, "The Church cannot uncritically take over structures from its own surrounding culture any more than it can uncritically import them from outside" (Snyder 1977, 142).

But can there be ritual without temple, sacrament without sanctuary, priesthood without priest class? A censure of contemporary temple ethos from a biblical-theological angle would have to be qualified by a strong affirmation of local art and architecture in the emerging expression of the new community of faith, or at least proper disassociation of the theological realities of NT "church" from the cultural excellencies to be affirmed in most arenas of societal life. The Roman Catholic Church in Thailand (in some cases) chose to adopt elaborate local Buddhist temple forms in the erection of major church buildings. Protestants largely rejected (and continue to reject) the religious associations of the

Buddhist context in favor of artless Western architecture and strictly utilitarian edifices. The trick seems to be how to create an understanding of separation between the artifacts of culture, redeemed or reaffirmed through conversion of the community to Christ, and the true nature of the new community, the nature of its worship and, indeed, its God.

The advent of a house church ecclesiology and method has been motivated primarily by concerns for more rapid growth over against cumbersome facility-based institutions and programs that avoid the separation of laity from ministry. From a missiological standpoint, house church planting provides a temporary sidestepping of the dilemma of temple both in terms of avoiding the physical imposition of an edifice with religiously ambiguous symbolism as well as re-centering the church around people as the temple, the loving community of the King. A building, to use the familiar sociological categorization, is a bounded set, a clear delineation of the holy from the unholy, the insiders from the outsiders. A mobile and non-facility-based, tightly knit group of people/family/friends illustrates the centered-set concept, without clear boundaries between the sacred and the profane, or between clergy and laity. Another strength of the house church movement as it matures is the contrast of the image of God portrayed through either place-and-event ecclesiology in the more established institution from the people-in-loving-community ecclesiology of the less rooted, mobile, and accessible younger networks. For it is humanity that in the end bears the *imago Dei*, and it is love that Jesus predicted would be the singular hallmark of his new community (John 13:35; 1 John 4:12).

Conversely in terms of structure, the persistence of especially urban megachurch superstructures with their attendant celebration or high worship imprint, has also had wide acceptance and set a model that many lacking the resources or leadership seek to emulate. A visit to rural Nepal will find youth groups scraping together their meager resources to put together an electronically wired praise band. Worship choruses composed in the West are often awkwardly translated/transliterated into local languages and have become a kind of *lingua franca* of the praise-and-worship movement globally. This propensity to praise is rooted in the Davidic monarchial model of the OT, a Christendom model of the church if you will. While the first months of the early church were attended by temple-court celebration, distinctly in the presence and under the watchful eye of the larger community, a clear distinction from what is now done almost exclusively inside four walls, this practice diminished of necessity after the destruction of the physical temple and Jerusalem as the holy city. One theological weakness of this particular expression is its tendency to equate worship with collective, enclosed praise celebrations, whereas both testaments present a very different picture of worship as fundamentally a social reality of obedient discipleship and lifestyle. This seems to be a leading rationale behind the simple church inclination of so many.

As physical structures will almost inevitably go up (or be shared or taken over within the existing community) in growing movements, the following might be considered parameters in sustaining a healthier ecclesiology and movement. Structures are incorporated into the larger sphere of the artifacts of a redeemed, redemptive community in dynamic continuity and discontinuity with the culture's history. They reflect the best in local art, an extension of the society's creative identity. As facilities for use by the church, they are commissioned fundamentally for multipurpose use within the larger community, a servant structure. As symbols, they are directed at and christened for the kingdom of God, designed for a church scattered as much as a church gathered. They are never called churches or temples, and they don't necessarily constitute the primary meeting places for the growing number of disciples or the primary residence or edifice for leadership. They could otherwise be erected or adopted as monastic way stations for apprentices/novices committing more fully for a time to the new faith; as service centers for administering aid to the poor, help for the sick, comfort for the bereaved; as community centers for generic community decision making and celebrative/festival functions—including larger, more public worship gatherings.

Where are our temples? Christians maintain they are simply "the body and building of Christ," wherever that is alive and intelligible. They are mobile like the tabernacle, dynamic like a building under constant construction, accessible like Jesus in the flesh, holy, set apart but utterly tangible, the salt of the earth, the light of the world, mistaken for Jesus, beautiful as a bride, intimate as a family, signposts of the kingdom—not of temporal wealth. Our temples are the only adequate this-worldly dwelling place of God, stable but anchored in eternity, visible but not perishable, the people of God wherever and whenever they gather in

Jesus' name; in other words, everywhere. To erect temples in an effort at religious dynamic equivalence seems a recipe for failure: on the one hand, a failure if we lack the resources to get it done competitively and, on the other hand, a failure to communicate the God on the move if we succeed.

References

Brueggemann, Walter. 1991. "Rethinking church models through Scripture," *Theology Today* 48 (July), 128–38.

Davis, John. 1993. *Poles apart: Contextualizing the Gospel in Asia.* Theological Book Trust, Bangalore, India.

Earhart, H. Byron, ed. 1993. *Religious traditions of the world.* Harper Collins Publishers. New York, NY.

Gellner, David N. 2001. *The anthropology of Buddhism and Hinduism: Weberian themes.* Oxford University Press, New Delhi.

Roetzel, Calvin J. 2002. *The world that shaped the New Testament.* Westminister John Knox Press, Louisville, KY.

Sharma, Arvind, ed. *Our religions.* 1993. Harper Collins Publishers, New York, NY.

Snyder, Howard. 1977. *The community of the King.* InterVarsity Press, Downers Grove, IL.

Stott, John. 1990. *The message of Acts: the Spirit, the Church and the world.* InterVarsity Press, Downers Grove, IL.

Tannenbaum, Nicala. 1995. *Who can compete against the world? Power-protection and Buddhism in Shan worldview.* Monograph published by The Association for Asian Studies, Inc., Ann Arbor, MI.

Walls, Andrew. 1996. *The missionary movement in Christian history: Studies in transmission of faith.* Orbis, Maryknoll, NY.

Weber, Max. *The religion of China.* 1951. (Hans Gerth tr.) The Free Press, New York, NY.

Wink, Walter. 1992. *Engaging the powers: Discernment and resistance in a world of domination.* Augsburg Fortress, Minneapolis, MN.

Wright, N. T. 1999. *The challenge of Jesus: Rediscovering who Jesus was and is.* InterVarsity Press, Downers Grove, IL.

PART II

BECOMING THE PEOPLE WHO REFLECT GOD'S KINGDOM THROUGH WITNESS OF WORD AND DEED

For the grace of God has appeared
that offers salvation to all people.
It teaches us to say "No"
to ungodliness and worldly passions,
and to live self-controlled,
upright and godly lives in this present age,
while we wait for the blessed hope—
the appearing of the glory of our great God and Savior,
Jesus Christ, who gave himself for us
to redeem us from all wickedness
and to purify for himself a people that are his very own,
eager to do what is good.
Titus 2:11–14

CHAPTER 4

CONTEXT-SENSITIVE EVANGELISM IN THE THAI SETTING: BUILDING CAPACITY TO SHARE GOOD NEWS

Alan R. Johnson

In my over two decades of service in Thailand I have had several what I call "light bulb" experiences where something happened and it was like having a giant spotlight suddenly shine on in my head. All of these experiences have shaped the way that I conduct my work in Thai society and with the Thai church. They have also led to trajectories of ongoing investigation and inquiry in trying to help further the proclamation of the good news of what God has done in Jesus Christ for humankind and to plant the church in this land.

One of the most important "light bulb" moments for me concerned message contextualization. In this chapter I want to present what I refer to as context-sensitive message contextualization in three parts. In the first part I describe the need for messengers to become cultural amphibians comfortable in two worlds. The second part describes my journey towards context-sensitive evangelism. The final part details a way of practicing context-sensitive message evangelism through (1) capacity building, (2) conceptual toolkits, (3) use of conversational bridges, and (4) environment building for evangelistic effectiveness.

The Need to Become a Cross-cultural Amphibian

The Thai church labors under a strong perception from their society that Christianity is foreign to the Thai; it is *sasana farang*, the white people's religion. Over the years it has become clear to me that this observation evokes radically different responses in local Thai Christians than it does from those who come as cross-cultural workers to share the gospel and plant the church. For local Christians it is like a baseline environmental operating condition. You may not like it, but it is the reality in which you live and work. This manifests itself in nearly a complete unquestioning approach to whatever style of "doing church" they inherited from somewhere else. To outsiders it seems stunning that attending a local church can feel so much like attending a church in North America with the exception that the songs are sung in Thai. There is this intuitive sense that church ought to at least feel a little Thai in light of how different society in general feels, sounds, smells, and looks when you are out in public. But for most local Thai churches the "version" or "mode" of faith they received (whether from bases in Europe or North America) is seen as the proper Christian way to gather as God's people.

This same observation of the Thai perception of the gospel as foreign evokes a much different reaction for cross-cultural workers. For many, it makes us start asking the question, "How do we change this perception?" It moves people to think about ways to help Thai people feel that the good news is for them and not some kind of foreign imposition. One of the big challenges in the Thai Christian setting is that, in general, there are two groups with radically different responses to this problem. On one side there are expatriates who come as cross-cultural workers interested in exploring Thai culture with the goal of helping make the gospel more relevant and understandable to Thai people. Then there is the Thai church that for the most part is uninterested in this subject.

There are several contributing factors that make up for this lack of attention to issues of culture and that make it such a challenge to have robust dialogue. Historically there was a strong element of rejection and demonization of local culture among Protestants, and this lingers today. Many Christians do not feel legitimated to explore how to relate to their society as Christians. The fact that there is no agreed-upon word among

Thai Christians to describe contextualization can make it awkward as you have to substitute a whole sentence or more where a single word in English suffices. There is a tendency for Thai converts to view Christian orthodoxy (being a "good" Christian) from their previous background ("people are not good Buddhists anyway") and thus avoid grappling with religious issues. On the pastoral side, there is such pressure for growth and use of the "right" method or technique that will produce it that there is little patience for concepts and abstractions that require thought and application.

The vast majority of cross-cultural workers that come to serve in Thailand commit to working with the Thai church. This of itself is a wonderful thing and very important to those of us who hold to the notion of a truly indigenous church. Outsiders work to strengthen the hand of the local believers so that they can do the work of ministry with their own resources. The downside, however, is that we all end up "tweaking" already-existing ministry values, philosophies, and structures inside of the Christian bubble and never get a chance to grapple with the bigger issues of millions of people for whom that version of the faith does not help them access the good news of Jesus.

My observation from being in the Thai setting, talking with colleagues in other Buddhist countries, and from reading the literature is that there is a big gap in the way that the whole issue of contextualization has been approached. That gap is what to do with the existing church in the Buddhist world. A major weakness in much of the literature about contextualization has been the unwritten assumption that outsider cross-cultural workers could work with people in what amounted to a hermetically sealed environment and freely experiment with various forms and approaches without hindrance. That is patently not true, because the church has already been planted. It has a history and a trajectory. It represents a mode of faith. God has used it (and continues to use it) to bring people into a relationship with himself.

In my thinking, one of the most promising directions for working on issues of context sensitivity is the potential found in partnering with the existing church. Rather than trying to deconstruct the whole enterprise, using insider knowledge can help build even more effective conceptual and practical methodologies than before! What would happen if Thai Christians in the existing church were equipped to simply communicate the gospel in a more sensitive and accessible fashion? Thai Christians have relationships with thousands of family members, neighbors, and friends. What if Thai Buddhists hearing the gospel from their Christian friends were able to better assess who Jesus is and begin to follow him in a way that creates less social dislocation and that communicates back to their social network their "Thainess"? Without changing everything, retaining all the strengths of what the existing church is doing, would this provide leverage to open doors to large numbers of Thai people who have to this point stumbled at the foreignness of the faith both conceptually and in practice?

This is what I am pursuing in my work on context-sensitive witness. My metaphor for cross-cultural workers is to be an amphibian. We need one foot firmly in the world of the church, to love it, work with it, and know it well. We also need one foot in the midst of Buddhist societies with millions of people who need to hear the gospel, and we need to understand them and their hopes, dreams, and rhythms of life. We then bring these two worlds together so that issues of context can be wrestled with in the church and not relegated to the realm of abstract theory.

Contextualization: "Because He Killed All Those Fish!"

I came to Thailand in 1986 excited to learn the Thai language so that I could begin to share the good news with my newfound Thai friends. It did not take long for me to realize that even though I was speaking Thai, and people for the most part were polite and respectful, creating understanding involved a great deal more than simply encoding words in the local language. Even when we know intellectually that people think differently, we still assume that our listeners understand what we are saying in the same way that we do.

Although there were a number of experiences over time that helped me understand the complexity of intercultural communication, one incident stands out in particular. I was conducting an English lesson with a couple of Thai high school students based on Luke 5 in the English text. We came to the point where I wanted to discuss the meaning of the passage and some of its implications. Since they were unable to converse easily in English, I said that we would switch into Thai. I then asked the question, "Why did Peter fall on his knees to Jesus and say that he was a sinful man?" Without a moment's hesitation one young man said, "Because he killed all of those fish!" I have to admit that his response caught me totally off guard. He was reading the text through his "Buddhist eyes." In that religion taking life is the principle sin. It made me realize in a much clearer fashion that the worldviews, beliefs, values, and assumptions of my listeners were creating in them different meanings than what I was intending, even when those understandings did not surface in conversation.

This started me on the process of trying to understand the meanings that people would be making in their minds from the terms and concepts that we use when we share the gospel. It became clear to me that Thais were not simply rejecting the gospel or Christianity, in reality the situation was much more complicated than that. At least part of their lack of response is a rejection of the linguistic and stylistic wrapping in which we as missionaries and local Christians were presenting the message. When the "wrapping" makes no sense, it keeps them from ever getting to the wonderful gift of the good news inside.

Later on I ran into a section in John Davis' book *Poles Apart* where he illustrates how John 3:16 sounds to the Theravada Buddhist ear. At every foundational point of the gospel, whether we are talking about the living God, the human condition, Jesus and his work on the Cross, or the human response of repentance and faith, there are issues that impede understanding and that sound extremely strange to a person steeped in Buddhist worldview (Davis 1998, vi–viii). These insights became foundational to my own personal quest to learn how to talk about Jesus in an intelligible and compelling way to my Theravada Buddhist friends.

I have wrestled with how to articulate clearly here what is needed in a way that avoids problems that weaken or truncate the impact of the good news or else make it irrelevant and obscure. I have found it helpful in trying to explain these challenges in gospel communication to cast it in terms of being context-sensitive in our sharing of the faith. Let me start by saying what context-sensitive sharing of the message is not. It is not making it in some way "easier" to believe. While we want to eliminate all nonbiblical stumbling blocks on the side of the evangelist and overcome the stereotypes and misunderstandings of our listeners, we must retain biblical stumbling blocks. Thus the work of the Cross (1 Cor 1:22–23) and repentance and turning from idols (1 Thess 1:9) are not pushed aside. It is not answering the sociological questions about what is keeping people from faith and then removing those things in hopes that people will ease into biblical faith and understanding down the line. Context-sensitive sharing is not simply recasting the message into local terms and worldview and leaving it there.

Positively, context-sensitive sharing or evangelism seeks to communicate the good news in ways that facilitate receptor understanding. In Matthew's account of the parable of the sower and its explanation, Jesus tells his disciples, "When anyone hears the message about the kingdom and does not understand it, the evil one comes and snatches away what was sown in their heart" (Matt 13:19). It dawned on me that "understanding" is one of our goals and that broadly this would have two strands in the Bible. On one side, you cannot figure out who Jesus is without divine revelation; thus, Jesus tells Peter that his confession of him as Messiah and Son of the living God "was not revealed to you by flesh and blood, but by my Father in heaven" (Matt 16:16–17). But there is certainly also a human element to this as well, and it is something that we all recognize in the use of language. When I am teaching people on this subject who are native English speakers, I will often break into Thai at this point and give a brief gospel synopsis. I then tell the audience that I just shared fantastic news with them—but it did not benefit them at all; they could not understand it. The issue is that, while we recognize this in completely different languages, we often assume if we have the language right that understanding will follow, even when the conceptual world of the listeners is completely different. Context-sensitive evangelism seeks understanding of the message on the part of the listener, not just correct encoding of the message on the part of the evangelist. It thus avoids the pitfalls on the opposite poles of the spectrum—putting it in a foreign conceptual form (even while using vernacular language), thus rendering it irrelevant or so obscure as to be difficult to understand, or completely subsuming it under local worldview so that biblical meaning is lost or distorted.

Over time in working on this "understanding" based idea of context-sensitive witness, I have run into several related ideas that provide a basis for this notion from the perspective of various disciplines, but all related to how humans make meaning, particularly when confronted with new ideas. When in evangelism we seek to tell the story of Jesus in concepts and the thought world of local people, we are not abandoning biblical meaning, but rather are inviting people to engage with the message and also to begin to explore tension points between the message and their worldview. Rather than requiring them to enter our thought world to understand Jesus, we are trying to show how Jesus is good news in their worldview and at the same time begin the process of engaging them with the core concepts of the Bible.

In communications theory this intersects with relevance theory and its concept of "cognitive environment," which has to do with a "set of assumptions which the individual is capable of mentally representing and accepting as true . . . [It] includes a person's current and potential matrix of ideas, memories, experiences, and perceptions" (Higgins 2010, 190). When new assumptions and thoughts occur in the communication process, they can reinforce or bring changes to the receptor's cognitive environment, which means that in relevance theory "accuracy in communication is described as an increasingly shared cognitive environment" (ibid.).

Missiologically this kind of interplay fits in well with Andrew Walls' ideas on the inherent translatability of the gospel. He reminds us that "none of us can take in a new idea except in terms of the ideas we already have" (1996, 35, 85–87). He illustrates how the proclamation of Jesus as *kyrios* (Lord) in the Hellenistic-pagan setting was critical because "it is doubtful whether unacculturated pagans in the Antiochene world could have understood the significance of Jesus in any other way" (ibid., 35). Yet at the same time, the natural association of Jesus with cult divinities through the use of this title did not happen among converts, because "those pagans who responded were brought into a community where the Septuagint was constantly read, and the biblical associations of *Kyrios* penetrated their minds and attached themselves to the cult divinity title" (ibid.), so much so that "in time much of the original loading of the word disappeared altogether" (ibid., 35, 89–90).

Here we see both elements of connecting with local worldview and the initiation of a process that challenges that worldview and reshapes cognitive environment. Two other authors have provided me with concepts that integrate well these two processes. On the side of connecting with local worldview, Timothy Keller talks about "cultural narratives," the "stories that a people tell about themselves to make sense out of their shared existence" (2012, 90). He says,

> When we contextualize faithfully and skillfully, we show people how the baseline "cultural narratives" of their society and the hopes of their hearts can only find resolution and fulfillment in Jesus. (Ibid.)

The other process that can reshape cognitive environment can be modeled on the way that we read a book. Benno van den Toren, reflecting on the work of Polyani on the nature scientific discovery, suggests a way for understanding how humans develop beliefs. He says,

> When we read a book, we all come to it with our proper cultural pre-understandings. This does, however, not mean that we are forever bound to these pre-understandings. If we read the book humbly and are willing to be challenged, our pre-understanding may be shown to be inadequate. This allows us to adjust them so that in a cycle of reading and rereading, our initially flawed understanding becomes gradually adapted to the content of the book itself. (2010, 100)

Thus what I am calling context-sensitive witness is not just a matter of finding linguistically encoded local reference points but is embedded in a process whereby those who wish to do so can engage their cognitive environment with that of the Scriptures. Putting it in these terms highlights the fact that this whole discussion about message contextualization is embedded in a broader process that includes both evangelism and discipleship. It also shows that the factors that bring people into faith are not going to be what sustains faith, and that the process of interaction with the biblical text must reshape the cognitive environment of individuals and their community of faith.

A Method for Context-sensitive Evangelism

My light bulb experience with the "killing of the fish" interpretation of Luke 5 set me on a personal quest to learn how to share the good news in a more understandable fashion. In the late 1980s, using resources that I could access at that time, I developed a presentation that took the same common points found in many gospel presentations and recast them in ways that could be more helpful for a listener coming from a Theravada Buddhist background. Many years later I presented the material at a SEANET forum, and it was published as "Wrapping the Good News for the Thai" in *Sharing Jesus Holistically with the Buddhist World* (Johnson 2005b).

When asked to teach others about sharing the gospel in the Buddhist context, it pushed me to think about ways to package this material into a model that would help people reproduce these ideas in different social and cultural settings. At the same time, my thinking was also stimulated by requests from people primarily in the West who wanted to know more about how to share with Buddhist neighbors. They always wanted to know more about Buddhism. However, I have come to understand that there are other critical factors more important than knowledge about other religious systems. I came to see that as important as a contextualized message is, it is not sufficient in itself to bring people to faith. In trying to diagram this, I have come to call these other elements the "environment" that facilitates evangelism where there is a large gap between the worldviews of the listener and the Christian community (see Fig. 2 below). Thinking in terms of the work of a local church, there needs to be an atmosphere of vibrant prayer, deep relationships with non-Christians, a way to expose them to the community of faith, and an experience with God's power. When that kind of atmosphere is combined with a more context-sensitive message, it increases the potential for positive response.

What follows here in the next four sections both explains and provides illustrative examples of what I call a capacity-building methodology for sharing the gospel in a context-sensitive manner. In the first section I explain the assumptions, values, and core elements of the capacity-building approach. The second section then describes components that can fill a "toolbox" with major topics that may be drawn upon to explain and clarify the meaning of the good news for the listener. The third section introduces conversational bridges to cultural concepts and objections useful in many evangelistic conversations. The final section expands the notion of building the environment that facilitates a positive response.

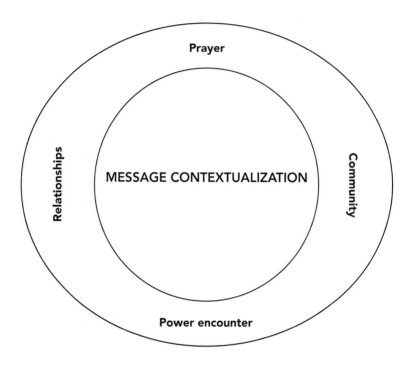

Figure 2: The environment that facilitates effective evangelism

Assumptions of the Capacity-building Approach to Contextualization

A capacity-building approach for sharing the gospel differs from other methods where there is a presentation that is serial in nature, moving through a relatively fixed set of points in a particular order. Such methods have a number of advantages; they are relatively simple for people to learn and thus easily transferable to others. The problem is that in real-life encounters with people there is often insufficient time to adequately present the good news, and people have questions and objections that need to be dealt with. The capacity-building approach means that the person bearing witness develops the ability to share clearly the various core ideas of the gospel from any starting point and in a relevant fashion to the cultural setting and worldview of the listener. Gospel content can then be shared naturally in the fragments of time that real-life relationships bring or in teachable moments.

What follows are a set of foundational ideas that make up the values and assumptions of this way of learning to share in a context-sensitive fashion.

- The whole approach is founded on dialogue rather than a monologue, and envisions a process rather than a point-in-time encounter. This is not something that you "run through in order," although it is easy enough to do a brief summary if that fits the situation. By building capacity to share on the various key points, it takes the rush out of things. It flows through intentional but natural conversation.
- Local Christians need to have a flexible track to run on when sharing the gospel. I have done interviews with people in Thailand who have experienced being witnessed to by a Thai Christian, and in many instances it was very unpleasant because it was pushy, monological, and it made no sense to them. This track allows for multiple entry points and the chance to ask questions and yet provides a way to share the message in a way that makes sense and has logical consistency.
- Each major point in the gospel becomes a self-contained module with its own explanations, arguments, and illustrations. Depending on where you engage a person, you can begin with a different module, but the point is that there is always the "track" to get back on so that your listener has a connected line of thought rather than random chunks of information.
- Paul's approach in Acts shows that he varied his explanation of the gospel with the worldview of the audience. We are not bound to a one-size-fits-all format for talking about what God has done for humans in Jesus Christ. The methodology here legitimizes the use of local terminology and concepts to show

how Jesus is good news in their worldview. Dean Flemming in his book on contextualization in the New Testament points out that Paul drew on terms like mystery, liberation, and gospel, all which had pagan associations (2005, 145). He says, "Paul seems quite willing to risk misunderstanding by co-opting language from the religious culture of his readers and infusing these forms with new meaning that in part alters and in part replaces the old" (ibid.).

- It views sharing the gospel as a process. We share content and check for understanding. If the people we are talking with do not easily understand the content of our message, instead of rushing through the points of the gospel and pressing for a decision to receive Jesus, we need to communicate the content of the gospel and then ask questions to assess what they understand.

- We need to help people probe the implications of a decision to follow Jesus. Because Buddhists focus on correct practice more than correct belief, they are often thinking about what the message means to them in terms of their social relationships rather than whether it is true or not. Taking time with people and allowing them to ask questions as they explore the implications of a decision to follow Jesus is critical to having them make an informed decision.

Figure 3 below shows the four core elements that become the major areas that we develop in order to tell the story of Jesus in a contextually relevant way. When Paul talks about what he delivered to people at Corinth as of first importance and what they responded to in believing, it had to do with God, the death and resurrection of Jesus Christ, and human sin (1 Cor 15:1–11). These in fact are the central items in many well-known gospel presentations such as the "Four Spiritual Laws," "Steps to Peace with God," "Evangelism Explosion," and so on. The difference in the capacity-building approach is that you can start at any of these points and loop back around to make sense of the whole over time with the listener.

The metaphor that I have used with English speakers in talking about the boxes in Figure 3 that make up the core content is the notion of "toolkits." We build our capacity to share the gospel in a relevant way by adding "tools" to our "toolkits" on each of these major gospel-content areas.

Humans and the problem of sin	God
Jesus, the Cross, and the Resurrection	Faith

Figure 3: The four "toolkits" for sharing the gospel

The model is designed to work in "real time" with the kinds of snatches of conversation and teachable moments that come in the natural relationships that we have with people. The entry points into spiritual conversations are the questions, objections, and scripts that people pose to us. When we have a set of "tools" to work with at each of these points, the doorways to conversation allow us to share gospel content. Because this approach can start anywhere and you do not serially go over a fixed presentation, the witness can work within the time and environmental constraints. So, for instance, if a person asks why Christians drink blood because they have seen a film that included the Last Supper or heard of Communion in some form without understanding, it is a fantastic starting point to look at Jesus' work on the Cross.

If time permits, you can then work back through the other points in the gospel to set the context for why Jesus' work on the Cross is so crucial. But if not, depending on the response and interest of the person, you can ask to come back and share in more detail, or wait for another teachable and open moment. The tools that we put in our "toolkits" (see Fig. 3) are composed of the following:

- A set of scripture verses foundational to that topic. This does not mean that we actually are quoting these verses in a given conversation, but they form the conceptual foundation and are central to the points we want to make.
- A set of indigenous illustrations that help to shine light on the concepts.

- A set of prepared answers for objections that listeners will have from their worldview. When we immerse ourselves in understanding local culture and worldview, we know the kinds of objections and red-flag issues that most likely will not be voiced in any given encounter. So methodologically we anticipate these mental objections and provide answers for them in advance of actually being asked. This is best done in an oblique fashion and never should make people feel like they or their religious beliefs are being denigrated.

My longer name for this approach is "ethnographically informed context-sensitive witness" because the person sharing the gospel has to do their homework in the local culture (the ethnographic part) in order to communicate clearly (the context-sensitive part).

Components for "Toolkit" Presentations of the Gospel

What follows here are some of the things that I have incorporated into my "toolkits" in the ongoing project of learning how to communicate about these points to people in the Thai environment. The material here is not exhaustive but only suggestive of the type of work that can be done to build a personal approach with a multiplicity of concepts and illustrations to draw upon. The content here is specific to the Thai setting, but illustrates the kind of process that could be carried out in another sociocultural environment.

Concepts about the Human Dilemma and Problem of Sin

Joseph Cooke has pointed out that for most Thais there is hardly ever a great sense of guilt because of wrongdoing (1978, 3). Their culture is oriented towards shame, not guilt. This is in part a consequence of the fact that the Thai Buddhist incurs guilt (in the legal sense of wrongdoing) only in one dimension, the manward side, since he has no belief in God (ibid., 7). However, Cooke notes that in this single dimension it is quite probable that those who take seriously the following of *sil ha* (the Five Buddhist Precepts) and other precepts, find themselves with a performance gap (ibid., 3). In other words, the behavior that they are able to produce and what they want to produce, is not the same, creating a gap. For those in such a situation, the performance gap is a good place to begin to discuss the universal human experience of falling short of our own moral standards. This can lead to discussion about the power of Jesus to grant new life that enables us to obey God's commands.

Since Buddhism and its concept of suffering begin with the human dilemma, I personally have found it most easy to engage Thais in talking about humanity's problem using the fruit tree illustration of Brasert Gusawadi (n.d.). He talks about how a mango tree that gives off sour-tasting fruit cannot change itself at all, but in order to get sweet fruit, we must obtain a variety or species that bears sweet fruit and plant those seeds. In other words, to solve the human problem of the performance gap, we cannot change on our own but need the impartation of new life.

Wan Petchsongkram talks about the common word *tujarit*, meaning dishonesty, as actually meaning evil action. When compounded, it can be used to speak of evil physical action, evil speech, and evil in the heart (*gaaytujarit, wajitujarit, manotujarit* respectively; 1975, 141). These words can be used in addition to *baab* (sin) to show concrete expressions of sin in our lives. In the fruit tree illustration, the sour fruit of our lives is expressed as evil physical actions, evil speech, and evil in our hearts. It all has its start in the seed, the sour specie that produces sour fruit. Using *tanha* (desire) to refer to something like the sin principle (biblical "flesh"), we can show that we commit evil deeds, because from within we have a problem, the *tanha* problem, and that we are in desperate need of a change deep from within if we are to truly change our actions.

The advantage of using these starting points and then talking about the human dilemma is that it can be done by connecting with a variety of terms and concepts such as karma, suffering, ignorance, or proverbs and sayings that are very common to Thais. This has the result of making people feel like you are "talking their language" and understand where they are at, and it opens the door for further conversation.

Concepts about God

Petchsongkram notes that the question of God's existence and the creation of the world are key hurdles; people who can say yes to those two questions usually are much more willing to see Jesus Christ as the

Son of God (ibid., 99–100). This is a very difficult area, for we are moving from the known (human experience in the world) to the unknown and unseen. Tissa Weerasingha suggests that since "Buddhist doctrine does not deal with the issue of a First Cause . . . the biblical doctrine of creation would fill a crucial cosmological deficiency" (Weerasingha 1984, 304).

One of the common objections about God being the Creator is that the world is in such a sorry state, it surely means that if someone did create the world, he must be *awicha* (ignorant) and a perpetrator of evil (Petchsongkram 1975, 84–85). When one does talk about God as Creator, there must be an emphasis that what God made was good and whole and that it was human disobedience and the entrance of sin that ruined things. Petchsongkram has a fascinating way of relating the creation story in which he shows how both *awicha* and *tanha* sprang up in human hearts and that this is the source of the world's problems (ibid., 85–89).

Also, in dealing with arguments for the existence of God, it is good to be conversant with concepts and evidences that point to the existence of a Creator. Dealing with the First Cause, the argument from design, and the argument from human personality and morality are all profitable ways to begin. Due to the fact that in Buddhism the ultimate reality is impersonal, Cooke recommends that we stress the personhood of God, since this is really one of the essential rock-bottom differences between Buddhism and Christianity (1978, 20). He suggests that this can be done through emphasizing the personhood of God in creation, using the realities of relationships in Thai society to develop analogies, and by demonstrating our own personal relationship with God (ibid.). One way that I have found to talk with people about the personality of God as a starting point is to talk about the term *singsaksittanlaituasakonlok*, which refers to all the powerful sacred things in the universe. *Sing* carries the idea of a "thing," and I will remark that this concept is almost right, but there is actually a *phu* (a person) who is the most high sacred one.

Once we have established that God exists, it is then necessary to talk about what God is like and to show that God is truly interested in us. This good news is that God, whom we cannot see, has revealed himself to be a God who is interested in us, who has not thrown us away, and who wants to restore us to the fellowship with him that God intended us to have. Normally, in a Western presentation of the gospel, these points are explained in terms of the love of God, which brings us salvation. Both of these ideas are red flags in the Thai setting. Where extinguishing desire is an ideal, the comment that God "loves" can be taken to mean that he is "hot" and connected rather than cool and detached. The Thai term used to talk about salvation in the Bible, *kwamrawt*, is not one that carries a great deal of meaning for the average person. Fortunately there are several excellent concepts that can be used to convey these truths.

We can talk about the mercy and compassion of God using the term *metta*. This is a very high word in Buddhism and can be translated as "beneficence" or "grace" (Petchsongkram 1975, 152–53). Also, the word used for "grace," *phrakhun*, is very important. These words can be used and illustrated to show that even though we ruined our lives through sin, and even though we have turned our backs on the One who made us, God is still seeking us out and does not abandon us. Cooke notes that this theme of grace and love that does not abandon us, even when it is awkward or inconvenient or when we fail to measure up, would most likely be very important to a Thai (1978, 13–14).

One illustration from Thai life that is helpful is the practice of the king releasing prisoners on special occasions. In the Thai language this is expressed as occurring *doy phrakhun*, or through the grace of the king. We can show how through our own efforts at doing good and making merit we cannot get rid of our evil heart and evil actions, but God through his grace, even though we do not merit it, brings us release and forgiveness, just as the king releases prisoners who deserve to be in prison.

Concepts about Jesus, the Cross, and Resurrection

When speaking of the substitutionary death of the Lord Jesus, it is necessary to emphasize the free and voluntary nature of his sacrifice as we see in John 10:18. As noted above, there is a tendency to think that, because Jesus died a violent death as a criminal, he must have had very bad karma in his past life. There must be positive teaching at this point and illustration of sacrificial acts that stem from a desire to help another. Alex Smith has pointed out a key historical story concerning the Thai queen Phranang Srisuriyothai (1981, 276–77). The substance of the story is that she disguised herself as a warrior to help her husband in the fight against the Burmese. As the Thai king was about to be killed in the battle, the queen rode her elephant between the two fighters and was killed, but her husband was spared. This type of true story, which illustrates vicarious sacrifice, can be very helpful in conveying the meaning to the Thai listener who has no background in his religious beliefs for such an act.

In speaking of the death of Christ, and using the terminology that his sacrifice enables us to be delivered from the effects of karma, we must also emphasize the broader scope that is included in his death and resurrection. This includes his victory over sin, over death, and over Satan and evil spirits. In this way we can make practical applications to the actual place that people live in. Christ's resurrection brings us power for living the new life, not the deadness of mere precepts and prohibitions, as good as they may be. It also frees us from the tyranny of death; and for the many people who are tormented or afraid of evil spirits, his victory over the enemy and his power to cast out demons is very important. In a similar vein, the inbreaking of God's kingdom rule, which is inaugurated in the ministry of Jesus and which is carried on by God's people, saw the demonstration of God's mercy in miracles of healing. All of these aspects must be given in order to show that the victory Christ has purchased for us through his shed blood touches on every area of our daily lives.

One question that the gospel communicator is sure to face when trying to explain about salvation by grace through faith and not through our works, concerns merit (*bun*). People are so accustomed to the merit/demerit system and the law of karma paying them back good for good and evil for evil, that the idea of being freed from the weight of our evil deeds without doing anything seems very foreign. I have experimented to a degree with using the concept of merit transference as a way of conveying this idea. It has to do with explaining the idea of our being justified by faith through Christ's death in the category of Jesus being our *bun* (merit).

The idea came to me while attending a Thai funeral. Prior to the cremation, there was a whole sequence of offering cloth that I did not understand. I asked a Thai friend sitting next to me what was happening, and he said that it was making merit. Then the question became, making merit for whom? Was it for the person giving the cloth or to the deceased? He replied that the offerings of cloth were to make merit for the person who had died. I realized then that although Thais do not talk about the transference of merit commonly, they do believe in it and it is found in rituals like this. So I have tried using that concept in the following way: I ask the question, "Why do you make merit?" The answer usually involves some concept of trying to gain merit for a better life both now and in the future. I then make the point that *bun*, either through ritual or through good actions, is done for a reason, and therefore there is some ultimate direction that it points toward. At this point I make the case for the fact that our own *bun* is simply not enough, because when we look closely at our lives we have more demerit (*baab*) than merit. In this way we can never, through our own actions, deeds, and *bun*, ever escape from our *kam* (karma) or make our way into heaven or be accepted into fellowship with the God who made us.

The verses I use come from the language of Paul in Ephesians and Colossians where he says that in Christ we were made alive, even though formerly dead in trespasses and sins (Eph 2:5; Col 2:13). Jesus, who committed no sin, was a perfect sacrifice and has become *bun* for us and has wiped out karma and delivered us from death and made us pure in God's eyes. We do not acquire his *bun* by our deeds but by trusting in him, and as we do so he transfers to us all the benefit of his *bun*.

It is obvious that the biblical term we are dealing with here is righteousness. The difficulty is that since there is no concept of God and no notion that sin breaks a relationship with God, there is not a sense of need for righteousness. The forensic sense of justification developed by Paul is not a motivating factor for a Thai Buddhist. The issue of merit, on the other hand, is right at the front of the average person's current thinking and experience and provides a starting point for talking about what Christ has done in his work on the Cross.

Concepts about Faith: Our Response to God's Gift

In the Bible saving faith has cognitive, emotional, and volitional elements. This can and should be explained in Thai. However, I have noticed that there are a number of words that express the idea of believing in the verb form and faith in the noun form: *chua* (believe, trust, have faith in, rely on), *sattha* (to have faith in, trust, belief), *luamsai* (to have faith in, believe in, be thoroughly convinced), and *waiwangjai* (have confidence in, trust in, rely on). More detailed study could reveal that in terms of their current usage, one of these words could fit the idea of volitional commitment better than mere cognitive belief in the facts. As an instance of this, I have heard people, when referring to losing a sense of faith and trust in another because of their poor behavior or example, say that they are *mot sattha* and not *mot kwamchua*. Perhaps *chua* is the broader term that includes and emphasizes cognitive assent, and *sattha* carries more of the idea of trusting or giving yourself to another. Where in English we would talk about "commitment to Christ," there are terms like *mawbhai* (to give oneself over, entrust, commit) and *jamnon* (to surrender) that can be used to convey the concept in Thai. Further research on the distinctions between these terms and how they are illustrated will help to sharpen the challenge of what it means to be a Christ follower.

In talking about saving faith, it is not enough to use correct vocabulary; we also must talk about the practical development of the life of faith. It is often difficult for people who are so indoctrinated into the works concept found in the merit and karma system to conceive of living a life "free from the Law" so to speak. They often feel that if there is no compelling reason to do good, then why should you do it? Hearing about salvation by grace through faith raises the same line of questioning that Paul addresses in Romans 6, and the Thai is prone to think that it is all "too easy."

However, I think there is an analogy to be found in the thinking of Thais as it relates to respect for and gratitude towards parents that helps us to change the emphasis in a helpful direction here. Showing gratitude (*jaikatanyuu*) to a parent is very important, and the child who does not show gratitude by sending money and taking care of his parents as they grow older is looked down upon. Parents have sacrificed for us, and we should sacrifice for our parents. We can use this concept to great benefit when talking about the practical outworking of the Christian life. We are saved and delivered by grace (*phrakhun*), but we live our Christian life by showing gratitude to our heavenly Father (*doysadang jaikatanyuu*). He has sacrificed his own Son that we might be restored to fellowship with him, and it is our duty to show gratitude by living our lives to please Him.

Conversational Bridges to Cultural Concepts and Objections

I have heard that one of the primary reasons given by Christians for not witnessing is that they do not know how to start a spiritual conversation.

Rather than utilizing witness introductions that answer cultural questions important to Western culture (such as God's plan for our lives or fear of death and desire to go to heaven), we should be looking for local cultural keys where we are working. Here I will illustrate with four different cultural concepts that have proven useful. These are only suggestive, and there are many other cultural concepts that can no doubt serve as entry points into sharing good news with the Thai.

1. Start with suffering: Keeping in mind what Cooke has said in regard to the lack of a sense of guilt that the Thai have concerning wrongdoing, it seems that rather than trying to create a sense of wrongdoing, we should begin where people are, with an understanding of *dukkha* (Thai: *thuk*), which is suffering. By using one of the three key terms that mark human existence in Buddhism, we can zero in on what our conversation partners commonly understand and experience—the frustration, suffering, and difficulties of life—and we can explain that this *thuk* comes because of problems that are within us rather than external to us. For another SEANET forum paper, I did research on how lay people understood *dukkha* and discovered in the course of the interviews that their broad term to cover the range of tangible experiences that comprise *dukkha* for them was the opposite of the answer given for why they practice *dharma* (Johnson 2011). I have found this to make a very good conversation starter around the inability to find true "quietness" (*sangob*) because of their experiences of *thuk* (suffering) .

2. Start with karma and ignorance: A missionary with the Overseas Missionary Fellowship (OMF) has developed a gospel presentation called "The Way to Freedom: The Way to a New Life," which has a similar starting point of dealing with humanity's problems. It looks at human life in three concentric circles from family and friends out to the hostile spirit world. It characterizes life using two key terms that the Thai Buddhists are familiar with: *awicha* (Pali: *avijja*) and *kam* (Pali: *kamma* or karma). Here humans are seen as locked in *awicha* (ignorance), and also reaping what they sow, which is the law of *kam*. This approach has much to commend it, because it ties the human condition into two common, key Thai word concepts that also have a contact point in Scripture.

Another method that starts off from the concept of karma is to use the introductory two questions of the "Evangelism Explosion" presentation modified for people with a karmatic worldview. Rather than asking if one would go to heaven after they die, you ask if they would be liberated from the law of karma (*pon jaak got haeng kam*). The follow-up question is to ask how they think that people are able to be freed from their karma.

3. Start with a Thai proverb: Another place to begin from in dealing with the performance gap is to use the Thai proverb *Khwamru thuam hua aow tua mai rawt*. This means that though knowledge floods one's head, a person cannot use it to save himself or herself. After setting the stage by showing how many problems occur both in society and personally, and by zeroing in on the listener's own perceived difficulties, this proverb can be very helpful in showing that even though we may possess lots of knowledge about what is right, we still cannot actually follow through on it and do it; we need power to act, not just knowledge. I found an illustration in a language study book years ago and found it very helpful. It shows a person drowning and having someone try to teach him to swim and having another pull him out of the water. When you ask people who they would rather have in this circumstance, someone who teaches you or who pulls you out and rescues you, they always affirm the latter.

4. Start with a common saying on good, evil, and the desire concept: Another possible place to begin in talking about humanity and our problems is to use the very well-known phrase *Thamdii daidii thamchua daichua*. This is a saying about the law of karma that means, "Do good, receive good; do evil, receive evil." We can use Galatians 6:7–8 to show that this principle of retribution is one that God uses in governing the world. The question can be asked, what happens if you do both good and evil? What do you receive then? This draws upon the fact of their experience that no one consistently does good. At this point, I think it is permissible to use the word *tanha* (craving, lust, desire) or *kileedtanha* (longing, passion, desire) to speak of the sin principle in humans rather than the word "flesh" (*nuanang*) as is used in the Thai Bible. *Nuanang* is made up of two words, one meaning the "flesh" or "skin" (*nua*), and the other "hide" (*nang*), compounded together. Just as the English translation of the Greek *sarx* as "flesh" is not understood by a first-time reader of Scripture as referring to the sin principle inside of humans, such is the case with *nuanang*. It has to be explained, and its meaning is made clear through its use in context. However, *tanha* (desire) is a religious word that is well known, and the concept that we cling to life and commit acts of sin because of *tanha* is well recognized by people. Thus in Galatians

6:8 we can show that because of *tanha* we consistently do not do good and cannot break the cycle of karma that we are caught in. However, the text says that if we sow to the Spirit we reap eternal life. This can become the bridge for showing how we can break out of *tanha* and karma. We need new life—life from God's Spirit.

While cultural concepts are generally used by the person bearing witness to direct a conversation towards the gospel, core objections that local people have to the Christian faith and message provide great bridges to evangelism if they are handled in a gracious and wise fashion. Rather than being conversation stoppers, they can be turned around to become doorways for sharing truth. What I have come to realize is that in any given cultural setting there are a limited number of primary objections that people have to the gospel. I have spoken with local Christians in different Buddhist settings, and they often express the difficult nature of sharing with friends and family due to all the objections and problems that their listeners have. I encourage them to start making a list of these, and it turns out that there are generally only a handful of objections that are widely shared within a given cultural setting. This means that if we can help people to develop responses to this limited universe of problem areas, it will open rather than hinder spiritual conversations.

These problem areas usually take two primary forms. One is actual objections (an example in the Thai setting would be that Christianity is the religion of white people), and the other is what I call "scripts." Scripts are passed on as culturally correct answers for situations that often are not related to real life, or that do not represent accurately a true belief or value. A Thai example would be the often-met saying that "all religions are equally good; they teach us to be good people." When pressed, however, people will indicate they believe that their religion is true. Practically, parents are often not at all happy to see their children convert to what theoretically should be another equally good religion. Thus this is more of a culturally scripted answer that has to do more with social cosmetic and defusing the tension that could come from disagreeing about religious convictions rather than an actual belief. The distinction between objections and scripts is not hard and fast, it is probably more useful as a tool to help us think about a particular problem area and how to craft a response.

Some of the more likely problem areas that you will encounter when sharing with a Thai will be the idea that to be Thai is to be Buddhist, that their family is Buddhist, that they must follow the ways of their ancestors, that they either do not sin at all or have not committed a big sin (such as killing someone), that Christianity is the religion of white people, that all white people are Christians (thus everything white people anywhere in real life or movies is what "Christians" do). Learning how to handle these problem areas can help to open many doors to fruitful gospel conversations.

I want to expand upon two major issues here to illustrate positive ways of engaging these critical questions that always arise when talking about the Christian faith in the Thai setting. The first is a saying that you are likely to hear at the beginning of starting to share the gospel with a person, and at the end after you have finished: "All religions are equally good; they teach us to be good people." If you do not have a way to gracefully work with this foundational response, it can put a quick end to further conversation. One day in discussing this with a Thai pastor, Rev. Wirachai Kowae, the founder of the Thailand Assemblies of God and Rom Yen Church, he shared with me how he handles this. I have found it to be a great door opener to sharing further.

When someone tells him this, he affirms the statement, but then goes on to make the following argument. Suppose you were out working or playing and got your face all dirty. When you come into the house, you go to the mirror, and it shows you the state of your face, how dirty it is. The mirror itself cannot help you. At this point you need the outside help of water and a cloth to clean up. In the same way religion, like the mirror, cannot clean us up either. Religion will help to show the state of our heart, just as the mirror shows the state of our face. Trying to keep the commandments of any religion will reveal that we have trouble doing so, the religion and the commandments show us the state of our hearts. However, just like the mirror, the religion itself cannot cleanse us from our sin. It takes help outside of us from Jesus Christ to be able to remove sin from our lives.

Another issue that comes up at the front end of many initial conversations about faith is "Do I have to change my religion?" This is related to the identity issue where to be Thai means to be Buddhist. There are a range of responses that can be made and which carry with them implications for how the relationship will proceed. Answers at the far ends of the poles (an unqualified yes or no) flounder on the meaning being made by the listener, while answers in the middle that reframe the issue have more potential for developing the relationship and fostering understanding of the uniqueness of the gospel.

When the evangelist answers, "Yes, you must change," the expatriate witness is usually thinking of the more restricted space of specific belief and ritual in the religious system and its claims to being soteriologically effective. But for Thai listeners it is heard as a wholesale rejection of everything Thai, and thus is a door closer to further conversation and relationship. In an attempt to grapple with this, some in the Buddhist world, who have been influenced by the literature of insider movements, advocate that a "no" answer is the way to go. Some streams of this way of thinking see the outsider as an advocate to tell people they can and should stay in their religious and social environment, and continue to identify themselves as a Buddhist.

The issue here again is the meaning the listener is going to create from this communication. If the evangelist says that coming to faith in Jesus does not mean you have to jettison your whole culture, this may be understood as legitimating the previous religious system and can easily lead to a mixing of incompatible beliefs and practices. In some cases Christian witnesses are advocating staying in the "socioreligious" system and are actually advocating that people continue in Buddhist practices but "do it unto Jesus in your heart." Biblically this is problematic at several points, a major one being the close linkage made between ritual practices and demonic elements involved in idolatry as we find in 1 Corinthians 10:14–22. On the social side such a response is fraught with difficulty. Even if the assumption that mature disciples committed to biblical faith can be developed using this approach holds true, on the Buddhist's side it will be seen as manipulative and an attack on their religion. Christians would find it grossly offensive if a Buddhist were to identify as a Christian and then propagate, as a "Christian," doctrines from Buddhism while denying core Christian beliefs and meanings of ritual practices. We need to be fair to our Buddhist friends and not engage in a practice that we ourselves would find reprehensible.

I have learned a different tack from my Thai pastor friends for handling the religious change issue. It keeps the door open for further relationship and focuses on meeting Jesus and experiencing his power. This is a reframing of the issue around the notion of relationship (*samphan*) and not religion (*sasana*). I will often add to this the idea that we want people to meet Jesus in the condition that they are in, and that he will guide them in what steps to take. Reframing avoids the pitfalls in listener understanding and opens the door to a positive presentation about what a relationship with Jesus Christ is like. This also allows us to explore, as the relationship develops, the social dimensions of what it means to come to faith in Jesus in a more nuanced fashion rather than a blanket "no" or "yes" to everything.

Building the Environment for a Positive Response

There are four major elements to what I am calling "environment": relationships, exposure to the community of faith, power encounter, and prayer. Before I briefly sketch out some ideas that relate to these four major elements, I want to talk about the relationship between environment and a contextualized message. My observation is that both are necessary, but taken individually, neither is sufficient to produce evangelistic effectiveness. If the environment is good but the message is not clear, non-Christians will back away or, if they believe, become evangelistically ineffective Christians who are unable to articulate the faith to their society. If you have a contextualized message, but the environment is poor, there is no attractiveness, and people will not become disciples, or they will synthesize elements from biblical faith and their local faith. I call these elements an "environment," because these are not discrete activities that are done serially, but rather commitments that are lived out all the time and form the backdrop for telling the story of Jesus in a contextualized manner. While my focus here is the Buddhist world, these environmental factors are important in any setting where there is a large gap between the worldview of the Christian community and local non-Christians.

Build Good Relationships with Buddhists

Christian demographers tell us that 86 percent of the Muslim, Hindu, and Buddhist world do not know a single Christian (Johnson and Ross 2009,

316). This highlights the need for all Christians to intentionally initiate and pursue relationships with non-Christians. Many have never met a single Christian, or never had a conversation with a Christian, much less developed a good friendship with a Christian. To reach a Buddhist with Christ's love requires making space for a genuine relationship. Our lives provide the interpretive background for everything we say about Jesus.

In the context of genuine, authentic relationships with people, there are a number of values and practices that should inform these friendships. I believe that we should bring issues of faith to the forefront of the relationship. Be upfront about your faith in Christ. It is disappointing for people when Christians pursue a friendship with them and then after a period of time spring on them that Jesus is the greatest thing in their lives. We need to genuinely love and serve people and not see them as objects of our mission. At the same time we need to let them know that our lifestyle choices are deeply connected to our relationship with Jesus Christ.

Telling stories from the Bible, reading the Bible with them, and letting them read it on their own is important. Folk Buddhists do not have a tradition of reading their sacred texts. At the same time, they often love stories. Much of the way they communicate their faith is via stories. This is a great opportunity to tell the stories of the Bible to people in answer to specific issues they may be facing or worldview issues.

Whenever possible, work with the entire family. Try to build a positive climate for the potential new convert by building trust with the family. In societies that highly value respect for elders and parents, for a Christian to lead a child or minor away from their ancestral path is the ultimate insult and a grievous offense. We set potential converts up for failure if we lead them to faith but then let them stand alone against the enmity of their closest social relations.

Bring Them into Contact with the Community of Faith

Much of my work on message contextualization has been done because of my observation that in general the only tool in the toolkit to help others hear the gospel is an invitation to attend church services. However, having said that, a critical piece of the environment is exposing the people we are in relationship with to God's people. This is not limited to formal church services, and in fact for many people that may not be the best place to start. Small groups and gatherings in homes—informal gatherings of Christians—give people a chance to overhear of God's grace at work in people's lives, rather than be told directly. This allows time for processing that can get derailed by more direct approaches, which actually stir up resistance.

Power Encounter

Buddhist people come to faith through experiencing Christ and not through verbal presentations alone. Normally in our Western tradition of witnessing, we talk about the gospel but do not often pray with people to experience the power of Christ. One of the "best practices" I have picked up from Thai Christian friends is integrating prayer for people into times of sharing faith. They ask people what needs they have, and they pray with them for healing, blessing, and provision right then. They also invite people to pray on their own as well. The experience of answered prayer often opens the eyes of folk Buddhists who will then be more open to learn about Jesus.

Prayer

At the end of the day, it is the work of the Holy Spirit that draws people to Jesus. One convert from a Buddhist country shared with a class I was teaching how her initial attraction to a church in her homeland was to the foreigners teaching English there. She began attending church services with them, but the preaching made no sense to her. Then one day while listening to a message on Revelation 3:20 she said Jesus knocked on the door of her heart and she invited him in. This is what Jesus does; he reveals himself to people. Persistent, prevailing prayer that probes the generosity of the Father's heart on behalf of peoples who do not yet know him is foundational. It is easy to talk about, hard to do.

Conclusion

Recently I shared this material on building capacity for developing context-sensitive witness in a graduate class. Most of the students were working cross-culturally, but one worked in the USA training leaders and facilitating new church planting. After I finished he raised his hand and said, "You have just told us bad news. This is too hard; nobody is going to do it." It is hard, but I do not see any other way around it. The Buddhist world for the most part has found the gospel message presented in terms of Western worldview issues unappealing. Large numbers of Buddhists and people in other religious systems are waiting to meet a Christian for the first time and to hear a relevant and compelling presentation of what it means to be a Christ follower. Local Christians and loving outsiders have the chance to position themselves to be vessels the Spirit can use by building environments conducive to evangelism and context-appropriate content as a part of their missional stewardship as they live among the Buddhist world. It will be worth the effort.

References

Cooke, Joseph. 1978. The gospel for Thai ears. Unpublished manuscript, July. Typewritten.

Davis, John. 1998. *Poles apart: Contextualizing the gospel in Asia.* Bangalore, India: Theological Book Trust.

Flemming, Dean. 2005. *Contextualization in the New Testament: Patterns for theology and mission.* Downers Grove, IL: InterVarsity Press.

Gusawadi, Brasert. n.d. Witi atibaay tang hang kwam rod doy chai ruub wongglom sung maaythung gaay jai lae winnyaan [A method of explaining the way of salvation using a circle with the meaning of body, mind, and spirit]. Bangkok: Overseas Missionary Fellowship. Unpublished manuscript. Typewritten.

Higgins, Kevin. 2010. Diverse voices: Hearing Scripture speak in a multicultural movement. *International Journal of Frontier Missions* 27, no. 4: 189–96.

Johnson, Alan R. 2005b. Wrapping the good news for the Thai. In *Sharing Jesus holistically with the Buddhist world*, ed. David Lim and Steve Spaulding, 205–48. SEANET 2. Pasadena: William Carey Library.

———. 2011. Investigating lay people's conceptions of *dukkha*: Groundwork for context-sensitive witness. In *Suffering: Christian reflections on the Buddhist dukkha*, ed. Paul de Neui, 147–62. Pasadena: William Carey Library.

Johnson, Todd M., and Kenneth R. Ross, eds. 2009. *Atlas of global Christianity 1910–2010.* Edinburgh: Edinburgh University Press, Center for the Study of Global Christianity.

Keller, Timothy. 2012. *Center church.* Grand Rapids: Zondervan.

Overseas Missionary Fellowship. The way to freedom: The way to a new life. n.d. Bangkok: Overseas Missionary Fellowship. Unpublished manuscript. Typewritten.

Petchsongkram, Wan. 1975. *Talk in the shade of the Bo Tree.* Trans. and ed. Frances Hudgins. Bangkok: Thai Gospel Press.

Smith, Alex. 1981. *Siamese gold—A history of church growth in Thailand: An interpretive analysis 1816–1982.* Bangkok: Kanok Bannasan (OMF Publishers).

Van den Toren, Benno. 2010. Can we see the naked theological truth? In *Local theology for the global church: Principles for an evangelical approach to contextualization*, ed. Matthew Cook, Rob Haskell, Ruth Julian, and Nathee Tanchanapongs, 91–108. Pasadena: William Carey Library.

Walls, Andrew. 1996. *The missionary movement in Christian history: Studies in the transmission of faith.* Maryknoll, NY: Orbis.

Weerasingha, Tissa. 1984. A critique of theology from Buddhist cultures. In *The Bible and theology in Asian contexts*, ed. Bong Rin Ro and Ruth Eshnaur, 290–314. Taiwan: Tai Shin Color Printing.

CHAPTER 5

APPLY CULTURAL CONTEXTS TO GENERATE MULTIPLE CHRIST-CENTERED COMMUNITIES

Alexander G. Smith

Donald McGavran called the patchwork quilt of the world's cultures a veritable "mosaic" of peoples (1970, 59). Each had its own characteristics and unique texture. Therefore, local churches should appropriately reflect the indigenous styles and nuances of communication of the specific cultures and peoples of which they are part. Drawn from a common community, they inimitably share close identity with that society. Thus because of faith, Christ-centered congregations will stand unique from other pieces of that variegated mosaic. But they should still reflect the obvious traits and clear continuity with their own community in indigenous life, dress, ceremonies, values, and so forth. The main purpose of maintaining close resemblance to their emic culture is so that they, as God's people, can be effective witnesses to those in the broader society around them by planting multiple fellowships of Jesus. By retaining close cultural identity with their relatives, friends, and fellows, Christ-centered congregations are able to share the gospel more naturally throughout their normal social networks. Their changed lives express God through transformed characters, lips, and love. These new powerful traits of living and belief in Christ will necessarily be observed by those in their local neighborhoods and society at large. This movement will best express itself in and through the multiplying of contextual congregations worshiping Jesus.

This chapter suggests the importance of retaining each people's unique contextual characteristics in the communities of Christ, for the purpose of relating to the general society and relaying the gospel clearly to them. Serious consideration must be given to incorporating indigenous culture into the life of fellowships, especially for the distinct clear communication of God's people to their surrounding unreached communities. The primary purpose of contextualization is good communication. Effective, efficient, local communication is predicated upon adequate and appropriate contextualization. As indigenous congregations are the natural product multiplied in their cultural soils, so their communication to family and neighbors should likewise be highly contextual too. Christ-centered contextual communities easily replicate themselves and multiply outwardly so as to become a dynamic movement saturating their environments with the transforming presence of Christ.

Reproduction: God's Purpose for Christ-centered Congregations

Christ's commission to his disciples clearly defines the congregation's primary duty to communicate Christ to their surrounding communities and beyond (Matt 28:18–20). Their clarion cry is initially to the people of their own kind. Their key message is Christ for the people, both locally and globally. While keeping their basic cultural context, all Christ-centered fellowships are to express the living presence and power of Christ through their lifestyle in word and deed, in faith and action, and in creed and conduct.

Professor Alan R. Tippett expertly expounded this function of the contextual congregation in representing Christ in all his fullness to their own community (1973, 145–63). Christ in and through his people, gathered as Christ-centered congregations, are to portray his living character, redemptive power, salvific purpose, and faithful blessing, initially in each community from which they arose. The body of believers is to reflect the love of God, the reality of salvation in Christ, and the healing of his reconciliation to those of their own neighborhoods, family, and social networks. They are to serve them, to proclaim God's providence for them, and compassionately help alleviate the human problems they face. Christ's congregations are to be both light and salt to the societies surrounding them. Though sometimes taken for granted, this vital fundamental process for transforming societies has often been neglected. Unfortunately, fellowships can become isolated, self-centered, self-serving subcultures instead of dynamically affecting their communal societies. Each Christ-centered congregation is to be involved intimately and practically with its community. Elsewhere, simply because of this assertion, I have argued for the parish church model to become the dominant functioning structure of truly serving congregations (Smith 2009, 28–35). The local church thereby impacts its immediate community or parish as its primary ministry.

Unintentionally, ignorantly, or deliberately, believers and fellowships frequently sabotage this primary purpose of the kingdom of God, instead of determinedly reinforcing it. Too easily God's missional purpose has been sidelined or sidetracked. This spiritual dimension is unchanging and must permeate all cultural, social, and contextual areas in which Christ's congregations are multiplied. Nor are they to be ignorant or naive about the possibility of spiritual fruit in their local secular communities. God has already allowed or ordained many preparatory seeds, pregnant with potential, latently awaiting his harvest. That preparation for producing fruit already exists in the context of Buddhist peoples, particularly in their penchant for the spiritual dimension.

Connecting with the Buddhist's Capacity for the Gospel

In his lectures during the 1970s, Tippett aroused the missiological community to an awareness of the capacity of the animist for the gospel. Whether or not modern mission has adequately applied this concept in contextualizing their communication remains questionable. Animism affects all religions of the world. Mahayana, Theravada, and Tibetan folk Buddhists incorporate strong flavors of animism into their religious concepts. These various assimilations include elements from Taoism, Shinto nature worship, shamanism, ancestral cults, familiar spirits, demons, hungry ghosts, hells, and many others. Although often contrary to Buddhist tenets, these accretions and interpolations that folk Buddhists practice enhance the ability of folk religionists to be impacted with the gospel. The Christian communicator's awareness and wise application of these subtle underpinnings from the animist world provide local congregations with potential bridges for connecting Buddhists with Christ. Wise application of them can become effective stepping-stones to the living Creator God. Significant connectors among Buddhists await thorough application for appropriating the gospel.

First, the predominant idea of prayer is integrated into regular daily practice. Buddhists pray in all sorts of situations, especially pleading for protection from demon forces, hungry ghosts, fate, and human enemies. They habitually seek help for blessing and prosperity. They use prayer beads (*mali*), prayer flags, prayer wheels, and stones with mantras engraved on them (*mani*) in their penchant for prayer. Many pray daily in front of Buddhist home altars, shrines, or ancestral tablets. Others intercede before images of Buddha, *bodhisattvas* (promised one), or animistic guardian shrines. Some pray before meals. In Japan and elsewhere they write their personal pleas and display them on racks before temples, *wats* (temple), or shrines. The festival of Purnima celebrating the birth, enlightenment, and death of Buddha emphasizes prayer. Generally, during this event prayers are recited, oil lamps lit before the images of the Buddha, Tripitaka scriptures read, and the statue of Buddha worshiped. "Meditation and offerings of flowers, silk scarves, incense and fruit are also part of the worship rituals" (Singh 2012, 50).

Second, Buddhists hold a high view of holy writings. They deeply respect their Tripitaka scriptures and their *sutras*. *Bhikkus* chant them on Buddhist holy days and quote them in sermons. I have visited numerous Thai rural homes where they have accumulated a pile of different Christian tracts given them over the years. Frequently, out of respect they keep them safely. Though they do not understand their meaning, they still honor them, because they respect holy writings. Because of this, Christians need especially to show respect for the Bible and the word of God and be available to their neighbors.

Third, Buddhists sincerely respect their religion, the *sangha*, and also numerous religious objects. Buddhism is an integral part of their lives. Even though they do not always follow it wholeheartedly, the sacred matters to them. Buddhism is deeply engrained into their nature since childhood. It affects every area of their lives—moral codes, values, education, social responsibilities, and respect for the king, temple abbots, high *lamas*, and *bhikkhus*. Respect for Buddhism is an essential and indispensable ingredient of national identity.

Fourth, religious symbolism has a highly significant emphasis in Buddhism. Symbols are meaningful and appropriate, particularly among illiterate or semiliterate populations. The creative iconography, the *mudras* (body positions), *mandalas* (artistic charms), *tangkas* (sacred paintings), Buddha's relics, temple murals, pictorial art forms portraying the history of the Buddha, the many variegated shaped images of Buddha, and *bodhisattvas* indicate a deep reverence for spiritual experience and a certain seeking for connection. Meditation is also an important regular practice in Buddhism, centered in looking for enlightening mystical experiences or spiritual answers to gain liberation from suffering.

Furthermore, philosophically, esoteric mysticism is another element that dominates Buddhist religion. In Buddhist worldview, all is believed to be interdependent, though constantly changing and impermanent. Hence many Buddhists attempt to find some mystical oneness with nature, a union with the impersonal universe. In Mahayana this becomes a call for a universal, simultaneous enlightenment of all life in the future, usually through the assistance of the *bodhisattvas*. This notion of seeking spiritual experience and mystical connection with the world or "mother earth" can become a possible talking point for a springboard to teach about the biblical mystical union with Christ in his role as Creator God and Redeemer. This leads into experientially knowing the personal experience of being complete "in Christ."

Another factor for Buddhists is an intense fear of malicious demons, malevolent spirits, hungry ghosts, and bothersome ancestral spirits. The prevalence of the spirit world is inescapable. This opens opportunities for proffering biblical responses of relief, assurance, and victory in times of spiritual need. Along with this is their abject fear of many Buddhist hells (1,088 with eight major hells and 135 subsidiary ones for each). Because of their bad karma, they are likely to be assigned to these in future reincarnations. Therefore, they seek protection from demonic powers, desiring healing from possession, disease, and sickness caused by the denizen of spirits. Beyond this is their hope for peace, quietness of being, prosperity, and happiness in life in the midst of suffering, the primary premise in their religious tenets.

Lastly, attention to spiritual and religious duty is clearly important to Buddhists. They devote themselves to the *dharma*, keep weekly "monk days," follow monks' instructions, attend activities at their *wats*, give offerings and food to the *bhikkhus* daily, make merit in multitudinous ways, and give resources to the *sangha* and the needy. All of these reinforce notions of duty in worship, relationship, responsibility, and reverence. Following the Buddha's code of morality (*sila*) also helps to maintain law and order in the community.

These seven contact points already exist in most indigenous Buddhist cultures. They are readily available for utilization as launching pads for connecting with the people, particularly at the level of their felt needs. They provide contextual bridges for local fellowships to proclaim the kingdom of God in all its fullness. The potential for touching nerve centers of real need is astronomical as is its power to multiply Jesus fellowships among those delivered from fear and the angry spirits. The question is: "How best can local congregations contribute significant spiritual impact on their surrounding society without being seen as a foreign appendage of Christianity?"

The Necessity for Contextual Indigenous Jesus Fellowships

For over two hundred years, Western theology, methodology, and cultural accretions affected Majority World congregations. How converts dressed, acted, or conducted their services was largely influenced by patterns from the West. Indigenous believers were expected to separate from their cultural world around them. Consequently the surrounding society viewed Christian churches, including congregations of extracted local people, as more foreign than native. Christianity was considered an outside, Western, overseas alien anomaly. Many methods that mission used ignored the basic fundamental means of communication inherent in local culture. Instead of introducing foreignness, sensitive contextualization utilizes local media for communication. Essentially it incorporates appropriate elements from normal culture for use in truly indigenous congregations. Observable differences in local believers exhibit the dynamic effects of the gospel on the quality of their lives, transformed by the presence of the Holy Spirit and by the principles of God's word. Thus indigenous contextual congregations enhance their ability to multiply new fellowships exponentially and more acceptably within culture.

The main vehicles of communication come particularly from the basic local anthropological, sociocultural context. Thus, true contextualization will best mirror significant marks of the host society, as well as apply the main dynamics of culture and communication within the indigenous church of their people group. Therefore crucial contextual dimensions should still permeate the lifestyles of the members' families and their cultural and locally related social interactions.

In prior and unfortunately current mission, attempts were often made to make the converts something other than, or totally different from, the norm fitting their cultural milieu. The results often produced a subculture, an alien one, distinct from their cultural compatriots. Extracted believers were "called out" from their indigenous contexts to be "separate from the world." They were not to be "unequally yoked" closely or intimately with unbelievers (2 Cor 6:14–17). Unfortunately this misinterpretation worked against dynamic multiplication of contextual fellowships. Jesus reminded his disciples that they were now not the same character and quality as the world, and therefore he sent them back into that world as light and salt (John 17). Jesus had no intention of isolating them or the congregations they later initiated from their culture. Paul frequently reinforced this teaching, calling believers to have a distinct difference of character in quality and living compared to their sinful society, without withdrawing from society. This refutes the misguided approach of extraction, isolation, and insulating, which misinterpreted Paul. Sadly, this missional error emphasized an unhealthy, artificial separation of believers from their human society. Usually this meant native converts needed to dress differently, receive Western-style education, becoming in essence more in keeping with the culture of the foreign missionaries and the churches they came from, rather than maintaining their indigenous heritage and cultural settings. Consequently this affected their communication with relatives and neighbors, and built barriers in society rather than bridges for the gospel.

Three historical landmarks in mission occurred in 2012: the two hundredth anniversary of American overseas missions through Adoniram Judson and others; the centennial of the first publication of Roland Allen's *Missionary Methods: St. Paul's or Ours?*; and the fifteenth anniversary of the founding of SEANET. The era of Judson and most agencies tended to emphasize the Western nature of the church in its followers. In keeping with John Nevius and others, Allen emphasized the need for the indigenous cultural character of the church so that its spontaneous expansion could be accelerated. He endorsed the 1886 Nevius plan to establish indigenous Three-Self churches (self-governing, self-supporting, and self-extending) from the beginning. Allen also

> wanted the forms of the church to be adapted to local cultural conditions and not be imitations of Western Christianity. To accomplish this missionaries would have to hand over responsibility to the local leaders in the community, who would not be professional clergy either in their training or in their compensation. (Anderson 1998, 12)

In the twenty-first century, SEANET has attempted to focus on depending on God while using contextual approaches for multiplying churches that maintain local sociocultural dynamics. That purpose was to produce church-multiplying movements within and in line with the social culture of the different peoples. SEANET emphasizes prayer mobilization, training for local church planters, strategies for multiplying church movements indigenously, and collaboration of resources from the global church to accelerate reaching this objective.

While retaining much of the flavor of the culture is recommended, not every iota of its indigenous context will necessarily be acceptable to new societies in Christ. Certain aspects of some cultural traits may so contravene Scripture that they may need to be adapted more than adopted, and transformed rather than transferred. This is particularly true of certain aspects of former involvements with the demonic world, false gods, and idolatrous images.

The true Creator God of the Bible is in diametrical contrast to these pseudospiritual entities and human-made idols. The whole tenor of Scripture affirms God's demand for his followers to leave these impotent objects in order to worship their Creator only. While the contextual forms of these spiritual entities may seem to be critical to cultural identity, the transformation of Christ's followers in all peoples will certainly mean their wholehearted transference of loyalty from idols to the worship of God alone. Paul emphasized this metamorphosis in transfer from idols to the living God as an essential evidence of genuine repentance (Acts 26:18). Christ's church is supracultural and multicultural, not bound absolutely to culture. Nevertheless, the congregation of believers still lives, works, and serves in a specific cultural context. So it is right that they retain much of their culture, even though they favor a new allegiance to the Lord Jesus. This is especially vital in order to reach as many of their own families, relatives, friends, and community members as possible. Therefore, local fellowships should reflect their own culture and not adopt outside foreign cultures, Western or Eastern, American or Korean, just because they follow the living Creator God. The reason I argue this is even more crucial, because the culture itself holds the relational keys, productive seeds, and normative processes for the most effective communication of the body of believers to its local, familiar community. This contextual approach also facilitates the best potential for multiplying Jesus fellowships throughout the whole people group.

Good Communication Arises out of the Cultural Context

In essence, contextualization is simply good communication. Marshall McLuhan declared the medium is the message (1964, 23–35). Contextual believers and contextual congregations provide the best mode for multiplication. As the medium is the message, so the context becomes the medium for communication. Using cultural forms of expression creates understanding more readily. Therefore moving from the known to the unknown, the familiar to the new, is accelerated. This follows the first rule of teaching; namely, know the primary audience and begin where they are. In working across cultures, applying this principle is crucial. It is equally vital for the indigenous fellowships of believers to apply these principles to reach their familial communities in multiplying new fellowships among them.

Deliberate prioritizing and nurturing are needed from the start to incorporate real indigenous communications into evangelistic, preaching, and teaching functions of the local congregation. This is particularly true for the speediest replication of house fellowships. William Rivers and Wilbur Schramm declare, "Mass communication helps us to transmit the culture of our society to new members" (1969, 15). The primary business of new societies in Christ is to transmit the gospel, replicate evangelism, and multiply new fellowships. Using local media such as drama, dance, and music styles, common native instruments, and songs in keeping with local tonal scales reflects an indigenous flavor. Read *Communicating Christ through Story and Song* (de Neui 2008) for more illustrations. Expressions of indigenous art, dance, and drama exhibit clear cultural compatibility in the internal worship and thereby the external outreach of contextual congregations (Smith 2010, 67–70).

Certainly, careful discernment must be exercised to achieve applied contextualization and avoid syncretism. A Western musician living in Thailand for several years learned to play the local Thai *ranat* (marimba) expertly. His skill and proficiency was equal to the indigenous celebrities. He followed meticulously the traditional *wai khru* rites related to the spirit master of the art. This included burning candles and offering incense to the spirits. He claimed to be a believer, but performed these cultural rituals without making appropriate adjustments. He needed to adapt part of those indigenous rites to transform them to fit a biblical framework, which would acknowledge God as the Master of his musical gifts. This omission tended to produce a mixed message to disciples in the churches and also among those in Buddhist communities. Even more confusion arises by accepting seemingly similar terms and religious jargon in interfaith discussions, without discerning context, meaning, and usage. This is so crucial to clear communication, it forms the basis of our next emphasis.

Overcoming Confusion of Conceptual Meaning Conflicts

One fundamental issue in the conversion of peoples to Christ is their contextual comprehension of biblical concepts frequently used in

Scripture and by Christ's followers. Too often Christ's congregations along with their leaders and workers erroneously think that communication is primarily what is said instead of what the hearer understands. Another error is to believe that they can transfer meaning to the hearers. In fact they are only sending bits of encoded information. These bits are then decoded and reformed in the minds of the audience according to their context, producing perceived meaning.

Frequently when communicating complex and foreign-like concepts, particularly concerning spiritual ideas alien to Buddhist minds and worldviews, confusion arises. Often Buddhists will put very different meanings on those terms. Therefore, using concepts unrelated to Buddhist *dharma* such as God, salvation, substitution, and eternal life generally adds to cultural misunderstanding. What are some principles that assist to overcome that problem? What is the process involved in checking the effective use of essential scriptural concepts? How can one understand the broader nuances of meaning in both host and biblical cultures? In what ways can they be applied and aligned with truth applicable to accurate doctrine? Certainly awareness of the problem is the first issue to be addressed. Careful research, thoughtful analysis, and studied experimentation are required before accurate meanings for simple and complex spiritual concepts can be obtained.

Contextualizing initial evangelistic terms and translating spiritual concepts demands much effort, time, study, and analysis. Three key principles are required to discern the actual meanings comprehended by hearers in indigenous communications. First, understand and evaluate crucial biblical terms for their nuances of basic meanings in Scripture and in the original languages. Concentrated studies of these key words and concepts help discover their true meanings and interpretations. Second, explore and comprehend accurate meanings of close or similar equivalents for those concepts in the local sociocultural-linguistic context. This is critical, particularly for those terms that initially appear to have approximate functional exchange. Such terms need to be fully understood as the local people perceive them. Third, select wisely those words and terms that closely express biblical concepts in the local language. Research and test these in the field. Conduct experiments followed by scientific evaluation, before finally adopting local terms for primary concepts in the Bible. While total equivalency may not always be obtainable, the closest conceptual heart of core meaning should be present in those words chosen for use in the local language. Avoid using inadequate words. Identify potential misunderstandings in vital terms in hope of obtaining precise conceptual communication. Accomplishing this also produces better gospel proclamation, well-informed converts, and enhanced extension of stronger knowledgeable congregations.

Before describing illustrative examples from Thailand, note a scintillating observation. Thai language is full of emotive words that relate to and are controlled by the heart concept *cai* (heart, mind, spirit). Combined with *cit* (mind, heart, soul) it becomes *cit-cai*, translated "mind and spirit," "heart and soul." The physical organ heart (*hua-cai*) refers to life as in *haai-cai* (to breathe) or *sin-cai* (to die).

Thai language tends to stress that communication is also a matter of heart: *khaw-cai* is to understand; *cai-khwam* is the meaning, essence, gist of the message (Haas 1964, 126–29). Dozens of Thai emotive heart words express the use of will and action through combinations with *cai*: for example, *tang-cai* (intend), *cai-det* (resolute), *cung-cai* (influence, persuade), *cai-ron* (hasty, impetuous), *cai-khaeng* (hard-hearted), *hen-cai* (sympathize), *cing-cai* (sincere, heartfelt), *wai-wang-cai* (trust, have faith in), and so forth.

Here I wish to illustrate and apply the process through which I struggled many years ago to find comparable terms to best express the biblical concept of faith and the verb for "believe" in Thai. The usual word Thai churches use for faith or belief is *chya*.

First, my study of the biblical *pistis* and associated words indicated a broader range of connotation than *chya* has in Thai. The Greek *pistis* means persuasion (that is, credence), moral conviction, faith, trust, and confidence in an active sense. Arndt defines *pisteuo* as to give credence to a person and to believe in, trust of religious belief in a special sense, as faith in the divinity that lays special emphasis on trust in his power and his nearness to help, in addition to being convinced that he exists and that his revelations and disclosures are true (1955, 915). J. I. Packer notes that *pisteuo* is a key word in the New Testament that "expresses the complex thought of unqualified acceptance of, and exclusive dependence on, the mediation of the Son as alone securing the mercy of the Father" (Harrison 1960, 208–9). *Webster's Dictionary* definition includes two interesting items: "inward acceptance of a personality as real and trustworthy" and "saving or practical faith or the acceptance of by the intellect, affection and will—of God's favor extended to man through Christ" (Webster, n.d.).

Second, this deeper emphasis of faith involving intellect, emotion, and will consequently moved me to research appropriate Thai words that cover those three dimensions. *Chya* was already adequate for the acceptance of the intellect as true, real, and genuine. Then *wai-wang-cai*, an appropriate emotive word, meant wholeheartedly to place one's trust and faith in someone. Furthermore, *phyng-pha-asai* indicated a deliberate action of will with the need to rely on or depend wholly on someone. Thus *pisteuo*'s breadth of meaning was best expressed by combining all three Thai concepts to make it full-orbed: *chya-waiwangcai-phyngphaasai*. Rather than use just *chya* for "faith" or "to believe," I began to utilize these three words separately, in triad combination or with acceptable contractions like *chya-phyng* or *wangcaiphyng*.

Third, I tested and experimented with these alternatives and found that teaching the concept of faith with all three elements produced clearer understanding, commitment, and determination in Thai believers. Furthermore, "repent" or "repentance" in Scripture also means a change of mind affecting intellect, emotions, and will. Confession, restitution, and forgiveness follow similar emphases. Understanding appropriate local equivalent linguistic terms and teaching them to local congregations produces positive maturity and better comprehension. It generates choicer biblical conceptualization among believers. It also helps local fellowships and members to more accurately proclaim from a biblical perspective as they witness to family and friends and multiply Jesus fellowships in their communities.

A similar process can be applied to ferret out meanings of complicated Buddhist terms and confusing connotations from the Buddhist worldview. Then local workers and their congregations can apply the best bridging words with enriched biblical meanings in teaching their constituent communities. This is important to make better informed choices in the closest dynamic equivalents for biblical or Buddhist concepts.

Discriminating Concepts of Cosmology, Heavens, and Nirvana

Tibetan Buddhists developed a *tangka* (pictorial circle) with an abbreviated sixfold view of the world. It showed six realms: gods or Brahmas, demigods including *boddhisattvas*, *asura* or titan demons (hells), *preta* ghosts, animals, and humans. The small crucial central circle portrays three animals representing the three fiery evils of greed (pig), anger (cock), and delusion (snake). Images of the head, hands, and legs of the Lord of Death protruded around the circle. Itinerant monks would unroll this painted portrait of the Wheel of Existence and, using a pointer stick, explain its various sections by word and song. By this simple method many rural and nomadic peoples learned Buddhism.

Classical Buddhist cosmology identifies thirty-one *bhumis* (realms of existence), which are divided into three worlds or regions (*traibhumi*). The brahmas or gods reside in the upper twenty heavens (*sagga*). Only males are here. No sex, greed, or sensuous feelings exist there. The uppermost four are realms of mind only, no matter, no spirit-soul just emptiness, where the miraculous rays of the Buddha are manifest. These four are world one, the formless *arupa-loka*. The sixteen heavens below them are realms of form and matter comprising the second world, the fine material *rupa-loka*. Existence in these twenty heavens is for many millions of years. These *bhumis* are extremely beautiful with jeweled palaces and riches. Below these brahma heavens is the third world, the sensuous *kama-loka*, made up of eleven levels of sensual desire. At the top are located six lower heavens, which are the abodes of *devas* (demigods), and *bodhisattvas*, again only males. Life span here is a million years. They exist playing out their full desires and lusts of their karma. But they must eventually pay for their own karma too through being reborn into the lower *bhumis*. Below the *deva* realms is the human *bhumi*. Beneath that are the four *apayas* or miseries: animals, *preta* hungry ghosts, the demon *narakas* or titans, and the hells (*niraya*). Residence in these hells can last trillions of years. Only from the human *bhumi* can one become enlightened. Even brahmas, *bodhisattvas*, and gods must pass through the human realm in their final quest for nirvana. Where then is nirvana (*nirodha, nipaan*)?

First, Burmese cosmology clearly notes that nirvana is not located in any of the thirty-one *bhumis* of existence, but depends only on ourselves. A wall painting in a Burmese temple in Myanmar notes, "Nibbana is not situated in any bhumis, nor is it a sort of heaven. It is a state which is dependent upon ourselves." Another Burmese picture of cosmology includes a special pavilion incorporating the national animistic *nats* or spirits, but shows no place for nirvana. The goal of Buddhism is liberation instead of salvation, or freedom from the endless cycle of life and rebirth, suffering and karma, all by means of one's own effort. What then is nirvana?

Leading Buddhist scholar and author K. Sri Dhammananda says nirvana "is quite unexplainable and quite indefinable" (1998, 127–28). It is not nothingness or extinction, nor is it paradise, a sort of heaven. It is not a place, but is more like a state or experience, "which is dependent upon ourselves." It is "an end of the craving which caused all the sufferings" and "the extinction of those relative physical and mental sources" (Ibid. 103–5). Humphreys writes that nirvana "means to the Theravadin the dying out of the three fires of Greed, Anger and Illusion. It is negatively expressed, being the extinction of undesirable qualities" (1958, 157). In Mahayana the "emphasis is laid on the Self to be attained, rather than the Not-Self to be stamped out" (ibid.). Note that both these Buddhist authorities, while stating nirvana is not extinction, still use extinction in their subsequent descriptions defining it! Nirvana is a state of lifeless emptiness (*sunyatta*), a release from impermanence, illusion, desire, craving, suffering, and the wheel of life. Nirvana is not a place, nor a heaven. Nor does soul, spirit, mind, body, God, or recognition exist in it—only everlasting death, emptiness, and neutral nonexistence. No life arises out of nirvana to be born on earth.

Second, the Bible defines what God's heaven is like. Scripture indicates that the heaven Jesus spoke of is the abode of God the Father, of Christ the resurrected Lamb of God, of the angelic hosts, and eventually all redeemed humanity. Jesus came down from heaven and returned there (John 6:38; Luke 24:51). It is a tangible place of mansions, light, beauty, and joy (Amos 9:6; John 14:1–3; Rev 21). No suffering, sin, curse, pain, disease, death, demons, night, crying, or sorrow will be found there (Rev 21; 22). Heaven is the final resting place of human spirits or souls (Eccl 12:7). It is a place of eternal life, full awareness, complete recognition, eternal light, spiritual perfection, living in new bodies like unto Christ's, and having unbroken communion with the Creator in the presence of God's glory. So what Buddhist term is best for translating the biblical concept of heaven? Is "nirvana," as defined above, adequate? Probably not, for it is seriously lacking. Is the Buddhist word *sagga* for "heaven" better? Again it is deficient in some ways too.

Third, several concerning issues raise cautions for contextualizers. Christ's congregations should start with the Bible and study precisely what particular concepts mean, not just speedily adopt a Buddhist term because it seems to fit the contextually fashionable "in" word of the moment. Ignoring the core of Scripture has allowed problems to creep into many fellowships over time. For example, Buddhist yoga and Buddhist forms of meditation are being used in churches today, without thinking through their unbiblical foundations or connections to unscriptural forces (Smith 2009, 32). In some Burmese folk Buddhist cultures, there may be some beliefs that warrant considering the use of "nirvana" for heaven, but this should not be quickly accepted and certainly not automatically exported as valid for all Buddhist people. Adopting such a practice should first be examined carefully in the light of the Bible as well as to its full precise definition and use in culture. Adopting "nirvana" in place of *sagga* (heaven) might lead to syncretism or to a later form of pseudo-Christianity that replaces living faith with one's own merit and self-effort. Often a thin line separates contextualization from syncretism. Because the definition and meaning of "nirvana" is so vastly different from the biblical heaven, Buddhists may rightly charge believers of deceiving them by lying when they present Jesus as coming from or being the fulfillment of nirvana. Biblical and personal integrity of believers and of Jesus congregations must always supersede entrepreneurial contextualization. Although believers need to be sensitive and wise in their proclamation of the truth, there is no virtue in avoiding the offense of the Cross through accommodation.

Overall the fundamental principle of dynamic equivalence favors the Buddhist term "heaven" (*sagga, suwan*) over "nirvana" (*nibbana, nipaan, nirodha*) for this biblical place of everlasting life where eternal God dwells. Overall the Thai *suwan* is preferred to *nipaan*. Since nirvana entirely depends on ourselves instead of on Christ's grace and substitution, a significant conflict in means of salvation is carried with it. Nyunt is correct in asserting that "salvation is impossible through human efforts but only the One who comes from outside of *Samsara*" can accomplish the redemption of fallen humankind (2012, 138). However, Nyunt's model of the "City of Nibbana" with two oval lines drawn between nirvana and *samsara* is incorrect for the starting point for Christ's incarnation and unsatisfactory as the ending point for his ascension (ibid.). While classic Buddhism postulates that nirvana is outside *samsara* as a state of escape from its cycle of life and suffering, it also adamantly affirms that nirvana is not heaven, nor the abode of God, Christ, or souls. Therefore by definition, nirvana cannot be that point of Christ's origin or return. Instead it is the highest heaven where God the Father dwells, not nirvana.

While Buddhist *suwan* (heaven) has shortcomings and inadequacies compared to the biblical concept, overall it has better dynamic equivalence in both content and context than *nipaan* (Thai: nirvana). Initially *Gott* was a close though incomplete Gothic German concept for God. But in time teaching enriched it sufficiently to carry the full connotation of God's character and attributes. Likewise, because of similarities inherent in *suwan*, Christ's followers can teach and develop deeper dimensions into the term to produce a higher, fuller concept equivalent to the biblical eternal heaven, not possible with "nirvana." Where experiments use "nirvana," it is essential that serious follow-up, research, and scientific testing be done to determine the responders' understanding of Creator God, Christ, and especially the means of salvation, works or merit, heaven, and eternal life. Christ's congregations must beware of using concepts with diametrically opposed meanings to Scripture, lest persistent outside forms of subtle error or idolatry erode believers' allegiance to God and faith in his Christ. That was the perpetual bane of Israel of old. Through his prophets, the Lord frequently declared judgment on their outside borrowing and incorporation of idols, Asherahs, worship of tree spirits, and of the planets into their worldview, beliefs, and worship.

Some practical means to speed efficient reproduction and assist accurate communication of God's plan for life's needs may be adapted culturally by transforming vital rituals and selective ceremonial practices by establishing functional substitutes.

Functional Substitutes for Expressing Christ's Message

A valuable area of communication adapts relevant cultural forms and ceremonies applicable to specific Buddhist cultures to help Christ-centered communities more acceptably relate the gospel to their constituent communities. This aids in transmitting Christ's message through familiar images and means that are readily comprehended in those societies. Cultural forms need to be studied, thoughtfully explored, analyzed, and applied. Functional substitutes for significant cultural ceremonies and even some festivals should be adapted and developed. Experiments could be conducted on their use and acceptance. Through them congregations can communicate to the societies in which they dwell, affirming their connectedness to the culture as well as expressing biblical values clearly. Some possibilities for appropriate functional substitutes that touch the felt needs of families are rites of passage such as birth, name giving, housewarming, weddings, and funeral ceremonies, or suitable festivals common to the surrounding neighborhoods and peoples. Often these are neglected in indigenous churches among Buddhists.

One example is Vietnam's Lunar New Year, called *Tet*. Everything shuts down at *Tet*. Even cities stop and folk return to their villages to eat *Tet* with their relatives and to remember their ancestors. They visit special temples, make offerings to the spirits, and have fun visiting and eating with their families. They try not to cause friction anywhere, because that may affect their prospects for the coming year. *Tet* is a most culturally and religiously significant time for Vietnamese. Christians tend to avoid celebrating *Tet* and so come under censure of the community (*TD Update* 2012, 1). Here is a case for creating a functional substitute for *Tet* within biblical norms for Christ-centered congregations. Maybe special worship ceremonies of Creator God their original Ancestor, who is God of their early ancestors, plus a unique Communion ritual could be developed to honor their forebears. Elsewhere in other SEANET volumes I have written on *buat naak*—Buddhist preordination (Smith 2005, 109) and other vital ancestral issues (Smith 2010, 161–82). These also warrant thoughtful functional substitutes.

Sickness is a major concern of folk Buddhists. Local healing rituals and practices concerning the spirit world should be studied along with research on their native practitioners and shamans. Believers should not ignore or summarily dismiss this as being the old way. Observation and analysis of them is needed to determine if and why appropriate functional substitutes with biblical principles and local cultural color may be required. Determine how they relate to the community's needs, what their specific role is, and what the populace's view of them is. Pentecostals, charismatics, and others employ various means of healing such as prayer, laying on of hands, words of faith, exorcism, the name of Jesus, and so forth. These may be partial functional substitutes, but has enough study and research been given to understand and adapt approaches of indigenous shamanistic functions so as to make Christ-centered congregations' means of healing acceptable to indigenous eyes? Do our practices seem too foreign to the local community? I do not mean we are to copy the shamanistic approaches, but rather that we might discover some acceptable principles and cultural bridging points to adapt and transform healing rites. Thus Jesus fellowships could serve the local peoples in ways they feel our healing approaches are compatible with culture and not foreign imports. Numerous kinds of Thai practitioners utilize different means for dealing with sicknesses in Thailand (Smith 1977, 89). Most relate to some area of the spirit world. Local contextual congregations should develop clear functional approaches from that spiritual perspective. Modify cultural models with adequate applications and sound biblical foundations. Unfortunately, often modern medicine becomes the substitute without adequately evaluating local spiritual dimensions of healing, which might identify clues for increased church growth.

Conclusion

The primary purpose for good contextualization is good communication. This is designed to reproduce Jesus fellowships across the spectrum of each *ethne* in an efficient and ever-widening dynamic movement. Efficient, effective native communication is predicated upon adequate, appropriate local contextualization. As indigenous congregations are the natural organisms of the cultural soil, so proclamation to family networks and neighbors should likewise be highly contextual. God's purpose for Christ-centered congregations is not primarily to focus on themselves, but to be his missional agents to those outside his kingdom. Contextual congregations exist to reproduce and multiply God's glory in their midst. They are the representatives of the Lord to their local communities. God wills that they communicate who he is in all his fullness, power, and provision to their societies. He desires them to proclaim his mighty word, exhibit his glorious works, and reveal his gracious will to them. They are beacons of godly communication and living savors of transformation throughout their communities. They also cross over to other *ethne*, saturating them with similar movements and multiplying house fellowships that worship and proclaim Jesus to all.

God allows inherent bridges for the gospel to be resident within the Buddhist peoples. They have a vast capacity for spiritual matters. Many practices are pregnant with potential possibilities to know Creator God. But this requires God's fellowships in their midst to become contextual in their communication to society. Contextualization at its best is good communication. Introducing adequate functional substitutes for crucial heartfelt needs like healing are means to better communication of the gospel.

The difficulties of communicating through interfaith dialogue revolve around conceptualization and interpretation of terms, particularly those that may seem similar but are really poles apart. Meaning discrepancy exacerbates this conceptual confusion. It is dangerous and unwise to use these concepts without thoroughly thinking them through, and evaluating and testing them before adopting those concepts and practices. A studied approach to linguistic and conceptual conflicts requires much study and discernment. The process of research, observation, analysis, application, experimentation, evaluation, and practical implementation is a wise way to preclude major pitfalls in communication for Christ's fellowships and their surrounding societies.

Missiologists should be careful to weigh both content and context in their interpretations and applications of cultural terms. This balance is crucial in order to avoid error. They must also consider quality not just quantity in developing strategies for multiplication of convert families and fellowships. Simplicity of tactics and approaches used should not overshadow depth in fostering spiritual experience and growth. It is safer to use an inadequate term as a point of contact than to adopt it as a functional fact. Care is needed not to give credence to questionable

Buddhist terms by accepting them unduly as equivalent in biblical meanings.

Maybe a warning against overly obsessing on contextual matters is in order. Recognize the danger of being enamored with contextualization, which may override priorities for spiritual development. Things may look quite contextual inside, but not be functioning adequately to impact the community outside. This can detract fellowships from continued evangelistic and mission outreach essential to their God-ordained central purpose. An overemphasis on being totally contextual can be counterproductive to multiplying and maturing fellowships. The hardest thing on earth is to keep balanced. Any unbalanced contextual focus must be resisted and corrected. The measure of efficient contextualization is maintenance and sustainability of both quantitative and qualitative spiritual growth and reproduction. The purpose of efficient contextualization is simply good communication and multiplication of like fellowships. Otherwise the focus on contextual issues becomes extraneous. Producing models of perfect contextual congregations is not an end in itself, but rather a means to more effective outreach, which influences the whole community and affects its transformation. Contextual congregations do not pride themselves in being showcases of adaptation, but rather model Christ in their genuine concern and efficient ministry to the general community from which they arose. Let the local Christ-centered fellowship look like a thing of the cultural rock from which it is hewn. Let the community eventually look like the mature church in its transformation through Christ in all the power and glory of his kingdom.

References

Anderson, Gerald H. 1998. *Biographical dictionary of Christian missions*. Grand Rapids: Eerdmans.

Arndt, William F., and F. Wilbur Ginrich. 1955. *A Greek-English lexicon of the New Testament and other early Christian literature*. Chicago: University of Chicago Press.

de Neui, Paul, ed. 2008. *Communicating Christ through story and song: Orality in Buddhist contexts*. SEANET 5. Pasadena: William Carey Library.

———, ed. 2009. *Communicating Christ in Asian cities: Urban issues in Buddhist contexts.* SEANET 6. Pasadena: William Carey Library.

———, ed. 2010. *Family and faith in Asia: The missional impact of social networks.* SEANET 7. Pasadena: William Carey Library.

Dhammananda, K. Sri. 1998. *What Buddhists believe.* Kuala Lumpur, Malaysia: Buddhist Missionary Society.

Haas, Mary R. 1964. *Thai-English student's dictionary.* London: Oxford University Press.

Harrison, Everett F. 1960. *Baker's dictionary of theology.* Grand Rapids: Baker Book House.

Humphreys, Christmas. 1958. *Buddhism.* London: Penguin Books.

Lim, David, and Steve Spaulding, eds. 2005. *Sharing Jesus holistically with the Buddhist world.* SEANET 2. Pasadena: William Carey Library.

McGavran, Donald Anderson. 1980. *Understanding church growth.* Grand Rapids: Eerdmans.

McLuhan, Marshall. 1964. *Understanding media: The extension of man.* New York: Signet.

Merriam Webster. "Believe". (n.d.). Retrieved August 6, 2014, from http://www.merriam-webster.com/dictionary/believe.

Nyunt, Peter Thein. 2012. *Missions amidst pagodas: Contextual communication of the gospel in Burmese Buddhist context.* Yangon, Myanmar: Myint Offset.

Rivers, William L., and Wilbur Schramm. 1969. *Responsibility in mass communication.* Revised ed. New York: Harper & Row.

Singh, Pallavi. 2012. Celebrating culture. *Spice Route.* May. http://www.spiceroutemag.com. Page discontinued.

Smith, Alex G. 1977. *Strategy to multiply rural churches: A central Thailand case study.* Bangkok: OMF Publishers.

———. 2005. Transfer of merit in folk Buddhism. In *Sharing Jesus holistically with the Buddhist world*, ed. David Lim and Steve Spaulding. SEANET 2. 99–124. Pasadena: William Carey Library.

———. 2009a. *A Christian's pocket guide to Buddhism.* Ross-shire, Scotland: Christian Focus Publications and OMF.

———. 2009b. Some historical views on Asian urban extension: Complexities of urban and rural relationships. In *Communicating Christ in Asian cities: Urban issues in Buddhist contexts*, ed. Paul de Neui. SEANET 6. Pasadena: William Carey Library.

———. 2010a. Family networks: The context for communication. In *Family and faith in Asia: The missional impact of social networks*, ed. Paul de Neui. SEANET 7. Pasadena: William Carey Library.

———. 2010b. The struggle of Asian ancestor veneration. In *Family and faith in Asia: The missional impact of social networks*, ed. Paul de Neui. SEANET 7. Pasadena: William Carey Library.

TD Update. 2012. Report. January 24. http://www.infomekong.com.

Tippett, Alan R. 1973. *Verdict theology in missionary theory.* Pasadena: William Carey Library.

CHAPTER 6

COMMUNICATION STRATEGIES FOR CHRISTIAN WITNESS AMONG THE LAO

Stephen Bailey

This chapter discusses a model of communicating the gospel among lowland Lao in the Lao People's Democratic Republic (Lao PDR). Given the limited response to the gospel after more than one hundred years of Christian witness, it is critical for expatriate and Lao Christians to take stock of the dynamics of communication in the Lao PDR. In addressing this problem, I have four objectives. First, I review some basic characteristics of the social context of the Lao PDR and the history of Christian witness among lowland Lao. Second, I consider the primary communicational model that Christians have used in witness among the lowland Lao people in the past. Third, I describe Lao worldview themes in order to discern what they say about Lao social relations. Finally, I suggest strategies for communicating the gospel in Lao society, which I believe hold promise for more effective witness. Given the similarities between the major cultural blocks of Southeast Asia, these strategies may also have implications for Christian witness outside of the Lao context.

Overview of Christian Witness in Lao Society

The social context of Lao society has been, and continues to be, marked by political, economic, and physical vulnerability. Throughout history, neighboring countries have used Laos as a buffer state to keep opposing, expansionist visions at bay, or they have sought to annex portions of Laos to serve the same purpose. Today the Lao PDR finds itself balancing its "special relationship" with Vietnam against the growing influence of China in Southeast Asia, their economic linkage with Thailand, and their fledging membership in ASEAN.

Roughly eighty-five percent of the Lao population are subsistence farmers. The topography and climate make it possible to farm paddy and upland rice as the staple food. But floods and insufficient rain often result in inadequate supplies of rice. Foreign rice grants have been necessary numerous times in recent years. Kitchen gardens and food products gathered from the forest supplement the diet, but the rapid depletion of forests and wildlife are adding to the difficulty presented by bad harvests.

Any description of the Lao PDR notes the general poverty, yet the past decade has brought rapid economic growth. The annual per capita income in 2012 was roughly $3,000, or about ten times what it was in 1990, and more than half the gross domestic product comes from subsistence farming. A recent U.S. Department of State report states,

> The Lao PDR is one of the ten fastest-growing economies in the world. Foreign investment has been increasing over the last several years and continues to flow to mining, hydropower, and agriculture. Vietnam, China, and Thailand are the largest sources of foreign investment, with each investing about $2.5 billion in Laos from 2000 to 2010 (*Asia 1998 Yearbook* 1998, 12–13).

In 2012, the ninth Asia-Europe Meeting took place in Laos and agreed to annual EU investment of up to EUR 25.5 million. Between 2000 and 2011, Laos' largest foreign investors were Vietnam ($4.7 billion), China ($3.4 billion), and Thailand ($2.8 billion) (Australia Network News 2013). But the biggest success in 2012 was Laos' inclusion in the World Trade Union. Tourism is

> one of Laos' biggest revenue earners: according to World Bank data, over 1.6 million people visited the nation of 6.2 million inhabitants in 2010. *The New York Times* named Laos the number-one travel destination of 2008. The country pushes its cultural capital: its temples, its stunning landscape. (O'Flaherty 2012)

However, this economic success has come at a price, and the rule of law and level of corruption continue to lag behind the positive economic growth. Charges of corruption and complaints of a lack of transparency are common among the international-aid and foreign-investment communities. But rural poverty persists, and although some medical workers in the country suggest there is evidence of malnutrition or insufficient nutrition among children, the poverty in Laos is not normally characterized by hunger.

Laos has been dependent on foreign aid since the early days of French colonial rule (Stuart-Fox 1986, 105). Today more than 16 percent of the gross domestic product comes from foreign aid (*Asia 1998 Yearbook* 1998, 12–13; Lintner 2001).

Beyond this, dozens of government, international, and nongovernment aid agencies operate in the country. This is significant because

> aid accounts for 18 percent of gross domestic product (GDP) and more than 80 percent of public investment . . . Whereas the infant mortality rate for Vientiane was about fifty per 1,000, in some remote rural areas it was estimated to be as high as 350 per 1,000 live births; that is, thirty-five percent of all children died before the age of one. (Library of Congress 1994)

The Lao government mandates that even small nongovernment agencies spend over $100,000 on direct project expenses. There are literally dozens of foreign aid agencies working in the Lao PDR today.

The poverty of the Lao people is more acutely felt in the areas of health and education. Traditionally health care was provided by one of several kinds of traditional healers. Today the Ministry of Public Health, with assistance from international aid agencies, is extending Western medical systems throughout the country. Despite these efforts, the "life expectancy at birth for men and women in Laos was estimated in 1988 at forty-nine years, the same as in Cambodia but at least ten years lower than in any other Southeast Asian nation" (ibid.).

Jesuit missionary Father Leria, who arrived in Laos in 1642, observed that the Lao typically had more than enough to eat (Stuart-Fox 1998, 95).

Although nutrition appears to be marginal in the general population, health surveys are of varying quality. Some data indicate that stunting—low height for age—in the under-five population ranged from two to thirty-five percent, while wasting—low weight for height—probably does not exceed ten percent of the under-five population. (Library of Congress 1994)

As the above overview shows, vulnerability has been a key characteristic of the social, political, and economic situation in Lao society for a long time. This context translates itself into a social system built on interdependence and allegiance to the social body, making Christian witness extremely difficult.

Almost half a century ago, William Smalley, former missionary to Laos, anthropologist and linguist, and editor of *Practical Anthropology*, wrote the following.

Apparently the gospel has never been made to seem relevant to the Lao. I feel deeply that a careful study should be made of the communication of the gospel in relation to the Lao culture . . . How can the Good News be made to seem good—to be something that people will really want—in this culture which does not, on the whole, see other needs than those met by its normal experience? Here the problem is not primarily one of language mastery. The missionaries are not worse than the average, and some are much better than the average . . . The communication problems here are cultural ones. (1956, 56–57)

For those who have traveled to Laos, or have had the privilege to live there as foreign guests, few have escaped falling in love with the ready hospitality of the people, recognized and referred to by the Lao themselves with the phrase, *nam chay* They value a relaxed and even-tempered attitude toward life that they refer to with the phrase *chay yen* (cool heart). They love *muan* (to have a good time), and are quick to forgive offenses with the frequently repeated words, *baw pen yang* (it was nothing). This unflappable style has served the Lao well during centuries of war and cyclical poverty. Many foreign powers have occupied Laos, but few have been able to effect significant change on Lao society.

Christian missionary efforts have not fared much better in their efforts to communicate the transformational message of the gospel.

The first missionary effort in Laos was attempted in 1642 by Jesuit missionary Jean de Leria. He stayed there five years before pressure from Buddhist monks forced him to leave (Roffe 1975, 392). In 1771 a Vietnamese catechist brought the gospel to the city of Thakaek, which has historically had a large Vietnamese population (Latourette 1939, 295–97). Later, in 1878, Catholic fathers tried again in northeastern Laos, but the mission came to a tragic end with the martyrdom of twelve priests in 1884 and five more in 1889 (Roffe 1975, 393-408). The most successful Catholic efforts occurred later in southern Laos.

The first Protestant missionary to Laos was Presbyterian Daniel McGilvary, who made several trips to northern Laos from Chiang Mai, Thailand, between 1872 and 1898 (Andrianoff 1991). In 1902, Gabriel Contesse and Maurice Willy began the work of the Swiss Brethren in southern Laos (David Andrianoff, email message to author, February 2, 2002). Later, in the early 1950s, Christian Mission in Many Lands and the Overseas Missionary Fellowship (OMF) entered southern Laos to work in cooperation with the Swiss (Oppel 1984).

The first resident Protestant missionary in northern Laos, G. Edward Roffe, was sent by the Christian and Missionary Alliance (C&MA) in 1930. In the 1960s, small contingents from Mission Aviation Fellowship (MAF), the Southern Baptists, World Vision, the Mennonite Central Committee (MCC), the Far East Broadcasting Company (FEBC), and Asian Christian Service arrived (ibid.).

Just before the Communist takeover in 1975, all foreign missionaries left Laos. The exception was MCC, the only Western mission that continued its presence into the postliberation era. MCC continues to do community development projects in the Lao PDR today. At the time of "liberation" both the northern and southern churches were self-governing and had worked together cooperatively for many years. The total number of Protestant Christians in the south was about two thousand (ibid.), and in the north the number was about seven thousand (Christian and Missionary Alliance 1973). The ethnic breakdown of the church was, at the time, roughly 60 percent highland Hmong from the north, 15 percent lowland Lao, and 20 percent midland Lao Khamu, with various other people groups making up the remainder.

The Protestant Lao Evangelical Church (LEC) was formed in the 1950s. It was a merger between the northern Protestant churches, planted by C&MA missionaries between 1930 and 1975, and the southern Protestant churches, planted by missionaries under the Swiss Mission Evangelique (between 1902 and 1975), the OMF, and the American Brethren.

Christian witness among the lowland Lao began and first bore fruit in southern Laos before World War II. Southern Lao have been relatively more responsive than Lao in the north, but there may have been social factors for this. First, many of these early converts were social outcasts, making conversion a more attractive option than normal. Second, in northern Laos, Christianity was associated with the French in Vientiane, and in the northern provinces with the Hmong, a group that the Lao generally look down on.

Today the LEC reports more than 654,000 members, but these numbers are difficult to verify since travel and communication between many provinces remains difficult. More than half of the LEC is made up of Khamu people (midland Lao). The Hmong (upland Lao) represent roughly another 35–40 percent of the church. There are several small, Protestant church gatherings not associated with the LEC, such as the Seventh Day Adventist Church, the church associated with a Lutheran mission; some small gatherings associated with Campus Crusade for Christ; the Assemblies of God; the Mennonite Brethren; the Sothern Baptists; the Methodists; and others. There are also a growing number of gatherings connected to mission organizations from Korea. There are small gatherings of Chinese and Vietnamese Protestants as well as several groups that connect themselves to the sending churches of various Asian missionaries.

Some property belonging to the Catholic community (mostly in the form of schools) was confiscated by the Communist government after it took control in 1975. After 1990, some Catholic churches were refurbished, and a new education and training home for village girls opened in Vientiane municipality. As of 1995, the Catholic Church was organized into four vicariates, overseen by three bishops. There were sixteen other ordained priests, seven of whom were ordained after 1975. Government pressure on the church, however, continues to hamper many Catholic efforts. There are roughly 635,000 Catholics, with the largest group in the church being midland Lao, followed in number by the lowland Lao. Several young men are being trained for the priesthood, and there is a vital youth ministry in Vientiane. Among Catholics the strongest foreign involvement is from Vietnam and the Philippines. After more than one hundred years of missionary witness among lowland Lao people, it is unlikely that there are more than seven thousand Protestant Lao believers in the Lao PDR. This translates into .23 percent of the lowland population in Laos. With the exception perhaps of Savannakhet, Lao Christians have made little impact on Lao society. In many cases, there simply has been no opportunity for the majority of Lao to hear the gospel. But even when they have heard the gospel, very few Lao have converted. Many who do convert, return to their traditional beliefs after a period of time. Lao Christians themselves seem unable to reverse this situation.

Among the problems confronting Christian witness in Laos is the fact that Christianity is largely seen as the religion of Western foreigners. Those who convert are seen as people who have chosen a foreign identity over their Lao identity. "To be Lao is to be Buddhist, and to practice and respect the traditions and customs of the ancestors," is a deeply held belief by the Lao People's Revolutionary Party, government officials, and the population at large. From at least 1994 to 2001, this attitude has translated into widespread and systematic persecution of Christians (U.S. Department of State 2001). While persecution continues in local communities, it has decreased in severity and frequency since 2001. What appears curious at first is that most non-Christian Lao voice approval of the teachings of Christianity while being clearly opposed to the conversion of Lao to the Christian church. This apparent contradiction is at the heart of the communicational problem I address below.

A Primary Communicational Model from the Past

In looking at this situation, it is not difficult to discern that Christian witness in Laos has been confronted with a high level of spiritual hardness. Among the general population, Lao Buddhism is more oriented towards the care of ancestral, guardian, and nature spirits than it is toward the moral metaphysics of the Buddha. Many people engage in contracts (*baphii*) with spirits for the things they need in their daily lives. Many also live in some level of fear of these capricious spirits. The Lao give offerings to the spirits as often as they feed the monks who come begging in the morning. A great number of concentrated prayer and power ministries are needed to address this situation.

From another vantage point, the situation suggests that the history of missions among the Lao calls for a more thoroughly contextualized gospel. Have the Lao really heard the gospel in a form they can understand? Perhaps if missionaries communicated the gospel more within the cultural assumptions and forms of the Lao it would make a greater impact. From my perspective, the churches in the city of Vientiane would certainly benefit from such an effort. For example, it is standard practice for the Lao to remove their shoes before entering a home or place of worship. Worship is also typically done while sitting on the floor. But in two Vientiane churches, worshipers keep their shoes on in the sanctuary and sit on Western-style pews.

While the church can always benefit from more concerted prayer, it should be recognized that there has been a significant prayer effort for Laos for some time now. Furthermore, prayer and power ministries already play significant roles in the life of the Lao Evangelical Church. In Vientiane all three local churches give considerable time to prayer and healing ministries. Testimonies to God's direct and powerful intervention in the lives of Christians for healing, provision, deliverance from the fear of spirits, and other needs are the norm among Protestants.

Looking at past efforts to contextualize the gospel is more complicated. There are two levels to contextualization: a level of form, and a level of meaning. In regard to the latter, I am convinced that the gospel is always contextualized in terms of meaning by local populations, whether local church leaders and/or missionaries give permission or not. People interpret the meaning of the gospel within the framework of their personal history and identity. How the Lao interpret the meaning of the gospel often has more to do with the perceived intentions of Christians than with the content of the gospel. I'll return to this later.

In terms of the use of local forms to convey the meaning of the gospel, the Lao have made periodic steps they are not fully at ease with. Cultural forms often mark the boundaries of a group's identity, and Lao

Christians often feel caught between wanting to be Lao while not wanting to mark their identity with allegiance to traditional religious rituals.

I know of at least three forms that the LEC in Vientiane has attempted to use in order to contextualize the communication of the gospel. First, in a rather unconscious way, the Lao have created a ritual they call the "Thanking God Ritual" (*Phithi Khapkhun Phra-chao*). This ritual mirrors a common type of household ritual known as *suukhwan*. It is performed to bring blessing to a person by calling their *khwan* (life essence). Lao Christians do not call their *khwan*, but in a similar way they use the "Thanking God Ritual" to mark blessing in their lives. A second traditional ritual, known as *soma*, has been incorporated into Christian wedding ceremonies. In this ritual young people seek the forgiveness and blessing of their parents or someone who has played the role of parent in their lives. Third, one LEC church in Vientiane now follows the traditional custom of taking off shoes before entering the place of worship and sitting on the floor rather than on pews. It is notable that all three of these forms entered into the worship life of the Protestant church after the Communist "liberation" of Laos and the departure of Western missionaries.

Even with these efforts, the majority of Christians in Laos are Khamu or Hmong. Thank the Lord for the growth of the church among these wonderful people! But we are still left wondering why the gospel is not impacting the lowland Lao.

From the beginning of Christian witness in Laos, a decision to give allegiance to Jesus has meant that converts cut off or seriously strain their relationships with key people in their lives by refusing to participate in the Lao religious ritual system. In the process, Lao identity has been replaced with membership in the small subculture of Christians. This small Christian community has their own specialized Christian language and ritual system. As in many Muslim, Hindu, and Buddhist communities, people who place their faith in Christ often face social death. At the same time, the small Christian community appears to have little to offer the rest of Lao society and is clearly linked to foreigners.

Christianity appears to be linked to foreigners in several ways. First, it is an imported faith that came with Westerners. Second, there are many foreigners who attend worship in the Vientiane churches and speak of their faith in their places of work. Third, the Lao are warned in the media that there are foreigners in Laos seeking to convert people to their religion using unethical means (e.g., providing economic incentives). Fourth, the LEC and the Catholic communities are able to carry out projects that obviously go beyond the financial strength of their local communities. The correct conclusion of many is that the financial strength of these Christian communities is supported by foreign Christians. Fifth, many of the forms used in church life are foreign imports. I have already mentioned the wearing of shoes and sitting in pews. Perhaps even more telling is the breaking of bread, *khaochii*, during the Communion service. *Khaochii* in the Lao mind is clearly linked to the colonial past and is understood to be the food of Western foreigners. For the Lao, rice is the stuff of life, not bread. Sixth, Lao Christians often use Lao words in ways that non-Christians do not understand. For example, the common word for "God" in Lao, *phrachao*, is often mistaken for one of the many gods of the Hindu pantheon. The word is more properly translated as "lord" and can relate to a person of royal or divine status. It certainly does not lead a Lao to think of the biblical Almighty Creator who is above and before all things.

The witness of local and expatriate Christians in Laos has not been without any effect. It has certainly been done with sincerity and, in some cases, even with sacrifice. My purpose here is not to criticize what has been done but to suggest that besides power ministries and contextualization of the cognitive content of the gospel, there is another issue that needs to be considered in Christian witness.

When Christian witness has been successful in Laos, it has not been primarily because of power—there is no shortage of power in traditional Lao religion—or because of good contextualization of forms and meaning. I believe the key to the communication of the gospel among lowland Lao is communication that engages Lao in terms of the structure of Lao relationships. This kind of communication taps into the issue of identity, which is so vulnerable in the context of the Lao PDR.

Charles Kraft suggests three levels of encounter in Christian witness (1999). First, there is the encounter with the power of the gospel. Second, there is an encounter with the truth of the gospel. Third, there is the encounter of relationship with and allegiance to Jesus as Lord.

Our first response to a lack of response to the gospel has tended to be prayer. This is appropriate and we should continue in these efforts. Our second response has often been to look for new ways to contextualize the content of the gospel. Contextualization has been concerned with translating the truth of the gospel accurately into the meaning systems of other cultures in order to achieve dynamic equivalence in meaning (Nida 1990; Kraft 1979). Clearly there is more work to be done in Laos in this area, but I suggest that this task will be done best with Lao Christians in the lead. Yet I wonder, along with Kraft, if the contextualization of the content of the gospel is as crucial as missionaries once thought. Particularly in traditional societies, but perhaps around the world, the contextualization of relationships is proving to be a more crucial task.

> God started with a Covenant, not with a book of doctrine. And Jesus came that the world might be saved through relationship, not through theology, as important as it is to think biblically. Theology then, is intended to serve relationship . . . Contextualization of relationship, then, has to become a major focus of our teaching, writing and witnessing. We need to learn what the contextualization of relationships is all about. (Kraft 1999, 8)

I turn now to a description of the Lao worldview. Worldviews are a model for social relations (Geertz 1973). In other words, I assume that the core assumptions and psychological images that pattern the perception and interpretation of the world for Lao people also shape, and are shaped by, the structure of their society.

The Lao Worldview and Social Structure

The worldview of the Lao can be described in terms of six worldview themes. These themes represent the core assumptions about the world that all Lao share to one extent or another. Figure 4 describes these assumptions for each category. What is important about these assumptions is what they reveal about social relations and how the structure of these relations impact communication.

I will use Mary Douglas' grid and group theory to relate these assumptions to Lao social structure. In her theory she compares societies in terms of two social dynamics. "Group," she defines as "the experience of a bounded social unit." It measures the degree of influence that the group has on the behavior of a member of the group. "Grid refers to rules which relate one person to others on an ego-centered basis" (1970, viii). In other words, grid measures, by comparison, the degree to which society structures the interpersonal relations of people in the group.

In Lao society it is possible to observe that group influence on individual behavior is quite strong in comparison to group influence in North American (U.S.) society. More particularly, the influence is experienced somewhat differently, depending on what level of Lao society you refer to. At the level of the household, the group influence is quite strong. Important decisions are always made in consultation with the members of one's household. Furthermore, households are oriented toward mothers, since they normally inherit the household property. Mothers are symbols of morality, because they tend to seek the welfare of the household group more consistently than others. A man generally lives with his wife's parents for the first few years of marriage.

At the level of the village, group influence is high, but not as high as in the household. Villages are largely made up of households related through maternal kinship ties. At the level of society larger than the village (what the Lao call *muang*), the influence of the group drops off, but is still significant when compared to North American society.

The high value placed on the group reveals a deep need for each member of society to play a role in seeking the well-being of the group. Given the very vulnerable social context in the Lao PDR, this is not surprising. Survival in the Lao PDR has historically demanded a high level of social interdependence.

The level of grid is highest in the opposite direction. The highest level of structure and ritual in relationships is found at the level of the *muang*. It decreases at the level of the village and decreases further at the level of the household. Nevertheless, relationships at every level depend upon a relatively high degree of structure. It is of particular interest to communicators to understand what this structure looks like and how it operates.

Worldview Theme Area	Orientation
Person/Group	Self as part of a web of household relationships structured in terms of older and younger obligations, male and female groups, and ritual specialists and lay people, within a muang power complex.
Time, Space, Matter	They are animated by spiritual beings and structured in terms of auspicious and inauspicious directions and times. They can be manipulated to manage the impact of karma, spirits, and gods on human success and failure.
Causality	The quality of social relations with the living, the ancestors, and the gods greatly impact human history. Moral and amoral power can be used to change life circumstances.
Human Nature	People naturally make mistakes, so they should be instructed on how to relate correctly to those who are older and younger. Society is a mirror of the sacred. People are not equal. Holiness is behaving properly in regard to the status of others. Sin is not behaving properly in regard to the status of others.
Meeting Human Needs	Needs and resources are assigned based on status in society. The primary strategies for increasing resources above needs is through alliances of mutual interest, established by token gift giving and final payment of the largest share to the older person in the relationship. Experts play a key role in managing natural and spiritual resources.
Preferences	Balance and harmony are highly valued, and envy is avoided to protect institutionalized inequalities. Blame is diffused and rarely attributed to the social system. Instead, blame is attributed to nonintegrated groups and individuals.

Figure 4: Lao worldview themes

Lao relationships are structured in terms of three basic categories. First, people always relate to one another in terms of an older to younger model. This is a kind of patron-client model that is defined first by the relative age of each person and then by factors such as education, wealth, and political power. This category is the fundamental building block for all Lao relationships. It is reflected in the worldview assumption regarding high and low space. The head is sacred. The feet are profane. North is auspicious. South is inauspicious. Mountains are good places for Buddhist temples, and valleys are not.

The second basic category in Lao social structure is that of gender. Women find their deepest friendships with other women, and men with men. The value for friendship that we see in North American marriages is not as high in Lao society. Men have ritual knowledge and have better karma than women. Women are a threat to the spiritual power of men and are not allowed to touch monks or the ritual objects that belong to men. Significantly, a primary reason for men to become monks is to make merit on behalf of their mothers.

Finally, Lao society is structured in terms of those who have ritual knowledge and those who do not. There is a clear and important distinction between clergy (ritual specialist) and layperson. Religion and society are expressed ritually, and while all Lao know how to act in each ritual, only some Lao (males) have learned the skills of actually conducting and empowering rituals.

What does all this say about communicating the gospel?

Strategies for Communicating the Gospel

There are many points at which engagement with the gospel of Jesus Christ will challenge the worldview of lowland Lao people. This engagement has cognitive implications regarding truth. It also has normative demands for the Lao context. But the cognitive and normative implications of the gospel must be discerned and decided on by the Lao Christian community under the guidance of the Holy Spirit as they reflect on Scripture. I suggest that this is not the primary task of missionaries.

The primary missionary task is to communicate the gospel in a way that allows the Lao to engage Jesus relationally. The intention of Christian witness is to bring people into relationship with Jesus. This can only be done effectively when missionaries themselves engage Lao people. Once people have engaged Christ relationally, the cognitive implications of the gospel will be interpreted based on the quality of relationships Christians have with non-Christians. This is at the heart of how the incarnation of the gospel happens in any context.

An incarnational model of Christian witness means that relational issues shape the informational truth issues of the gospel for each context. In contrast, the struggle to do contextualization well is often motivated by the desire to define the gospel in terms of transcendental truth statements. Since all our knowledge is bound up in our culture, these supposedly transcendental truths are actually reflections on what missionaries have found to be crucial for their own identity and context. The gospel does not call for objectivity in interpretation. The gospel calls us to interpret our context in terms of our relationship with Jesus Christ and the ethic of his kingdom.

Jesus lived in a particular time and place. He lived on behalf of others and died on the Cross on behalf of others. His life and death established the vision of the kingdom of God. When Christ died on our behalf, he not only offered us freedom from sin and a means to be in relationship with the Creator, but he also established a new way for us relate to one another. From that point on, the kingdom ethic declared that disciples of Jesus were to live on behalf of others. This vision, in like manner, establishes the interpretive key for the meaning of the Cross in each context.

The missionary task is to bring people into relationship with the Creator through a relationship with Jesus. This is a social message and can only be communicated in the midst of social relations. In Lao society, missionaries must incarnate Jesus following the social structure of the society. One of the key issues in this regard is to communicate in such a way that it protects and enhances the welfare of the household group and respects the older to younger pattern of relationships. It cannot be communicated by opting out of the social system altogether as has been the primary pattern for communicating the gospel in the past.

Communicating within the Group

The dominant issue (especially in the village) in Lao society is the interdependence of the social group. Individuals have freedom to choose their own path as long as they act in ways that do not endanger the well-being of those in their household, village, and nation. The influence of the group is strongest at the level of the household, where maternal kinship ties and obligation are strongest. Consequently, the first communicational strategy is to communicate within the structure of the interdependent social group, giving special attention to the household.

Communication of the gospel within the household should be done within relationships that allow Christians to relate in ways that have been transformed by the ethic of the kingdom of God. In the Lao context this means living on behalf of others in ways that recall the moral power of mothers and monks. Mothers and monks are important symbols of living selfless lives on behalf of others. Mothers and monks are the primary ones who enable people to experience *khwamsuk* (happiness, well-being). Here, the vision of the Lao captured in the word *khwamsuk* overlaps with the vision of the kingdom of God.

Christians must mark their relationships with others by living on behalf of others. In this way, the nonverbal message of the gospel will be found more acceptable, because it will affirm the group in morally powerful ways. Christian lives should even affirm the well-being of the group beyond normal expectations. Of course the worldview of non-Christian Lao will lead them to conclude that the intention of this kind of communication is to address and affirm the traditional moral quality of mothers and monks within the Buddhist context. This highlights the need for nonverbal communication to be supplemented by verbal communication.

Communicating the gospel within the group demands that the whole household unit be taken into account and that witness not result in disenfranchised individuals. Very often, young people have converted to Christianity as individuals, without the consent or input of their households. While it can be acknowledged that removing an individual for a time from their normal social group often opens them up to new ideas and ways of living, the failure to take into account the household group often results in a short-lived faith. The pattern in these cases has been for households to ostracize, persecute, or even abandon young converts. At the age of marriage, many of these young converts marry other Christians who are also cut off from their household network, or they leave their Christian faith to return to the household's care and provision. While the household unit should be the main focus, special attention should be given to the heads of the household.

Pastors Nantachai and Ubolwan Mejudhon have modeled a household approach in Bangkok, Thailand, where the social context is similar to that of Laos. Upon meeting a young person interested in the gospel, they ask for an opportunity to be introduced to the members of their household, especially the parents and elders. At this meeting they go out of their way to recognize the authority of the household structure in the young person's life and explain who they are. They also make sure that what the young person hears is the same as what all the members of the household have an opportunity to hear. Furthermore, they are careful not to dominate the time of young converts with church activities. Instead they instruct these new converts to take every opportunity to fulfill their obligations to their household. If a time comes when the new convert is ready to be baptized, the church then invites the young person's family to the service to participate in the service by presenting the newly baptized Christian with his or her first Bible (Mejudhon and Mejudhon 2000).

Christians can also communicate within the group through a Christian witness characterized by hospitality. This should be a hospitality that works toward the integration of every person who attends the local church. Lao villagers traditionally deal with the danger they feel from outsiders by encouraging outsiders to come in and take a role as an insider. Christians should do the same by finding ways to include non-Christians in their worship.

Societies that are high group want to protect their boundaries. The gospel critiques this tendency. The boundaries of the local church need to be porous. Every effort should be made to include others in Christian worship. Non-Christians should be invited to read the Scriptures, lead the singing, and assist in the preparations for common meals. It may also be appropriate to invite non-Christians to the Lord's Supper if they are willing to recognize the Lord's death in the Eucharist ritual. While Christians may balk at this suggestion, it should be remembered that non-Christians practice this kind of hospitality as a matter of course. Social integration of interested non-Christians within the Christian household of faith is a key to communicating the faith in Lao society.

Another means of communicating from within the group is to model local churches on the Lao household. The kinship relationships of the household, the sense of moral obligation to one another, and the priority for the well-being of the kin group are all appropriate models for relationships in local Lao churches. Institutional models of the church that reflect hierarchy and relationships of authority without kin-based relations will recall the amoral use of power (force) at the *muang* level of social experience. In cases where local churches are plagued by competition for control of foreign resources, they are already reflecting the *muang* power system.

Communicating the gospel within the group structure of Lao society also suggests the possibility of a "churchless" model of Christianity. Herbert Hoefer has made an argument for this model in the Hindu society of India (1991). He shares the advice he received from a Brahmin believer in Christ, whose ministry is to visit the *Jesu Bhaktas* (believers in Jesus who remain part of the Hindu community).

His first advice is, "If anyone asks, tell them you are a Hindu." It is acceptable to worship the god of your choice as a Hindu. The statement also indicates that you have identified yourself with the culture, history, traditions, and cause of the nation. Secondly, he advises *Jesu Bhaktas* never to go to a church. He warns that they (Christians) will usually come after you immediately, embarrassing both you and your family. This will cause unnecessary misunderstanding and opposition with your family. Thirdly, he advises avoiding going into full-time "church work." Rather, one should stay within one's family and fulfill one's social responsibilities. One's primary call and opportunity is to be a witness there (Hoefer 1999, 37).

Communicating within the Structure

Christian witness within the household group will require communication that follows the structure of Lao relationships. This strategy requires structuring communication to flow in terms of older to younger relationships, male and female groupings, and through the use of ritual.

Patron-client Communication

Communication will be best when it flows within the structure of older to younger relationships. Missionaries will need to be concerned not only for the communication of information but also for the social obligations involved in the communicational relationship. For the most part, Christian witness should flow from the older one in the relationship to the younger one. But older communicators will need to be aware of and live up to the social responsibility to provide advice and security for those who are younger. They should not be surprised when the younger one converts rather quickly. But neither should they be surprised if these younger converts abandon the faith just as quickly, should the older one in the relationship not provide the kind of care expected of them. For foreign missionaries this creates a problem of establishing expectations they cannot live up to in the long term.

One method of dealing with this is to connect converts to Lao Christian "older brothers and sisters" within the household of faith who can live up to these expectations. Another, more critical strategy, however, is to teach the younger one to look to God as the one who can provide for all his or her needs.

At the same time, converts should be instructed to continue to give their allegiance to the household to which they belong. Living up to their obligations in the household is important because (1) the Scriptures teach us to honor our fathers and mothers so that things will go well with us (Eph 6:2–3), (2) it will be a means of avoiding persecution for the wrong reasons, and (3) it will be a means of winning some social space necessary for further Christian witness.

Christian witness that flows from the younger one in a relationship to the older one is also possible. Mejudhon suggests that younger people in a relationship engage their older brother or sister in witness through meekness (1997). Witness in this context requires time and even more careful attention to fulfilling social obligations. In this context, witness begins by demonstrating obedience and loyalty. It requires that witness be primarily in nonverbal and nonconfrontational formats. All Lao realize that older people know better than younger people, especially in the area of religious knowledge. It is likely that the older one in the relationship will counsel the younger one to abandon their Christian faith and return to the traditional religious rituals. In these cases polemic refusals will be unproductive. Younger Christians should prayerfully discern with the counsel of other brothers and sisters what parts of the ritual system they can participate in, and at what level. Participation in the ritual system at some level, even if at a low level, coupled with apologies and extra efforts in fulfilling other obligations will win tolerance. This is especially true if the younger party shows loyalty in spite of small returns from the relationship. Some level of ritual participation is crucial in this context, because it demonstrates respect and honor for those involved.

Male and Female Communication

Communication in Lao society is best when it is between people of the same gender. This recognizes the male-female classification of Lao social relations. This is probably true around the world, but it is stressed in the social context of Laos to a larger degree than in some other societies. This is especially true with married adults since friendships are strongest between married women and between married men. Unmarried young men and women, on the other hand, are often found socializing together (in groups, not alone). Communication can flow from an unmarried male to an unmarried female as long as it is done in a group setting. A man and woman are not allowed to speak alone unless it is public knowledge that they intend to be married.

Ritual Communication

Communication will be best when ritual shapes the media of communication. The emphasis on order in Lao relationships gives ritual a crucial place in the maintenance and transformation of relationships. This emphasis on ritual requires that communication often be shaped in a formalized code. Communication in Laos is often more concerned with *how* (relationally) something is said than in *what* (content) is said. Speeches generally follow an expected pattern. Meetings open and end with ritual words. Even humor follows a strict structure. Formalized communication can be a means of integrating the members of the group and clarifying roles.

The communication of the gospel needs to be done in terms of ritualized language, whether it is done in storytelling, the manipulation of symbolic objects, or in stylized speech.

Christians should also carefully consider when traditional rituals can be used, when traditional rituals can be used in altered form, and when there is a need to create new rituals. One of the most stressful times for converts to Christianity in Laos is when they are asked to participate with their household in *khwan* or Buddhist rituals. Protestant Christians are consistently instructed not to participate in traditional rituals. While I believe that this is a way of clearly marking their allegiance to Christ, on a social level it cuts off opportunities for further witness that would naturally be there through household relationships. Failing to participate in traditional Lao rituals communicates that a person has opted out of the group. The implication is that the person no longer feels obligated to the needs of the group.

Many Christians obey the instruction of the Protestant churches and end up cutting themselves off, or seriously straining their relationships. Other Christians find the prospect of social death more than they can accept and end up participating in rituals, spiritually and socially unprepared. Afterwards there is a good deal of remorse, and they are careful to not let other Christians know about their participation. Another group of Lao Christians are experimenting with ways to participate in traditional rituals in a way that satisfies social obligations to the household and yet identifies them as Christians. Can a Lao person participate in traditional rituals in ways that demonstrate the proper respect to the structure of the household, village, and nation, while communicating their exclusive allegiance to Jesus Christ? I believe they can. Lao Christians need to prayerfully discern this path.

A key to participation is the ability to identify roles in the ritual performance that allow Christians to meaningfully participate and identify themselves as Christians. For example, when a Christian's non-

Christian brother is being ordained as a monk, it is a serious issue to completely refuse to participate. A young man's ordination is a rite of passage to full adulthood. Men are referred to as "raw" (*dib*) before they are ordained, and they receive titles (e.g., *Tit* adult male) afterwards, depending upon the level of ordination they attain before they remove their robe and return to secular life. According to some Lao Christians, the very lowest level of participation, but an appropriate one, would be to assist with the cost of the ceremony, the preparation for the feast, and to attend the ritual as an observer.

Attendance at *khwan* rituals can be done in a similar way. In my own experiments in this regard, I have found there are normally ways to meaningfully participate. For instance, at the end of a *suukhwan* ritual everyone is given an opportunity to verbally bless the recipient. I do this with a short Christian prayer of blessing in Jesus' name, while I follow the custom of tying cotton string around the person's wrist. This tends to communicate my intention to respect and bless the individual and their household, thereby establishing a solid basis for relationship and further communication.

Low-level participation in traditional Lao rituals raises the issue of spiritual power and dual allegiance. Given the social context, I believe Christians can and should participate in Lao rituals in low-level ways as a means of providing a witness to the gospel. But religious rituals should not be participated in without careful consideration of the spiritual powers involved. It should also be remembered that the power of Christ is stronger than any spiritual power that may be present, and that the power Christ used is available to his disciples (Luke 10:19). Paul Hiebert writes, "We must avoid two extremes: a denial of the reality of Satan and the spiritual battle within and around us in which we are engaged and an undue fascination with, and fear of, Satan and his hosts" (1994, 214).

There are two crucial issues involved here. First, prayer for spiritual protection and discernment should precede and accompany any participation in traditional Lao religious rituals. Second, believers should be firm in their faith in the presence and power of Christ for the situation. Without this kind of faith, Christians would do better to refrain from some levels of participation. In any event, it should be recognized that ritual is a key factor in establishing, maintaining, and transforming relationships in Lao society.

For better or for worse, the media is very often the meaning that Lao people attribute to the message that Christians deliver. Strong kinship (household) level relationships are the most effective media for communication of the gospel to Lao people. The gospel is a relational message that requires covenant between humans and the Creator, and covenant keeping with each other. Spiritual power and cognitive truth will also be involved in communicating the gospel to the Lao. How the power and truth of the gospel are interpreted, however, depends upon how our Christian witness engages others relationally.

References

Andrianoff, David. 1991. Daniel McGilvary and early Protestant missionary outreach into Laos. Unpublished manuscript.

Asia 1998 yearbook. Hong Kong: Review Publishing.

Australia Network News. 2013. February 2.

Christian and Missionary Alliance. 1973. *Annual report.* New York: Christian and Missionary Alliance.

Douglas, Mary. 1970. *Natural symbols.* New York: Pantheon Books.

Geertz, Clifford. 1973. *The interpretation of cultures.* New York: Basic Books.

Hiebert, Paul. 1994. *Anthropological reflections on missiological issues.* Grand Rapids: Baker Books.

Hoefer, Herbert. 1991. *Churchless Christianity.* Madras, India: Gurulul Lutheran Theological College and Research Institute.

———. 1999. Follow-up reflections on churchless Christianity. *Mission Frontiers* 21, no. 3–4: 36–41.

Institute for Cultural Research. 1999. *Vientiane social survey project 1997–1998.* Vientiane, Ministry of Information and Culture, Government of the Lao PDR.

Kraft, Charles. 1979. *Christianity in culture: A study in dynamic biblical theologizing in cross-cultural perspective.* Maryknoll, NY: Orbis Books.

———. 1989. *Christianity with power: Your worldview and your experience of the supernatural.* Ann Arbor, MI: Servant Publications.

———. 1999. Contextualization in three dimensions. Inauguration lecture of the Chair of Global Mission, Fuller Theological Seminary, Pasadena, October 20.

Latourette, Kenneth S. 1939. *A history of the expansion of Christianity: Three centuries of advance.* New York: Harper & Brothers.

Library of Congress. 1994. Laos. http://memory.loc.gov/cgi-bin/query/r?frd/
cstdy:@field(DOCID+la0078 (accessed March 2, 2000; page discontinued).

Lintner, Bertil. 2001. Laos: Gifts from above. *Far Eastern Economic Review*
(August 30): 51. www/feer/com. Accessed November 20, 2001

Mejudhon, Nantachai, and Ubolwan Mejudhon. 2000. Contextualization
workshop. Presented at the Lao Day of Prayer, Bangkok, November 3.

Mejudhon, Ubolwan. 1997. The way of meekness: Being Christian and Thai in
the Thai way. DMiss diss., Asbury Theological Seminary.

Nida, Eugene. 1990. *Message and mission*. Pasadena: William Carey Library. First
published 1960.

O'Flaherty, Bridget. 2012. Is the party over in Laos? The Diplomat, October 5.
http://thediplomat.com/2012/10/05/is-the-party-over-in-laos/?allpages=yes
(accessed March 17, 2013).

Oppel, Lloyd. 1984. Laos: Church and state report. Unpublished manuscript.
Typewritten.

Roffe, G. Edward. 1975. Laos. In *The church in Asia*, ed. Donald Hoke, 391–408.
Chicago: Moody Press.

Sanneh, Lamin. 1989. *Translating the message: The missionary impact on culture*.
Maryknoll, NY: Orbis Books.

Smalley, William. 1956. The gospel and the cultures of Laos. *Practical
anthropology* 3, no. 3: 47–57.

Stuart-Fox, Martin. 1986. *Laos: Politics, economics and society*. Boulder, CO:
Lynne Rienner.

———. 1996. *Buddhist kingdom, Marxist state: The making of modern Laos*.
Bangkok: White Lotus.

———. 1998. *The Lao kingdom of Lan Xang: Rise and decline*. Bangkok: White
Lotus.

U.S. Department of State. 2001. Laos: International religious freedom report.
http://www.state.gov/g/drI/rls/irf/2001/5607.htm (accessed November 11,
2001; page discontinued).

PART III

BECOMING THE PEOPLE WHO REFLECT GOD'S KINGDOM THROUGH WELCOME

"Look," said Naomi, "your sister-in-law is going back to her people and her gods. Go back with her."
But Ruth replied,
"Don't urge me to leave you
or to turn back from you.
Where you go I will go,
and where you stay I will stay.
Your people will be my people
and your God my God.
Where you die I will die,
and there I will be buried.
May the LORD deal with me,
be it ever so severely,
if even death separates you and me."
When Naomi realized that
Ruth was determined to go with her,
she stopped urging her.

Ruth 1:15–18

CHAPTER 7

CREATING CHRISTIAN FUNERARY CULTURE: AN INVITATION TO JAPANESE CHURCHES

Katsuhiko Seino

In Japanese society, Shinto rites are primarily for the living, and Buddhist rites are for the dead. Japanese Buddhist funeral traditions are so strong that many feel change is impossible. But the reality is very different. Funeral customs are changing rapidly, and funerary culture is being reformed every year. Once this fact is known, one will recognize the urgency for Christian funeral customs to be established in Japan. Churches throughout Japan must band together and create a Christian funerary culture. If the Japanese church of today cannot dynamically create such a funerary culture befitting her society, then Christianity will be literally buried beneath the franchised forms of Buddhist and secular funerals. This chapter invites Japanese (and other) churches to learn with us from our church's attempt to create a Japanese Christian funerary culture.

Shinto and Buddhist Rites of Passage

Traditionally, Shinto rituals surround all phases of life in Japan. At birth there is the naming ceremony of the newborn. Later there is the *Shichi-go-san* ritual that celebrates the growth of young children. At many hotels there are still Shinto-style wedding rooms available, although

Western wedding ceremonies are very popular. When a new building is being constructed, there is a Shinto ground-breaking ceremony and a framework-raising ceremony. In the summer there are many regional festivals that have their basis in Shintoism. The local Shinto shrine plays an integral part in the communal life of neighborhood and regional associations. On a national level, Shintoism has been tied with all the rituals of the emperor and in the past held a high degree of social influence.

At death is when Buddhism becomes important. Many morgues in Japanese hospitals are decorated in a Buddhist fashion. From the wake to the end of the funeral, many parts of this rite of passage are Buddhist. Crematoriums incorporate Buddhist influences into their design. Depending on the region, the partnership of the local Buddhist monks and the neighborhood association will handle all the details of the funeral. The location of burial is usually within the *Danka* (local region) Buddhist temple grounds or at a Buddhist cemetery or park graveyard. On the forty-ninth day following the funeral, there are many other Buddhist mourning rituals that can take place.

The Function of Rites of Passage

Funerals are one of the most important rites of passage in every society. According to French cultural anthropologist Arnold van Gennep, the function of rites of passage are separation, transition, and incorporation (1961). In the first stage, the individual going through the rite gets some sort of special treatment and becomes separated from the community (separation). Then once this level has been attained, some change occurs over time (transition). Finally, the individual realizes his or her new state of being and responsibilities and resumes a place back in society (incorporation). Completion of the rite of passage is society's acknowledgment of the process of change in status or position and the reentry of the individual into that new role (Van Gennep, 1961).

How does this play out in a funeral? If someone passes away at a hospital, the body gets placed in a coffin. Then there is a wake; this is the separation period. The funeral ceremony is the transition period, and the cremation and burial is the incorporation period. In this way the one who was alive is accepted as a deceased person through the ceremony.

Proposal for Functional Substitution

There are three primary components to all rituals: form, meaning, and function. These three aspects are especially significant for those who are trying to bring the good news of the gospel message into Japanese Buddhist culture through the use of local rituals of any kind. After having analyzed Japanese rites of passage, a Christian can preserve the good parts of the rite, while removing idolatrous aspects and changing unrighteous parts. If the ritual's meaning is idolatrous or the form is inherently immoral, these cannot be left alone as they are. If the meaning of said rite opposes the Bible, then rejection or abolition of it should be considered.

However, before a complete rejection or abolition is determined, it is important to consider the function of the rite. Here there is need for careful thought, because all rites of passage have a particular purpose within society. To completely reject a rite of passage is to also deny the function that it serves. Naturally people would experience great unease if a long-standing rite or custom were to be abolished. To destroy a long-standing rite implies that everything done before was meaningless, and this could breed much personal anxiety and social distress.

The rejection of a custom is a serious matter to a culture. The society that has had its customs rejected by Christians feels animosity towards those that abolished their traditional practices. In such a case it would be only natural that people would reject anything that a Christian or Christianity might say. Long-standing practices of customs and rituals should not be tossed aside lightly. If a certain rite needs to be rejected, it is imperative that another rite or custom with the same functionality be prepared in advance. When rejecting a rite of passage that opposes the Bible both in meaning and in form, there is the necessity to create a new rite of passage that performs the same function for the local society that the original rite of passage fulfilled. In missiology this method is called "functional substitution."

Functional Substitution by the Japanese Church

I believe that functional substitution has been used often in Japanese churches. Here are some examples: When it comes to rites of passage, temple visits for newborns have been changed to dedication services in churches. Instead of *Shichi-go-san* (November festival with a visit to local shrines to celebrate the well-being of young children), a children's memorial service is in place. In the place of *yuino* (Japanese engagement ceremony), there is an engagement ceremony within the church community. Instead of a Shinto wedding, there is a church wedding; and instead of a Buddhist funeral, a church funeral is performed.

Functional substitution is especially evident in the church when it comes to the Buddhist funeral process. Rather than bringing money to the funeral for incense, attendees bring a gift of money for flowers. Rather than going forward and offering up incense and prayer to the deceased, attendees go forward to place flowers in the casket as they say their last goodbyes. In the place of an all-night vigil over the body, a wake and service are held the night before the funeral. Instead of a temple funeral, a church funeral is held; and in the place of *hoji* (Buddhist event), a memorial service takes place. This is seen in other areas too where on New Year's Day church members will gather for a New Year's service as opposed to going to the local temple to offer the first prayers of the year (*hatsumode*), and in the place of a ground-breaking ceremony a cornerstone ceremony is conducted.

Contextualization Is a Work of Dynamic Creation

The work of indigenization and contextualization becomes the mission front within the cultural sphere, and through this shines the power of God through the church to the local culture. However, this work is constantly a difficult and risky one. It also does not end after one choice but rather is a continuous, creative process and effort. This work cannot be avoided if one is to preach the gospel to people in a certain culture or for those desiring to build a church that speaks into her cultural sphere. Indigenization and contextualization is a continuous, creative, and dynamic process.

The Process of Culture Becoming Sanctified

When we think about desired (and undesirable) outcomes of functional substitution, we soon realize that what is most significant is not progress in missions or indigenization or even what immediate reactions might arise after choosing a new method. The real question is in regards to long-term impact upon the culture. When we talk about individual sanctification as Christians, we know that the sanctification of our personality, the development of our gifts, and our devotion are all part of a long-term process. In the same way, we desire to see Japanese society move towards righteousness and become a culture overflowing with love. We recognize that the sanctification of culture also takes time.

Whether it be the sanctification of an individual Christian, or of a non-Christian society's culture, it is all a process. Indigenization is a process that cannot be decided by one choice in a mere moment. There is need of the practice and growth of righteousness and love with Christian discernment and consistent passion. Just as a believer needs to continually renew their faith when in a non-Christian culture, so the church needs renewal through ongoing confessions of faith and reformation.

Rites within the Funeral System

In general, all rites that involve death and the deceased are put in the category of the funeral system (*sosei:* 葬制). The range of all that this includes methods of handling the body, to periods of mourning, taboos on the topic of death, memorial events afterwards, and other long-term events. Amidst all of these, there is one that cannot be ignored: the treatment of the corpse. Currently in Japan in some remote regions burial in the ground is practiced, but this is as an exception to the rule; cremation and interment of the ashes are the common practices. Burial in a tree or washing of bones may be conducted even in this day and age, but according to a report by the Party for Freedom in Burial Rights, these cases are extremely rare, less than two hundred in number out of the 1.3 million annual burials in Japan. A significant change happening more recently in Japanese society is the rise of smaller nuclear families where grandparents and other relatives live elsewhere. The rising number of unmarried singles has led to individual internment not in family tombs.

In the midst of this great shift, what kind of funeral system can Japanese Christians develop? What does the church have to offer?

Spirits of the Dead and Ancestral Spirits

According to findings from cultural anthropology, many cultures have the following general understandings about death: that a deceased person will be, at least for a time, a spirit and will try to cause some kind of ill will upon the living out of jealousy or spite. Because of this many cultures have developed rituals to protect the living from the spirits of the dead. For example, when the ashes or a body are going to be taken to the cemetery for interment, it is customary among some cultures to take the urn or the body, not through the front door, but through the back or side door of the house. Along the way there may be coins scattered at each intersection, and the body may be turned around along the way to the graveyard. This is explained as being done in order to dizzy the eyes of the spirit of the dead and to confuse it. There are also some customs in which people will take the long way home when leaving the cemetery. This is in order to get the spirit of the dead lost and unable to return to the home easily.

On the other hand, it is conceived that ancestral spirits exist to bless the descendants. Therefore there is time needed for the spirit to become an ancestral spirit, and this differs depending on the cultural sphere.

From where did the belief that the spirit of the dead would become an ancestral spirit to protect its descendants originate? Did it come from experiences people have reported about interactions they've had with a recently deceased love one? Or did it come from the stories of those who saw an ancestral spirit protect them? Or is it that the living sometimes feel their own limits and therefore turn to their ancestors for guidance through prayer? Regardless of its origin, faith in ancestral spirits is still quite common amongst a variety of spheres in Japanese culture. The festival of *Obon* is an example of a tradition that hits upon this, as it incorporates rituals to invite ancestral spirits to return and then to send them back out every summer.

Analyzing Japanese Funerary Culture

We will now learn more about Japanese funeral rites, specifically the Buddhist funeral ceremony, and also funerals in the church of Japan. There are many parts and levels that directly concern the death of an individual. There are the physical aspects, which include handling the body, cremation, and burial. There are legal aspects, which involve such things as a report of death, a will, and the distribution of assets. Finally there are the societal aspects, where the members of society affirm the death of the individual through the funeral and memorial services. In Japan the common ritual progression is the wake, funeral, cremation, and finally laying the ash urn in the family burial plot.

Changes to Buddhist Funerals

In this chapter I will not attempt to review the history of Japanese funerary rites. Fifty years ago, however, the Christian church was not well known, and among farming villages funerals were simply processions towards cremation and burial in an allotted place in a communal field. Within the cities there would be an ornate Japanese shrine-like gold casket on the back of a hearse. But over time this has changed due to the wishes of various communities. Now there are numerous Western-style sleek black hearses running through the streets. It used to be that white altars were the primary type used, but now over time many altars of different original designs are being used. Today among the tall Buddhist-style tombs some Western-style tombs can now be spotted. Many new cemeteries are being arranged in the style of a nature park with fresh new designs.

The Buddhist funerary rite has also been changing quite drastically. Ceremony halls (funeral meeting halls) have expanded to accommodate these changes. Until 1990 there were only 360 of these halls nationwide. Only ten years later in the year 2000 that number increased to 3,075. In 2009 there were an astonishing 6,102.

Due to changing housing situations and the shrinking of family size, Buddhist funerals have increasingly been held at these secular ceremony halls rather than at the *Danka* (neighborhood) Buddhist temple. This is now a major industry, and its impact is evident nationwide. Funerals have moved from the religious temple to the public hall. All the arrangement for funerals are now in the hands of funeral directors and their staff. The monk is now no longer the officiate but is relegated to only a minor role as the chanter of the *sutra* (oral chant) during the service.

Funeral Businesses and Other Contractors

According to the All Japan Funeral Directors Co-Operation (AJFDCO), all existing businesses that actually contribute in some way to the Japanese funeral industry can be categorized in one of four ways. First, there are the "Funeral Specializing Businesses" (members of AJFDCO), long-established businesses and organized groups that participate in various aspects of industry throughout every region of Japan. Next, there is the "Family Ceremony Benefit Society," which has built ceremony halls throughout regional or suburban cities and towns that handle all types of ceremonies for families, not limited to funerals. Then there is JA, which stands for Japanese Agricultural Cooperatives, which has designed and built ceremony halls throughout the nation focusing primarily on the funerary business. Lastly, there are the rest of the funerary businesses not belonging to any of the previous groups. An example of this are the number of hotels that in recent years have begun handling funerals in various forms (All Japan Funeral Directors Co-Operation. n.d.)

From their inception funerals have been religious rites, so qualifications and appointments to lead funerals traditionally came from within religious organizations and did not need administrative approval from national organizations. This history has led to the ability for the funeral industry to freely build up its own line of business unimpeded by the government. This independence makes it extremely difficult to ascertain the exact number of funerary businesses and corporations actually operating in Japan.

Currently the funeral directors at ceremony halls handle all matters alone. Surprisingly, the funeral director position, since 1996, no longer requires a civil qualification but receives authorized qualification through the Ministry of Health, Labour, and Welfare. In order to obtain the qualification of funeral director there are academic and practical skill exams that lead to two levels of licensing. In 2010 it was calculated that there were between four thousand and six thousand funerary businesses. The number of employees was approximately seventy-two thousand, and out of those people there were 20,300 people who had funeral director qualifications. Ceremony hall funerals have rapidly increased, and in recent years there have been fewer monks who come to funerals, but now there are ways to get qualifications as a monk via correspondence courses. Various temporary staff recruitment agencies will send lay monks to ceremony halls. This is all further evidence that Japanese funerary culture has changed at a dizzying pace.

Graves

For a long time temples had the monopoly on graveyards. However, various municipalities have been building cemeteries with plots open for sale, while privately owned cemetery parks are being formed. All of this has been slowly crumbling the Buddhist temple monopoly. In addition to this, new businesses that make a wide variety of tombstones are creating a highly competitive market as these new cemeteries develop.

In the past the cremation and burial was done at the local *Danka* temple, and the stone would have the family name engraved upon it. However, in recent years the number of single individuals passing away, divorces, and remarriages have increased, which has caused complications in family relationships. Burial in a family grave is not always welcome. Due to the changing times, individual graves have become more prevalent.

There is a giant Buddha statue at the Ushiku cemetery, inside of which are personal graves for placing urns of ashes. Between eternal interment fees and preservation fees, one plot costs ¥600,000 (roughly $6,000). There is a personal interment space known as "The Garden of Water" at the *Tocho* temple in the Yotsuya ward of Tokyo. Within the pond are names engraved on a stone slab. Beneath this is where the ash urns are kept. Reservations may be made even while an individual is alive. This massive personal grave enterprise is all undertaken by the temple.

The Practical Parts of Funeral Rites

When it comes to burial rites, there are various laws regarding graves and burial. The church that receives and carries out the request for a funeral must be aware and learn the legal basis and regulations of these laws.

The main constituent in funeral rites up until recently was the head of the household. Since the Second World War the eldest son or the surviving spouse usually took this place. This main person would have every single right and duty regarding the funeral and related ceremonies. Under normal circumstances this main individual would request the clergy (monk or pastor) to oversee the funeral rites, while the funerary business would handle the practical details. There are legal rights, separate from claims to assets, which give rights regarding funerary decisions and authorize the use of assets set aside for various funeral expenses. These are rules about protecting the grave and the Buddhist household altar. Unlike financial or other material assets, these duties cannot be partitioned between people, so therefore this responsibility is often decided by custom.

The Need for and Cost of Funerals

Look at the numbers. It is now known that Japan has the oldest population of any country in the world with almost 30 percent of its population over sixty-five years of age (World Population Review 2014). In 2014 the estimated population of Japan was 126,981,371 (ibid.), down from 127,787,000 in 2004. By the year 2046 it is estimated that the total population of Japan will be just above 100 million. By 2060 the population is estimated to be down to just over 86 million (Lah 2012). The number of deaths in 2004 was 1,029,000, but this has been growing and the projected number of deaths in the year 2047 will be at least 1,663,000 per annum. In other words, over the next sixty years there will be between 1.2 million and 1.6 million deaths annually, and the need for increasing numbers of funerals will no doubt be there.

According to the surveys conducted by Japan Consumers' Association, in 2007 the costs of funerals in Japan could be categorized in the following ways: amount paid to funeral business: ¥1,423,000 ($14,515); cost for drinks and refreshments: ¥401,000 ($4,090); offering given to temple: ¥549,000 ($5,600). Total: ¥2,373,000 ($24,205). The total cost differs in each region, but the averages have been calculated here (All Japan Funeral Directors Co-Operation. n.d).

Secularization of Funerals

From time immemorial weddings and funerals have been religious rituals, but over time Japanese weddings have become more secular. Without any connections to the church, chapels are being constructed within hotels; wedding halls are making chapel- or church–sanctuary-style rooms. The shape and form of wedding ceremonies have diversified and secularization has continued, having moved from a Shinto or Buddhist form to a Christian form, but only in appearance and in style. In actuality, faith is not a factor. On top of all this, there are weddings being held without any form of clergy present.

It is not only within weddings that we are seeing a secularization, but also within the funerary culture. As we enter into a society with a large elderly population, ceremony halls are being erected even in rural communities. It could be that this is a carefully calculated business effort for the coming era of the growing elderly population. Wedding chapels built many years ago during the boom of such business endeavors may very well be remodeled to meet the increasing demands of Japan's aging population.

The secularization may very well continue. Funerals held at ceremony halls will be monopolized by the funeral director, with monks coming only to read the prayers. In time even Christian funerals may only require the pastor to read from the Bible. Funerals, which were from the start a religious ritual, may very well come to be without any type of clergy, whether Buddhist, Shino, Christian, or other.

Reframing the Function of Japanese Funerary Culture

As discussed earlier, rites of passage hold significant meaning in the life of every culture. These customs become foundational rules for the members that make up each society. At the same time, rites of passages often involve ritual prayers of thanks offered up to powers higher than humankind, usually tied to the local religion or faith. Thus, it is quite natural that the majority of rites of passages are carried out as religious ceremonies. So then, when the gospel of Jesus Christ is proclaimed in a culture, it is important to know how to interact with the customs and rites that already exist in that society.

Many questions will arise. At a church funeral, is it necessary to make a pronouncement whether the deceased went to heaven or hell? Must the church confirm at a funeral the existence or nonexistence of the deceased's faith? Is it a requirement for the church to explain where the deceased departed to? Again, if a church places the ashes of a deceased nonbeliever into the church's *Nokotsudo* (storage location of ashes), will this signify that the deceased went to heaven? Or if a nonbeliever's remains were to be placed inside the communal church crypt, would it somehow be violated? Is the presence of the physical remains (ashes) of a nonbeliever in a church crypt something that truly displeases God?

There was a time when I met someone who said that only the ashes and remains of Christians were to be allowed in a church's communal crypt. At this individual's church they had a splendid crypt prepared, but they only performed funeral services for Christians and only performed ceremonies of *Nokotsu* (placing the ashes in the crypt) for Christians. At this church they could not perform services or ceremonies even of the parents of believers if they were non-Christians. When I commented on how sad I felt this was, this person responded, "All of our church members have consented to this, so there is no issue." In this case, if a church member lost his nonbelieving father, and this member happened to be the eldest son, he would be forced to have a Buddhist funeral. Also, this would mean that he would be giving the ashes and remains over to the temple with all the Buddhist traditions, ceremonies, and expenses required within that system.

Is it right to push church members into conducting their family's funerals at Buddhist temples or even in secular institutions? This will mean that the Japanese church is forcing her Christian members not only to perform non-Christian ceremonies, but it is also entrusting her members into the ritual care of another religion (or nonreligion) because she is not caring for them herself. Is this not a weighty issue for Japanese Christians? How has the church helped in these instances? What would the church gain in this regard? This is indeed a significant issue. Let us consider how a church would conduct a nonbeliever's funeral.

The Church as Means of God's Comfort for the Bereaved

There is one thing that cannot be forgotten. The judge of the dead is not us, but the creator of life, God. Christians have been given the mission to preach the gospel, but we have not been given the mission or the right to judge a person's life nor what happens to them after death. In the church funeral, what we ought to do is to help the family and friends as they walk in the midst of confusion in the face of losing a loved one. The church must be there to provide some kind of societal ceremony for those who are grieving; speaking comfort and encouragement to the family, relatives, and friends; learning something from the life of the deceased; and helping all find meaning in God's presence. That is to say that we as Christians do not speak to the dead but rather to the living. We are not speaking into the destination of the deceased, but we speak to give hope to the living. We do not speak judgment on the life of the deceased, but instead introduce God's gift of grace to the living.

The Church as Means of God's Life for the Living

The church funeral is fundamentally to give comfort and encouragement to the living. In addition, I believe it is for the sake of sharing the new life found in Jesus Christ to the living that Japanese Christian churches must be willing to perform funerals for nonbelievers. It should be clearly understood that Christian funerals are not for the sake of the dead but for those who remain. To perform a funeral service for a nonbeliever at a church is to give the hopeless and despairing relatives liberty and release. It is the chance to introduce the one and only Creator God to nonbelievers who have come to pay their respects. Church services for nonbelievers can set those who attend free from the hopelessness of Buddhist or Shinto funerals and can introduce people to the Christ-centered community of the church.

The Church's Opportunity in Mission

Currently in Japan the funeral, the procession after burial, and the *Nokotsu* are not unrelated. If one were to have a Buddhist funeral performed and the ashes given to a temple, this would cause the relatives to place the annual burdens of *Houji* and *Danka* (social obligation and financial payments) upon themselves and their descendants for many decades to come. On the other hand, if the services are performed in a church context and the ashes were placed within a church's *Nokotsudo*, then the family would be set free from these burdens completely. Additionally, a Christian funeral, *Nokotsu*, and other future memorial services all give opportunities to testify about God. This is imperative in speaking into a society such as Japan. Through these functional substitutes the social obligations of obstinate systems of *Danka* and *Houji*, perpetually entrenched by Buddhist funerals, will be appropriately addressed by the Christian church.

Consider this very real possibility. The nonbelieving father of a church member passes away. Let us say that the church then receives a request from the family to perform the funeral and all the services including the *Nokotsu* and does so. Later, when the mother passes away, the relatives will again approach the church requesting her funeral and services as well. Her ashes will be placed in the same *Nokotsudo* as the father. The outcome is absolutely assured, 100 percent! Years, even decades later, when remembrance services are held once again, the church has the opportunity to offer comfort and hope to all in this family network. Currently in Japan, however, many churches are unwilling to hold funerals for nonbelievers. The Japanese church has thrown away this unfathomable evangelistic possibility. What have they gained from it? Performing church funeral services and *Nokotsu* for nonbelievers may be the opening of the floodgates to what God wants to do next in Japanese culture.

Missional Funerals and *Nokotsu* at Tsuchiura Grace Church

We have looked at how the church of Japan should proactively do not only Christian funerals but also services for nonbelievers as well. But, for a pastor, performing such a ceremony can most assuredly be worrisome, thinking about what to actually say or do. To address some of these worrisome questions, I will share three actual examples from our fellowship, Tsuchiura Grace Church.

Funeral for a Church Member's Mother

A church member's mother suddenly fell, and the doctors said she had no chance of recovery. She was very far away, but I visited her in the hospital a few times. It was during those times that the brother of the church member gave me the opportunity to meet his uncle (the eldest son). The brother also introduced me to the pastor of his church. Together all of us prayed and planned for how we might move forward. After some intimate fellowship, the uncle, understanding his nephew's wishes, agreed to have the funeral be a Christian funeral. The aunt and the rest of the family also agreed in the end. Two weeks later the mother passed away.

The funeral was performed at the local town's ceremony hall. We put a lot of hard work into the design and symbolism of the plants and flower arrangements at the service. The deceased was a calligrapher, and so we decorated the hall with one of her pieces of work that was about the size of a *Fusuma* door (traditional Japanese sliding screened door). Her husband had passed away more than fifteen years previously. The sermon was prepared and based upon general grace. Church members played the organ, violin, and the cello. Other church members came via the church bus in order to pay their respects.

The son came to say farewell at the end of the ceremony. "I had the ceremony arranged to be a Christian one because of my being a Christian. My mother might have said, 'There you go again doing something selfish.' However, she did accept my faith, and was glad in the end we had our wedding at a church, so she might also have smiled and said that 'it makes sense.'" After all of the funeral had finished, family and relatives were comforted, encouraged, and received some relief.

Six months later, we planned to have the mother's *Nokotsu* ceremony. The eldest brother went to the temple where the family had traditionally laid their deceased family members' remains. He explained that the mother's funeral was performed as a Christian funeral, that the *Nokotsu* was also going to be taking place at the church's *Nokotsudo*, and conveyed his desire to transfer the ashes of his other family members so that they all might be in the same place together. The temple responded very well and provided the appropriate forms, with the agreement that the grave plot would be made empty again. Thus in this way the Christian brother was able to also have the ashes of his father, aunt, uncle, and brother all brought to the church's *Nokotsudo* with those of his mother.

We invited all the relatives and performed a *Nokotsu* ceremony for all the deceased family members. The uncle said, "I'm quite relieved that the couple got to be placed together. I'm quite amazed at what the church can do."

Through the church funeral and *Nokotsu*, this young Christian couple cut off their connection with the Buddhist temple system. This was a great achievement. From now on they are relieved of the requests from the patron of the temple for *hoji* or donations. They will never have to concern themselves with these things again. In another way it can be seen that these brethren were successful in putting a wedge into the obstinate *Danka* system. Later the couple invited their relatives once again to an anniversary memorial party for the deceased parents, held at the church's *Nokotsudo*. What is even more important is that from henceforth the family can hold these memorial parties as many times as they want *in the context of the church*. Each time they hold such an event, the church can speak comfort from the Word and share testimonies of the great worth in knowing Jesus Christ.

Funeral for a Nonbeliever

I would like to give another example of the church holding a funeral for a nonbeliever. The deceased had two daughters; however, the youngest, Mrs. K, and her husband were church members. Mrs. K had hoped that the funeral and *Nokotsu* could be held at the church and spoke with her nonbelieving sister. In the end they agreed upon it together, and I was able to perform the ceremony at the church.

I actually was quite troubled over whether I should perform this funeral or not. The truth of the matter is that the father who passed away was not only a nonbeliever, but he was also quite an enthusiastic observer of traditional Japanese religions. He collected *kumade* (decorated symbols of good luck) from an *Asakusa* (famous Buddhist) shrine. He obtained charms from the *Anahachiman* (famous Shinto) shrine and on New Year's Eve would put his heart into placing one in a given direction (based on Fengshue beliefs). On the twenty-eighth of every month he would faithfully go to the nearby *Jindai* (ancient Japanese) Temple to offer prayers up to the *Ofuda* (protection amulet). At *Hatsumode* (Shinto New Year's festival) he would go to the famous *Narita-san* (Shingon Buddhist temple). On top of all this he begged for his daughters to have a *Happi* (traditional Japanese straight-sleeved) coat from *Zenko* (seventh-century Buddhist) Temple be placed with him in his coffin. In spite of all this, he had no specific faith or allegiance to any of these, rather that he was passionate about all kinds of faiths, following within the sphere of the amalgam of traditional Japanese religions.

His enthusiasm towards all faiths and lack of allegiance to any particular one allowed him to welcome new circumstances with joy when his youngest daughter, Mrs. K, became a Christian and married Mr. K, a passionate Christian. Even afterwards, he developed a deep understanding for the church activities of the Ks, even the developing faith of his grandchildren, and had a kind and accepting posture towards it all. I was still unsure for a time about performing this ceremony but, seeing the relationship of the family and my relationship with them, I took on the responsibility of performing the funeral and *Nokotsu* ceremonies. Afterwards, each time a memorial party was held, the relatives came to attend at my church, and I am pleased to say that the bond of the family has still remained.

A Funeral Involving Suicide

The last example I would like to share is a church funeral service for a young man who had committed suicide. Within Japanese church history, a church funeral for a person who committed suicide has most often not been permitted. Burial in a church cemetery would also not be allowed, and thus there were harsh dealings for such cases. However, for us we had a dear relationship with the parents and even with the individual. Therefore we held the wake and funeral service at the church. I understand that there are varying opinions on such a topic; however, please consider the sermon below at least as an example.

As was explained earlier by the deceased's mother, young TS passed away on October 8, 11:57 a.m., finishing his short thirty-nine years and returned to God, the creator of life. I pray for God's special comfort over the family and relatives. Young TS often came to this church with his parents. A year ago he said that he also believed in God and wanted to be baptized. So we began preparing for that. However, his illness began to get worse, and so we decided to wait until he got better.

Since we had a close relationship with him, we also are grieving his death. In view of the sadness and pain of his parents, I am at a loss for words. I did not want him to go before us. I wanted to talk, eat, and spend more time with him. I know that all of you who came to attend today feel the same way. You all have known about the illness that young TS had been fighting. His parents had been fighting hard with it for a very long time in order that they might protect him. That is why it is so sad that he had lost his strength to fight. We are all saddened. We don't know what to do. We groan in sorrow.

Indeed we all groan in this sorrow. But that is because his parents, his relatives, and the rest of us all love him. He was special to us. Who we lost was precious, and so it is truly sad. We have to say good-bye to one we love, and so that is why we are saddened. This day, we grieve the reality of this parting. We grieve at this sudden farewell. But this sadness is a testimony of our love. This funeral itself is a ceremony to pour out our love for him. Our voices and the hymns of this service are not sorrow but rather are a symphony themed with our love for him.

Young TS lost his strength to fight this illness. This is very painful for his parents. But please, both of you, do not blame yourselves. Please do not condemn yourself with words such as, "If I had only not done that," or "If only I had done this for him." This may be a severe expression, but for us humans there is no way we can completely control another and push them either to take their own life, nor can we completely control another to prevent them from taking their own life.

His father has written and explained the details of the death of TS. Let us commend this courage and truth. In church history, there has been a rigidness and an unwillingness to take care of situations of suicide. However, we have chosen not to keep this man far away from us. How could we push him or this matter outside of the church? He was in our fellowship. We will not push him out. It is because the Bible says so!

Romans 8:38–39 "For I am convinced that neither death nor life, neither angels nor demons, neither the present nor the future, nor any powers, neither height nor depth, nor anything else in all creation, will be able to separate us from the love of God that is in Christ Jesus our Lord." Neither life nor death can pull us away from the love of God. And in Romans 14:8 it declares that whether we live or die we belong to him. That is why we have chosen not to let this man be placed far away from us. What is most important before God is how he lived, not how he died. We will not know the full extent of the matter. But we do know for certain that our young friend TS lived with all his might. Let me show you this.

TS had within himself a certain talent. As you see in the bio of his life, he had many picture books read to him as he was growing up. Later on he went into a critical point in his life, but he came alive again through picture books. Most certainly through this experience he found that he loved children and began to write stories for children. Unfortunately they did not come out in time before these moments, but very soon they will be fully published. He loved people and was loved. It has only been three days since his passing, yet here are friends from America, Switzerland, France, Africa, from all over the world who love him and have come to be here this day. This is proof that TS indeed did live.

Through his character he taught us, showed us, and let us experience kindness. About a year ago he was coming every day, his mother's homemade lunch in hand, to help out at the kindergarten here at this church. The little ones would gather all around him, and they had fun playing with him. To those very children he would often read picture story books. Children have the natural genius to distinguish types of people. They must have sensed his gentleness. They had a nickname for him, T-chan ("Little T," a term of endearment), and he enjoyed that nickname. He lived sharing his kindness.

Romans 14:8 declares it clearly. "Whether we live or die, we belong to the Lord." Let us entrust our beloved T-chan to the creator of life, who says, "Even if you are among the dead, you belong to me." And let us continue to live before God. "Even in living, you belong with me." Let us pray.

Whether we live or whether we die, we belong to the Lord. So we shall live. And we can trust in God to live tomorrow as well. Let us sing this last hymn together. Please stand with me.

Finally we will have a farewell flower offering. The relatives will come to the front first. To the left please take a flower and then place them on the flower stand next to the coffin. This flower offering is not a religious act but rather an expression of respect and love for the deceased. Those who belong to other faiths, please feel at ease to participate. The family will be at the right. After the flower offering, please say a word to the family members. Now, may the relatives come first for this flower offering.

In order to have the atmosphere and the pace understood, I have included the full sermon text and the instructions about the flower offering segment of the service as well. Being that the deceased was a young man, we did not sing a traditional hymn but something more modern with hope and comfort—a "worship song." My hope is that this story might be a helpful reference.

Christian Funeral Ceremony

The church funeral should be carried out and founded upon Christian doctrine. That is, the burial of a precious body created by God. It is also the solemn end of an individual who lived within the grace given by God. Therefore, to the Christian the funeral is a time to bow down and worship the Creator, who is the ruler over life and death. There is also hope beyond death. That is the eternal life through Jesus Christ, and the hope found in heaven. So then, to the Christian the funeral is a time to confess the promises and hope found in the word, and it is a ritual to seek comfort in that hope. That is the kind of funeral we ought to set out to do, a funeral that expresses these things from the Bible. Now let us think more specifically about how a Christian funeral can be carried out in reality.

Discretion towards Nonbelievers at a Church Funeral

When a loved one has passed away, family members need grief counseling. Once all the events of the funeral come to an end, very serious questions will rise up in their hearts. Why did my loved one die? Why did it have to be him? Why did it have to be her? Why did they have to be taken away in this manner? What are they doing now? In other words, the meaning of death will start to be questioned. The afterlife will be imagined. In these instances that the church will face, the questions are: Can the church be discrete? Can the church show care to the family? Can they empathize with the grief and loss of others? The church funeral also becomes a demonstration of how Christians accept death; it is an opportunity to testify about how to handle death.

Normally when the funeral is carried out at a Japanese church, even if the deceased was a Christian, it is very common for there to be non-Christians amongst the family and relatives. Among those who attend the church funeral are many who are entering the inside of a Christian church for the first time. Then there are those who most likely belong to a faith that is not Christian. For all these people there is a very real need to appropriately explain the Christian ideologies behind the church. At our church we have been handing out, along with the funeral program, an explanatory pamphlet titled "To those who are in attendance at a church funeral for the first time."

Consideration towards Nonbelievers in the Sermon

When it comes to consideration of nonbelievers, oftentimes evangelically passionate clergy will prepare an evangelical sermon. In the past I have attended many church funerals where nonbelievers heard a sermon preached about the sin of humanity and the judgment of God. This is close to terrorism for people in attendance. Those present at such funerals were left with unpleasant feelings and resistance towards the church. This will only push Japanese people away from church. Speaking the gospel to non-Christians is not what is right, but rather having them understand the gospel should be considered what is right.

For a non-Christian being present at a family member or friend's funeral, listening to an evangelistic sermon must be unpleasant. These people came to attend a funeral and did not come to listen to a sermon. While using the time and place of a funeral to teach about Christian doctrine might seem normal to a Christian, it would be quite natural for a nonbeliever to feel that it was coercion. To speak to an audience who are stuck in the atmosphere of the funeral about something that they had not been expecting could be described as lacking consideration for the attendees. This is "sender-centric communication." This instance pushes unpleasantness, and therefore the message will not be received.

In opposition to this we have tried to put the care of the feelings of those in attendance as a priority and plan the funeral carefully. There is much effort needed to avoid having the attendees feel that they had been coerced at a church funeral. To begin with, first-time attendees will be tense and nervous. Will funeral offerings be received? Will there be a flower offering? Which direction should I face? Where do I place the flowers? Must I say, "Amen"? Normally, visiting non-Christian individuals come to church feeling uneasy. It is necessary to take into consideration the feelings of attendees and to convey matters to them in a way that will put them at ease.

Considering how the listeners will hear and interpret our message is called "receiver-centric communication." We want to bring this to bear and testify to the greatness of our faith as well. The sadness of family, relatives, and friends is great. The reality of death is also very great. Let us not push forward our own selfish agendas but be considerate. Let us not fail to allow people to grieve and to be comforted appropriately, simply because of the hope we have in heaven.

Still, we want to share the greatness of our faith and of the gospel. That is why in the instance of the Christian's funeral I included the testimony of the deceased in the sermon. Rather than using the words of the preacher, I try to use the words of the deceased to share the greatness of the gospel. Those who come in attendance may be opposed to the words of the preacher, but the words of their friend or family member may open their heart. To this end I try to collect a file with as much as I can learn of testimonies or significant facts about my church members. In a funeral there is nothing as strong as the deceased's own testimony.

An Invitation to Create a Christian Funerary Culture

We have looked at the current state of Japanese funeral affairs. New traditions are being created for funerals. Funerary culture is being formed. Can the church in Japan remain silent? It would be truly unfortunate if the church could not create a significant Christian funerary culture. Let us pray that we can creatively create a funerary culture rooted in the Word and one that shines the light of Christ to every regional culture of Japan and beyond.

References

All Japan Funeral Directors Co-Operation. n.d. http://www.zensoren.or.jp. Accessed 15 August 2013.

Lah, Kyung. 2012. Japan's population faces dramatic decline. CNN, January 30. http://edition.cnn.com/2012/01/30/world/asia/japan-population-decline/index.html. Accessed 20 Sept 2013

Van Gennep, Arnold. 1961. *Rites of passage*. Chicago: University of Chicago Press.

World Population Review. 2014. Japan population 2014. http://worldpopulationreview.com/countries/japan-population/. Accessed 30 August 2013.

CHAPTER 8

CHANGES IN THAI CHURCH: MOVING TOWARDS A RELATIONAL MODEL

Ubolwan Mejudhon

I taught Buddhist philosophy in a Thai university before I became a Christian in 1971. In 1973 my husband and I were called to plant an indigenous church, the Muangthai Church. However, we used Western ways of approaching and witnessing to Thai Buddhists. The church slowly expanded. We found many split-level Christians among the believers, those who changed only their behavior but not their inner values. We also found that hundreds of those who prayed to accept Jesus did not follow him.

During the years 1994 to 1998, my husband and I furthered our study at the E. Stanley Jones School of World Mission and Evangelism, Asbury Theological Seminary, in Wilmore, Kentucky, in the United States. There we encountered an important turning point in our ministry when we studied anthropology, religious studies, and contextualization. I learned to open up Thai culture, Thai belief systems, and Thai relationships, as well as using the principles and methods Christians have used to spread the gospel in the past.

I discovered that Thai Christianity seemed Westernized. Carl E. Blanford commented about Christianity in Thailand as follows:

> Christianity has been introduced into Thailand by Westerners and is generally regarded as a "foreign religion." Its institutions

are foreign. The architecture of its buildings is foreign. Its music is foreign. Its emphasis on individual conversion and the separation of its members from their original social relationships also cause people to regard it as foreign. This foreignness of Christianity as introduced and practiced in Thailand constitutes a difficult barrier for the present-day missionary to overcome. (1985, 84)

My study revealed the negative attitudes of missionaries toward Buddhism and Thai culture. Dr. Dan Beach Bradley arrived in Siam on July 18, 1835. On September 24, 1835, he wrote in his diary:

Lectured my people on the falsity of their religion and the many ways in which they sin against Jehovah. A good degree of seriousness manifested. The people stare when I tell them plainly the rottenness of their religious system, but they seem to say that what I say is probably but too true. (Feltus 1936, 46)

The research of Philip H. Hughes (1989) also illustrated that the Thai way of understanding religion was much different from that of the missionaries. Moreover, I found that Thais accepted messengers before they accept messages. However, missionaries wanted the Thais to quickly receive the gospel message. Eugene A. Nida (1954, 251) mentions, "It is not primarily the message but the messenger of Christianity that provides the greatest problems for the average non-Christian."

I, therefore, propose a new hypothesis, one I pretested in 1998. From January 1999 to January 2002, I tested this hypothesis in the Muangthai Church. The research findings are very encouraging.

In this chapter, I will present the statement of the problem; the conceptual, practical, and theoretical framework; the data; and the methodology of research testing. I will conclude with the summary of research findings, which confirms my hypothesis given in the statement of the problem. I personally believe that my theoretical framework can be most effectively used with Buddhists in Southeast Asia. However, I also believe the principles and methods should be applicable to most contexts in the new millennium, because this theoretical framework manifested itself in the life and work of our Lord Jesus.

Turn, Turn, Turn

There is a time for everything. For over two hundred years, Buddhists in Thailand (formerly Siam) have not widely accepted the gospel of Jesus. Thailand is less than 1 percent Christian and has become the headquarters of Theravada Buddhism. In the past, Christians have ignored the context of Buddhist belief and culture. We have not studied the personalities of Buddhists in each context. We have been ignorant of the ways in which Buddhists learn religion. We have also overlooked the ways Buddhists create deep relational bonding.

In this chapter, I use Thailand as an example for learning how to witness to Thai Buddhists. I would like to propose a more effective method for discipling Thai Buddhists, one which comes from: (1) a better understanding of the personality of Thai Buddhists, (2) knowing how Thai Buddhists learn religion, and (3) learning how Thai Buddhists create deep relational bonding.

By discipling I mean evangelizing, nurturing, and disciplining. I believe this definition of discipling is congruent with biblical discipling. I supported this conclusion in my dissertation, "The Way of Meekness: Being Christian and Thai in the Thai Way" (Mejudhon 1997, 321–40). A. H. Mathias Zahniser (1997, 23) also holds that God's discipling of individuals has already begun before their spiritual birth.

In my dissertation, I examined the personalities of Thai Buddhists, their religious learning methods, and their ways of deep relational bonding. These research findings in 1997 broke fresh new ground for theories of discipling. I used these new theories to find new methodologies in discipling. I then pretested the theories and methodologies for one year in a local church in 1998. After that, I tested the theoretical framework and methodology for three years, from 1999 to 2002. Having presented my introduction and stated the problem, I will now illustrate my theoretical framework, which is the criterion for measuring the effectiveness of my thesis. Next, I will elucidate the data collected from the local church as well as the methodology I used. At the end, I will present a summary of the research findings. Now we will go directly to the theoretical framework.

Theoretical Framework

Here I devote this part of the chapter to the theoretical framework. My conceptual theoretical framework consists of three main parts: (1) the Thai way of meekness, the Komin model, as stated in my dissertation (Mejudhon 1997); (2) the Thai way of meekness in religious discipling, mentioned in the same dissertation; and (3) Thai ways of relational bonding, as described by Lauriston Sharp (1978) and my additional research findings (Mejudhon 1997) concerning this matter.

Komin's Theoretical Framework of Thai Personality

Psychology of the Thai People: Value and Behavior Patterns (1991) is the result of Komin's ten-plus years of studying Thai values. Her empirical research reveals the Thai national character in the form of nine value clusters: (1) ego orientation, (2) grateful relationship orientation, (3) smooth interpersonal relationship orientation, (4) flexible and adjustment orientation, (5) religio-psychical orientation, (6) education and competence orientation, (7) interdependence orientation, (8) fun and pleasure orientation, and (9) achievement-task orientation. Anyone who violates these nine value clusters is considered to be "aggressive."

Komin presents the Thai as a people who have a strong self-identity and who use the Thai way of meekness to avoid confrontaion in order to keep smooth relationships and to protect their identity. Komin's theory presents the way of Thai meekness as the avoidance mechanism that fends off unnecessary clashes. Thai meekness is not used out of fear, rather the Thai are first and foremost ego-oriented and characterized by the highest ego value. They are independent, and self-esteem is a very high value for them. Moreover, the Thai emphasize relationships. Therefore, the Thai way of meekness functions socially through a strong self-identity, grateful relationships, smooth interpersonal relationships, flexibility and adjustment, interdependence, as well as fun and pleasure. It seems to me that the values mentioned above exhibit themselves also in the Thai religio-psychical orientation. Komin does not mention much about the Thai worldview. Her research findings of nine Thai national value clusters seem to point to the Thai worldview of "power and weakness."

This worldview is exhibited by a strong self-identity as well as by the gentle and indirect ways of Thai social interaction.

Komin also presents Thai behavior patterns as follows: (1) Thais can react aggressively if their self-identity is violated; (2) Thais use indirect ways to soften a negative assertion in order to avoid public confrontation that challenges the inferior, the equal, and the superior; (3) Thais use reciprocity of kindness between givers and receivers; (4) Thais cherish a nonassertive, polite, humble personality, expressed through appearance, manners, and an interpersonal approach; (5) Thais have compromising and warm personalities, but are lax in principles; (6) Thais learn religion from ceremonies, rituals, and festivals; (7) Thais emphasize the forms of education more than the knowledge; (8) Thais cherish assimilation and communal cooperation; (9) Thais enjoy fun and pleasure, but are able to work hard; and (10) Thais work most successfully when they are able to balance hierarchy and relationship.

Komin's research seems to suggest that Thai society is structured around three core elements: hierarchy, relationship, and individualism. Moreover, she proposes that these Thai characteristics come from Thai culture and not from Buddhism, because Thai Muslims and Thai Christians demonstrate the same traits of meekness. However, since Buddhism first arrived in Thailand, it could have been the source of meekness in all three groups.

Her research also demonstrates that the Thai believe more in Buddhist folk religion than in the high religion. This assumption can be argued from the point of view of religious studies. Buddhism, Islam, Hinduism, Christianity, and traditional religions all emphasize the concept of meekness. Buddhism confirms the "mid-*en win* die way." Islam elucidates "submission to God." Hinduism emphasizes "unity and nonviolence." Christianity cherishes "love toward God and humankind," and traditional religion suggests "harmony with nature, supernatural beings, and powers." Therefore, it is partly true that the Thai way of meekness comes from culture. The additional factors of geography, history, and economics, in the past provided the tranquility needed for the Thai way of meekness to develop. Additionally, it is also probable that the syncretism of the various religions mentioned above is also an important source of the Thai way of meekness, because the mentality of a people is affected by its worldview, religion, and mythology (Luzbetak 1988, 252).

Komin's research concerning the Thai value system, which she proposes as being in the form of nine value clusters, seems to suggest that the Thai worldview is focused on power and weakness. I, therefore, proposed in my dissertation that the Thai personality consisted of binary oppositions; in other words, power and weakness, according to Levi-Strauss' theory of structuralism of culture (1953).

Therefore, the structure of the characteristics of the Thai personality is presented below. The structure is a theoretical model for evaluating data from the research testing.

Thais have a "both/and" worldview, structured as power and weakness, which is presented below in figure 5 The power and weakness components of worldview are the mental eyeglasses Thais use to see the world around them. Closely related to this center worldview are arranged the nine value clusters, represented by the next concentric circle in the diagram. The Thai value system carries nine value clusters: (1) ego orientation, (2) grateful relationship orientation, (3) smooth interpersonal relationship orientation, (4) flexibility and adjustment orientation, (5) religio-psychical orientation, (6) education and competence orientation, (7) interdependence orientation, (8) fun and pleasure orientation, and (9) achievement-task orientation.

Moving out to the next concentric circle we come to Thai behavior patterns. The purpose of practicing Thai behavior patterns is to keep the Thai's nine value clusters intact, especially ego-orientation cluster. The worldview of power and weakness influences the Thai to use humble attitudes and gentle behavior patterns in Thai social interaction. However, when the Thai's self-identity is violated, he or she reacts aggressively.

The next concentric circle in the diagram contains the sources of the Thai way of meekness. Primal religion, Buddhism (Buddha's life model), Hinduism, and Thai relational culture each continue to make an impact on Thai personality. The final circle represents the tangible expressions of Thai society, structured as it is, by the elements of hierarchy, relationship, and individualism.

The theoretical framework for Thai personality reveals some important practical theories for discipling Thai Buddhists. Effective discipling is vulnerable, progressive, and cooperative. Discipling moves from where non-Christians are to where Christ is. These practical theories help keep the egos of Thai Buddhists intact. As a result, Thai Buddhists become more receptive to the gospel of Jesus Christ. Now we are ready for the theoretical framework for Thai Buddhist ways of religious learning.

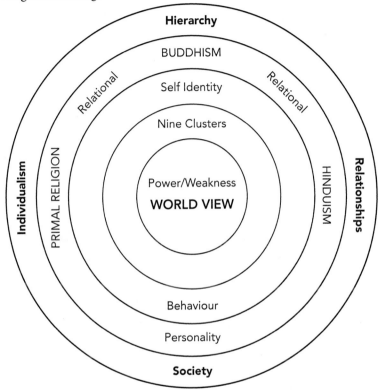

Figure 5: Structure of characteristics of the Thai way of meekness

Theoretical Framework of the Thais' Religious Learning: The Thai Way of Meekness in Religious Discipling

I spent a year and a half researching Thai ways of religious discipling. I studied Buddhist *Jataka* (ancient narratives of the previous lives of the Buddha) and modern Thai literature concerning Buddhist monks. I also conducted interviews with non-Christians. The research yielded an important theory about the ways the Thais learn religion. The research findings elucidate the Thai Buddhist way in religious discipling as follows: (1) religion is affective; (2) religion is applicable to the present felt needs; (3) religion is practical, solving life's problems; (4) religion emphasizes rituals, ceremonies, and festivals; (5) religion has integrative functions; (6) religion is concrete, experiential; (7) religion is bonding; and (8) religion does not force faith.

The theoretical framework of Thai Buddhists' ways of religious learning demonstrates the practical theories mentioned above. These practical theories enhance the theoretical framework of Thai Buddhist religious learning. Now I will move directly to the theoretical framework of Thai Buddhist ways of deep relational bonding.

Theoretical Framework for Thai Buddhist Deep Relational Bonding

Lauriston Sharp explains about Thai Buddhist ways of deep relational bonding in *Bang Chan: Social History of a Rural Community in Thailand* (1978). Sharp believes that the Thai kinship system selects potential kinsmen in three ways: (1) they must share some difficult experiences in the natural ways of living; (2) they must exchange services and favors to the extent that an investor in or reciprocator of services lays aside all conditions to ensure that love and respect dominate the relationship; and (3) they must accept a long-term commitment of fixed obligations beneath the easily contracted arrangement. After these steps the two people, whatever their origin, become kinsmen.

My interview research (Mejudhon 1997) illustrates some Thai ways of creating deep relational bonding: (1) participation in the communal activities, (2) sharing difficult experiences in the natural pattern of life, and (3) togetherness and long-term commitment. Effective discipling should be vulnerable, cooperative, progressive, and move from the familiar to the unfamiliar.

I believe the practical theories mentioned above are congruent with Scripture. Reading the Scriptures from the perspective of a believer from a Majority World country, I believe Jesus was vulnerable, progressive, and cooperative in his ways of discipling the apostles. Our Lord accepted people as they were. Then he moved them to where God wanted them to be. His attitude in witnessing poured first from his heart (Matt 9:36; Mark 6:34). Jesus asked for help; he asked for water from a Samaritan woman. He borrowed a boat from Peter. Our Lord was vulnerable. Jesus allowed Nicodemus to take time to make a decision. Our Savior worked progressively. He cooperated with Andrew, as well as other disciples, in discipling Peter. His discipling behavior pattern was cooperative.

Dr. A. H. Mathias Zahniser emphasizes the important role of vulnerability in witnessing (1994). John Paul Fieg argues that the Thai concept of time is longer than that of Westerners (1989). Paul G. Hiebert's (1985) book *Anthropological Insights for Missionaries* states that members of Majority World cultures cherish cooperation among people in groups. Their self-actualization and personal growth gives way to the best interest of their group. Moreover, their identity comes from community. Lamin Sanneh (1993) agrees that familiarity breeds faith.

The Task of Testing: Data

I have presented the introduction, the statement of problem, as well as my conceptual and practical theoretical framework. In this section, I will support them with my research data. First, I would like to briefly explain the background of the Muangthai Church, where I conducted the testing of my theoretical framework and methodology. I will explain who the participants were. Some were my Christian teacher's aides and some were non-Christians who had been brought to our church. I started the pretest of my theoretical framework in the Muangthai Church in 1998. I then launched the full research test concerning the Thai way of witnessing to Buddhists from 1999 to 2002.

The Muangthai Church, Bangkok, Thailand, is an indigenous church. It was started by six lay people in 1973. It was founded by Rev. Nantachai Mejudhon (who is now the pastor), myself, and three others. The church used Western ways of witnessing, teaching, and training from the very beginning until 1998. The church experienced a crisis during the years between 1994 and 1997 when Rev. Mejudhon furthered his studies in the USA. Attendance dropped and fewer people were enthusiastic about evangelism. Those who prayed to accept Christ did not attend the church. When I started my research pretesting, the attendance was around eighty people.

The data collection was conducted as follows: First, I chose three congregants to be participant-observers in my Sunday school class for non-Christians during 1999 and 2000. Two more lay people were chosen to be teachers among slum preadolescents between 1999 and 2001. These five took over the teaching of all the classes in 2001. Second, I encouraged members of the Muangthai Church to invite people from their social networks to visit our church.

The Task of Testing: Bonding with People

The Muangthai Church encouraged congregants to bond themselves with members of their social networks. The pastor educated members about the nine values of the Thai. Christians learned to reengineer their values and behavior patterns to fit more within the Thai context. We learned to be Christian and Thai. As a result, significantly more non-Christians visited our church during regular worship services and Christian festivals from January 1999 to January 2002.

Moreover, the pastor educated the members concerning the biblical perspectives on social concern. The church property is next to a slum area in Bangkok. Two members, Pen and Pong, started to care for orphans and slum children who were neglected from our neighborhood. Both of them volunteered to do the job, and they used their own money. Soon more members joined to support the work. The church became like a foster family to about twenty children. We did not force them to listen to the gospel or attend the church. However, they wanted to come because they were loved and forgiven, time and again, for their mischief. After a year of bonding, in January 2002, fourteen of them voluntarily committed their lives to Christ.

A record conversion of fourteen slum students confirms the validity of our theoretical framework. Among the twenty slum children taken care of by Pen and Pong, five boys were seemingly hopeless. They were orphans whose parents had either died of AIDS or had been murdered. Some of them sold drugs. They regularly skipped school. Their ages were between eight and twelve years old. Our church was their favorite playground. They ate dinner at the church with Pen and Pong, who were like their foster parents. We had problems with their vulgar language and violent fighting. However, one boy, Bee, said, "I know teacher Pen still loves me." Every Friday they came to listen to storytelling. Pen and Pong gradually told them about Jesus according to a rough lesson plan. Many times they adapted the lessons to help their audience better understand the gospel.

Many people reached out to these slum children. Sunday school teachers took them to a children's museum. A minister took them to stay overnight in his home when the government cut electricity to Bee's house. Three people tried to teach them English and help them with their homework. Other members taught them to draw pictures and play football. We also involved them in playing Thai folk music during the Christmas 2001 program. These youngsters freely moved in and out among us. Pen and Pong devoted themselves to them by taking them to run and play around in a public park each Saturday. They even taught the children how to take a bath using soap, at the church. These kids stayed with their relatives in the nearby slum.

Drug traffic was spreading in the slums. The wicked system of drug trafficking especially trapped students who skipped school. We began to feel hopeless, because we knew time was running out.

On January 6, 2002, the "gang of five" attended our worship service for the first time with the other children. They sat through the Children's Day celebration. The pastor explained how precious children are by showing stars hidden in apples. In the afternoon Pen and Pong presented all the children with the gospel of Jesus. Realizing they did not have a father model, Pen presented Jesus as their Father, and she gave them time to make a decision. Fourteen of them wanted to follow Jesus. The following evening, they came by themselves to confess their sins. Some great changes in behavior took place. The gang of five returned to school. They also regularly attended the church and the class to prepare for the baptismal service. Their violent natures were completely transformed. The church and non-Christians in our neighborhood have noticed the changes and are very happy.

This primary stage, mentioned above, validates the important roles of vulnerability, cooperation, and progression in bonding with non-Christians. Christians carefully help their friends move from the familiar Thai Buddhist context to the unfamiliar context of the gospel. This research testing confirms the validity of our theoretical framework.

The Task of Testing: Worship Services

After the primary stage of bonding, understanding the field of religious studies introduced many good changes in our Sunday worship services. The research findings from my dissertation concerning the Thai Buddhist way of learning religion indicated the need for many changes in the decorations of our sanctuary, worship songs, and the style of preaching. The Muangthai Church has made some experiments, which I will briefly explain below.

First, we found a Thai traditional music teacher in our midst. We also bought some Thai traditional musical instruments. Then some children, students, and adults paid a teacher to learn *Saw-ong*, an art which has been lost among Christian churches. We researched how to develop proper Thai tunes and songs that would open up Thai feelings. We also invented some Thai ways of reading Scriptures. Moreover, we introduced a new way of giving a testimony. The one who gives the testimony dances to a Thai music tune, and a singer chants the testimony.

Second, we tried our best to make each Sunday worship service festive. The sanctuary was decorated with sights, sounds, symbols, and fragrances. One Good Friday service, we arranged the tables and chairs in the form of a cross. On each table we put a candle and a vase of white flowers. A full-sized wooden cross was put up in our sanctuary. Three big nails and a crown of thorns were passed around among the congregants. The preaching message was concretely near, now, new, and narrative to the audience's ears. After the service, the church gave each member a small bag of Thai potpourri, which was made at the royal palace. That night many members mentioned how they had encountered Jesus' presence. Such an experience is very important because, as Peter McKenzie comments about encountering Jesus,

> Religion, including Christianity, is not philosophy, not worldview, not theology, but intercourse with the sacred. This intercourse is a twofold one. It comes to expression very clearly in the dialogues between the soul and Christ as they are found

in the most beautiful and popular writings of the German mystics: *The Booklet of Eternal Wisdom* of Henry Suso and the *Imitation of Christ* of Thomas a Kempis. (1988, 310)

Third, we added variety to the worship services. On the first and third week, we have different teams of youth lead the worship. On the second week, we have traditional worship services for elderly people. On the fourth week, we have worship services for young adults. Every two months, we have a special service focusing on the Thai way of worship. Our church also organized a church choir.

Fourth, the preachers tried to preach the Scripture at the deep level of attitudes and values, rather than at the behavior pattern level. Sermon delivery became more concrete, concise, and constructive. Listeners laughed and participated more while they listened to the word of God. After worship services, Christians and non-Christians preferred to spend time discussing the applications of the sermons they had heard.

Fifth, we held evangelistic meetings during Christian festivals and some other Thai festivals. The most popular Christian festival is the Christmas celebration. Popular Thai festivals are Children's Day, Teacher's Day, the Chinese New Year, Valentine's Day, Mother's Day, the Thai New Year, and the King's Birthday. We rarely had "altar calls," but we encouraged seekers to attend Sunday school class. Our church aimed at progressive and cooperative witnessing. After seekers met Jesus Christ in Sunday school classes, the pastor gave altar calls for them to come forward. Then new converts publicly confessed their determination to follow Christ.

An example of our Christmas 2000 outreach will demonstrate the effectiveness of our theoretical framework. During the Christmas 2000 celebration, we planned to use the Thai way of witnessing, using Victor Turner's (1969) book *The Ritual Process: Structure and Anti-structure* and William E. Paden's (1988) book *Religious Worlds: The Comparative Study of Religion* as our guidelines for the program preparation. We therefore planned four important stages: (1) presenting the story of Christ's nativity in a Thai way, (2) inductive preaching for a verdict, (3) preparing a counseling team, and (4) having a love feast after the Christmas worship service. The committee tried to design ways in which we could repeatedly and artistically present the story of Christ's nativity to non-Christians who were unfamiliar with the Christmas story. We also wanted to present the theme of Jesus' incarnation, explaining how he left heaven to live on earth. We also expected a lot of participation from the audience. As a result, we narrated the story through Thai traditional ways of dancing and singing, which symbolize a high level of hierarchy. We then immediately used Thai folk dances and singing to repeat the narration. The folk ways symbolize a low level of hierarchy. Over two hundred audience members participated in singing the folk songs. A lot of non-Christians celebrated the Christmas narration at the end of the program by walking forward and dancing a Thai folk dance. The program indirectly indicated that the high class met the low class in Jesus' birth.

Then the pastor inductively preached an evangelistic sermon. Ten non-Christians responded to the invitation. Most of them are now members in our church. During the love feast, the pastor interviewed non-Christians concerning the presentation of the Christmas narration and the sermon. The pastor could not find even one negative response. However, one Christian family was quite annoyed with the way we presented the Christmas story. Most non-Christians repeatedly commented that they clearly understood the gospel. One non-Christian who had attended our Christmas programs for the past ten years said, "This is the best Christmas program."

Research testing illustrates the validity of our conceptual and practical theoretical framework. The knowledge of religious studies improves our worship services. Vulnerability, progression, and cooperation play important roles in effectively witnessing to Thai Buddhists. The presentation of Christmas 2000 confirms that Christians should lovingly and gently move non-Christians from their familiar Thai Buddhist context to the unfamiliar context of the gospel of Christ.

The Task of Testing: Presenting the Gospel

We now come to the very important part, presenting the content of the gospel to Thai Buddhists. During the past twenty-five years, the Muangthai Church has encountered two problems: (1) there are many split-level Christians who converted only at the level of behavior patterns, not at the worldview or value levels; and (2) there are those who prayed to accept Christ, but did not become Christ's believers. With the help of my theoretical framework, I planned the course and the methods of dialoguing about the content of the gospel.

The course I designed coincides with what Asbury Theological Seminary professors Dr. Darrell Whiteman and Dr. J. T. Seamand have presented. Dr. Whiteman (1994) spoke of culture and the gospel in his lecture at the E. Stanley Jones School of World Mission and Evangelism at Asbury Theological Seminary, USA, as follows:

> Gospel traverses culture. Gospel judges and saves culture. Gospel dedicates and sanctifies culture. Gospel beautifies culture. Gospel exorcises demons in culture.

Dr. J. T. Seamand agreed that the gospel of "The Four Noble Truths" is the best way to witness to the Buddhists. He suggested:

> "Four Noble Truths" and the "Eight-fold Path." The Four Noble Truths are:
>
> a. Suffering is a fact of life.
> b. The cause of suffering is sin.
> c. The cure for sins is the suffering of Christ.
> d. The way of deliverance is through faith in Jesus Christ.
>   (1981, 175)

Moreover, cultural anthropologists believe culture functions as an interrelated whole. Technology, economics, politics, kinship, and religion remain important institutions of culture. Stephen A. Grunlan and Marvin K. Mayers confirm the idea. They write:

> Culture is the integrated system of learned behavior patterns characteristic of the member of a society. Cultural anthropology deals with the sytem as a whole, how the parts fit and function within the whole, and how whole systems relate and compare. (1979, 56)

Therefore, during witnessing, any discussion about the topic of the suffering of human beings will always include concern about materialism, relationships, and idealism.

The course of presenting the gospel to Thai Buddhists consists of two steps:

1. The eradication of the wicked parts of the worldview and values, and the preservation of the good in the Thai Buddhist worldview and values.
2. The presentation of the gospel context consisting of:
   a. the suffering of human beings in materialism, relationships, and idealism
   b. the suffering of Jesus Christ as 100 percent man
   c. the cause of suffering: the sins of mankind
   d. the cure of suffering: Jesus Christ's death and resurrection as 100 percent God
   e. the call to reconciliation with Christ: faith in Jesus Christ

The method of teaching is comprised of seven important elements as follows:

1. Christians create a friendly and family-like atmosphere in the Sunday school class for non-Christians.
2. Non-Christians are welcomed to ask questions and criticize Christianity, Christians, and Christian churches. Teachers and teacher aides pay focused attention to the non-Christians' ideas.
3. Non-Christians are included in sharing their opinions concerning the topics being discussed. Arguing and debating are not encouraged on the part of Christians.
4. Christians usually give explanations after non-Christians give their opinions. Christians use illustrations, testimonies, and the Scriptures in answering questions or objections. Christians can simply say they cannot answer every question.
5. Christians end each session by encouraging non-Christians to directly ask Jesus and read the Scriptures to find the answers on their own.

6. The course is not a fixed model. Teachers can adapt the content of the lesson plan according to the guidance of the Holy Spirit and the context of the non-Christians present.

7. Prayer is important for the effective witness of the gospel to Thai Buddhists. The church should pray for both teachers and non-Christians.

Some testimonies of those who became Christians in this class will exemplify the efficiency of the theoretical framework. I will record the conversion of two persons, Pung and Sutkate.

Pung was a lady who was twenty years old. Her father had died of alcoholism. Pung ran away from home at fifteen. She had a young son, but she had broken up with her husband, who took her son away. At the point when she was deeply depressed, a Christian relative came to help. Pung attended our Sunday school class for seven months. She loved Christians, but she could not believe Jesus was God. One night she prayed that God would help her know about her little son's situation. On the following day, she received a letter from her husband who had not communicated for about a year. He shared about their son's situation. God had answered her prayer. She knew he was real. Pung became a Christian. She witnessed to her younger sister. Her younger sister became a Christian. Moreover, now her older sister wants to be a Christian too.

Sutkate was an architect of Thai architecture. He lost one arm in an accident when he was eight years old. Sutkate asked many difficult questions in the Sunday school class. He had experienced having a Hindu idol answer his prayers as well as Jesus. He wondered why he should believe in Jesus as the one and only way. Christians tried to answer, but Sutkate was not satisfied. Therefore, Sutkate sought answers on his own from the Bible. He also prayed directly to Jesus. Sutkate found the answers that satisfied his soul. He became a Christian within seven months. He now actively serves among slum orphans.

The record of the course of presenting the gospel content as well as the methods of dialoguing about the gospel confirms the efficiency of our theoretical framework. The roles of vulnerability, progression, cooperation, as well as moving non-Christians from the familiar Buddhist context to the unfamiliar gospel context are obvious in dialog about the gospel with Thai Buddhists.

The task of testing illustrates positive results in the Muangthai Church. By January 2002, fifty-eight of sixty regular seekers became Christians. Only two men did not make decisions. They continue to attend our Sunday school class for non-Christians. The percentage of converts is 96.67. Between 1999 and 2001, there were seventy-five non-Christians who attended the Muangthai Church's Sunday school for nonbelievers. The percentage of converts among those who attended the class was 77.33. Average attendance at the church is now 150, which is 87.5 percent more than the attendance in 1997. We now have two Sunday school classes for non-Christians. Ten more congregants are being trained to be teachers and teacher aides. Baptismal classes have expanded to three.

Moreover, the test of our theoretical framework has also greatly affected our Sunday school curriculum. The church has produced five hundred Sunday school lessons for children from two to fifteen using the conceptual and practical theoretical framework. We aim at preparing children to progressively and cooperatively absorb and encounter Jesus within three years as they learn the New Testament and the Old Testament. Children actively participate in their Sunday school classes. The church has also opened a training center for cross-cultural communication. We have trained about seventy missionaries. Many have reported the effectiveness of the theoretical framework we have taught, when applied to their ministry situations.

The Task of Testing: A Summary of Findings

At this point, the test of the witness in the Sunday school class for nonbelievers and the witness among slum children confirms the effectiveness of our theoretical framework.

As noted in the theoretical framework, Thais have a unique personality and a unique way of learning religion, as well as the uniqueness of the Thai way of deep relational bonding. The conceptual theoretical framework consists of: (1) the structure of characteristics of the Thai way of meekness as mentioned in the diagram, (2) the Thai way of religious learning, and (3) the structure of Thai deep relational bonding. Number 2 and number 3 were mentioned in detail in the discussion of the theoretical framework. The conceptual theoretical framework comes from anthropology and religious studies. The practical theoretical framework suggests that vulnerability, progression, and cooperation are all vital in witnessing to Thai Buddhists. Moreover, more Thai Buddhists will understand, as well as accept Christ and his gospel, if Christians gently help them move from the familiar Buddhist context to the unfamiliar context of the gospel.

The conceptual and practical theoretical framework exemplified themselves in the process of creating deep relational bonding with non-Christians, and in the process of improving worship services, as well as in the process of witnessing the gospel. Moreover, the theoretical framework affected the children's Sunday school and our practice of social concern. We created an effective three-year Sunday school curriculum withlessons using this theoretical framework. The theoretical framework has helped us expand social and humanitarian work among our slum neighborhood. The church now fits better within its context.

I therefore confirm my statement of the problem, that there is a time for everything. For two hundred years, Buddhists in Thailand did not widely accept the gospel of Jesus. Less than 1 percent of the population accepted Christ. Thailand became the headquarters of Buddhism. In the past, Christians ignored the context of Buddhists. We did not study the Buddhist personality in each context. We were ignorant of the ways Buddhists learn religion. We also overlooked the ways Buddhists create deep relational bonding.

In this chapter, I have used Thailand as an example for learning how to witness to Buddhists. I have proposed a more effective way of discipling Thai Buddhists, which comes from: (1) a better understanding of the Thai Buddhist personality in each context, (2) knowing how Thai Buddhists learn religion, and (3) learning how Thai Buddhists create deep relational bonding. The task of testing demonstrated the validity of my solution to the stated problem.

References

Blanford. Carl E. 1985. *Chinese churches in Thailand.* Bangkok: Suriyaban Publishing House.

Feltus, George H., ed. 1936. *Abstract of the journal of Rev. Dan Beach Bradley: Medical missionary in Siam 1835–1873.* Oberlin, OH: Multigraph Department of Pilgrim Church.

Fieg, John Paul. 1989. *A common core: Thais and Americans.* Yarmouth, ME: Intercultural Press.

Grunlan, Stephen A., and Marvin K. Mayers. 1979. *Cultural anthropology: A Christian perspective.* Grand Rapids: Zondervan.

Hiebert, Paul G. 1985. *Anthropological insights for missionaries.* Grand Rapids: Baker Book House.

Hughes, Philip H. 1989. *Proclamation and response.* Bangkok: Payap University Archives.

Komin, Suntaree. 1991. *Psychology of the Thai people: Value and behavior patterns.* Bangkok: National Institute of Development Administration.

Levi-Strauss, Claude. 1953. Social structure. In *Anthropology today*, ed. Alfred L. Kroeber, 524–53 Chicago: University of Chicago Press.

Luzbetak, Louis J. 1988. *The church and culture: New perspectives in missiological anthropology.* Maryknoll, NY: Orbis Books.

McKenzie, Peter. 1988. *The Christians: Their beliefs and practices.* Nashville: Abingdon.

Mejudhon, Ubolwan. 1997. The way of meekness: Being Christian and Thai in the Thai way. DMiss diss., Asbury Theological Seminary.

Nida, Eugene A. 1954. *Customs and cultures: Anthropology for Christian missions.* New York: Harper & Row.

Paden, William E. 1988. *Religious worlds: The comparative study of religion.* Boston: Beacon.

Sanneh, Lamin. 1993. *Translating the message: The missionary impact on culture.* Maryknoll, NY: Orbis Books.

Seamand, J. T. 1981. *Tell it well: Communicating the gospel across cultures.* Kansas City: Beacon Hill.

Sharp, Lauriston. 1978. *Bang Chan: Social history of a rural community in Thailand.* Ithaca, NY: Cornell University Press.

Turner, Victor. 1969. *The ritual process: Structure and anti-structure.* Rochester, NY: Aldine De Gruyter.

Whiteman, Darrell. 1994. Anthropology. Lecture presented at the E. Stanley Jones School of World Mission and Evangelism, Asbury Theological Seminary, Wilmore, KY.

Zahniser, A. H. Mathias. 1994. Close encounters of the vulnerable kind: Christian dialogical proclamation among Muslims. *Asbury Theological Journal* 49, no. 1: 71–81.

———. 1997. *Symbol and ceremony: Making disciples across cultures.* Monrovia, CA: MARC.

CHAPTER 9

APPROPRIATE TYPOLOGIES FOR THAI FOLK BUDDHISTS

Paul H. de Neui

Is it possible for Thai Buddhists to remain within their cultural context and faithfully follow Jesus Christ? In a Buddhist country such as Thailand, national identity is closely linked with religious identity; good citizenship is equated with being Buddhist. This religious patriotism seems problematic for the cause of the gospel of Christ. As a result cross-cultural missionaries have often viewed Buddhism as the enemy of evangelism and have sought ways to counter it with Christianity. This approach has not only served to alienate people socially but has also reinforced the misunderstanding that Jesus is a foreigner, the leader of the foreigner's religion. For too long following Christ has been presented in the Buddhist world as "more western than Christian" (Wisley 1984, 128).

The goal of this chapter is to extrapolate from the Thai Buddhist context a range of appropriate typologies that might broaden a perspective on that which can be both the greatest witness and greatest hindrance to the presentation of the gospel of Christ within the Buddhist world: the church itself. It must be noted that the Thai Buddhist context varies greatly from urban to rural to hill-tribe perspectives. The appropriate typologies proposed in this chapter grew out of a desire to promote a greater unity of purpose while at the same time increase the range of diversity acceptable within the body of Christ to present the gospel in Buddhist contexts in ways that communicate and transform lives holistically in power, truth, and relationship.

Some cross-cultural missionaries consider Thai Buddhism as a purely philosophical religion and therefore strategize accordingly. Some spend time studying the *dharma*, the Four Noble Truths, the Five Precepts, and the Eightfold Noble Path in order to convince people why Christianity is better. My experience living in the context for a number of years is that Thai Buddhism as understood at the popular level incorporates an increasing number of non-Buddhist elements within its purview for a variety of reasons: to reinterpret tradition, to provide broader social appeal, to indicate its relevance for daily life, and to insure religious sustainability. Some of these elements relate to veneration of local spirits and Brahman practices that predate the introduction of Buddhism to Southeast Asia sometime in the fifth or sixth century AD. To outsiders the accommodation of primal (and other) religious traditions, practices, and beliefs may appear contradictory but is perfectly acceptable to all but a handful of elite Buddhist monks who seek purification of the religion, and those Christian missionaries well-studied in Buddhist philosophy who find their favorite approaches falling on deaf ears. Popular Buddhism is pragmatic and cannot be boxed within a solitary entity. "Such elementary forms of the religious life offer immediate attention and a holistic approach to acute individual problems where solutions may not be available otherwise" (Heinze 1992, 28).

It is time for those within the body of Christ serving in Buddhist contexts to recognize the pragmatic reality of popular Buddhism that embraces a diversity of approaches and to learn from it. A diversity of approaches is needed in Christian mission and particularly within God's chosen agent in mission: the church. Existing models that focus on countering elite Buddhism with Christianity on the intellectual level have a role to play in reaching those who are truly followers of an elite form of Buddhism or high religion—but what about the majority who are practitioners of popular Buddhism and will have nothing to do with a Westernized Jesus?

Biblical and Historical Precedent

From the beginning of recorded Scripture, God was calling a people out of animism. Joshua 24:2–3 records God's words: "Long ago your ancestors, including Terah the father of Abraham and Nahor, lived beyond the Euphrates River and worshiped other gods. But I took your father Abraham from the land beyond the Euphrates and led him throughout Canaan and gave him many descendants." Two generations later, Jacob's wife insisted upon stealing her father's household gods (Gen 31:19) to take with her for protection as she traveled (Barker 1995, 52). In the Exodus account, God specifically states that the final plague was a judgment upon the Egyptian gods, an act of power encounter and a calling out, to be celebrated by generations to come (Ex 12:12–17). God's first commandment, "You shall have no other gods," significantly ends with the words "before me" (Ex 20:3) or "in hostility toward me." God acknowledged the existence of other gods (after him) in the lives of his people but instead of demanding their immediate repudiation allowed time for the transformation of their allegiances (Kraft 1996, 210).

Certainly, the history of the Israelites, an animistic people in the midst of other animistic societies, shows the disastrous results of confusing secondary with primary allegiances. Elisha's tacit approval to Naaman in 2 Kings 5:15–19 seems to indicate that God understands when social obligations require certain actions that might appear compromising to faith. For God, the condition of the heart always has priority over external ritual. God rejects rituals, even of his own command, when offered out of hypocrisy of the heart (Amos 5:21–24).

It is often noted how Paul used animistic Greek images and forms to speak to Greeks (Acts 17:16–23; 1 Cor 9:19–23). It was the actual inclusion of non-Jewish animistic Gentile believers into the family of faith that brought about the most revolutionary transformation of the church. To the hearers of its day the term "Gentile believer" was an oxymoron. "Being Gentile surely carried implications of religious consequence, deeply ingrained in the psyche of every Jew and Judaizer who objected to their inclusion in the church without first converting to Judaism" (Massey 1999, 190–91). To say "Gentile believer" was akin to our saying "Buddhist follower of Jesus," "Muslim believer," or even "Non-Christian Christian." The term "Christian" was never required of the followers of the Way; all three usages found in the Bible are pejorative (Acts 11:26; 26:28; 1 Pet 4:16). Nowhere in Scripture is there any indication of an agenda to erase the distinctives of the various peoples gathered into the family of God (Roxburgh 2002). Instead, every nation, tribe, people, and language will ultimately be represented and somehow miraculously joined together in a gloriously comprehensible tribute of praise to the Lamb (Rev 7:9).

Believers in the first centuries of the church had to come to an understanding about their animistic heritage. Who were they if they were not Jewish? What did they discover?

> Early Gentile Christianity went through a period of amnesia. It was not so critical for first-generation converts: they responded to a clear choice, turned from idols to serve the living God, accepted the assurance that they had been grafted into Israel. It was the second and third generations of Christians who felt the strain more. What was their relation to the Greek past? (Walls 2000, 13–14)

Greek theologians would borrow from their animistic tradition in order to communicate the gospel in ways to which their people could relate and respond.

> They used the Greek epics; they used the Homeric myths, and also Stoic and Epicurean philosophy when it suited them. We even find Clement of Rome, after arguing for the reasonableness of the resurrection from the fact that seeds die and come to life again in new flowers, laying enormous stress on the phoenix. This Eastern (mythological) bird was said by the poets to die and be reborn from its own ashes every 500 years. Clement really believed this! It is the climax of his argument. He was in this respect as others a child of his age. Even so, it was not the phoenix he was interested in, but Christ. Anything in Greek thought that would help his listeners to lay hold of the wonder and the reality of the resurrection was good enough for Clement. And this is the characteristic aim which the Greek exponents of the gospel set themselves: to embody biblical doctrine in cultural forms which would be acceptable in their society. Not to remove the scandal of the gospel, but so to present their message in terms acceptable to their hearers, that the real scandal of the gospel could be perceived and its challenge faced. (Green 1970, 142)

The earliest missionaries to the pagan animist inhabitants of the British Isles in the early sixth century questioned their own interaction with the animistic context. What from animism, if anything, could be used for the gospel, and what must be rejected? They received the following response from Pope Gregory I:

> The heathen temples of these people need not be destroyed, only the idols which are to be found in them . . . If the temples are well built, it is a good idea to detach them from the service of the devil, and to adapt them for the worship of the true God . . . And since the people are accustomed, when they assemble for sacrifice, to kill many oxen in sacrifice to the devils, it seems reasonable to appoint a festival for the people by way of exchange. The people must learn to slay their cattle not in honour of the devil, but in honour of God and for their own food; when they have eaten and are full, then they must render thanks to the giver of all good things. If we allow them these outward joys, they are more likely to find their way to the true inner joy . . . It is doubtless impossible to cut off all abuses at once from rough hearts, just as the man who sets out to climb a high mountain does not advance by leaps and bounds, but goes upward step by step and pace by pace. (Thomas 1998, 22)

Numerous examples, possibly from every continent and culture, could be given to illustrate the historical interaction between a politically dominant Christianity that attempted to eradicate animism merely to drive it underground. Religious-oriented evolutionary thought gave rise to the notion that animism would eventually die out to the higher religions, preferably Christianity. As recently as 1973 missions anthropologist Allan Tippett wrote, "I give it [popular folk religion] tens years, at the very utmost twenty, to disappear" (1973, 9). Many Christian missionaries admit that this is unrealistic but continue to act as if it were true. In fact, popular religions with primal religious practices have had a recent resurgence (Van Rheenen 2002), particularly in modern urban contexts (Hard 1989, 45–46).

It was not required of early believers that they attend "Jewish" classes in order to become full-fledged church members. Why are we requiring the same thing from people coming from other religious and cultural backgrounds? Bruce Heckman describes this from the Muslim perspective in which he worked:

> Muslim believers need a community which is distinct from the Christian community. Their community cannot be simply a "new believer" class which is attached to an existing church, nor a temporary arrangement which hopes to eventually bridge them into the Christian community. The Muslim believers' community will need the freedom to critically examine their Islamic background and decide upon the inclusion, exclusion or alteration of old religious and social forms. The style, location and scheduling of meetings needs to be a result of their communal choice rather than based upon Christian patterns (Arab or expatriate). (1988, 128)

In an effort to address these issues, John Travis developed the C1 to C6 spectrum "to assist church planters and Muslim background believers to ascertain which type of Christ-centered communities may draw the most people from the target group to Christ and best fit in a given context" (1998, 407). This highly debated spectrum has generated numerous conferences provoking thought about the definition of "chuch" among mission groups working within a Muslim context. I believe that this spectrum, with modification, has application for those working in the context of popular Buddhism as well.

One Mission, Many Models

The C1 to C6 spectrum presents six typologies of church and Christ-centered communities that exist in the context of the popular Buddhist world as well as in the Muslim world. The spectrum is not intended to judge one method of church planting over another; it serves as a model of typologies. It is unfortunate that it has been described as a continuum that seems to imply positive movement upward and negative going down. In fact, there is no particular "up" or "down." Such terminology tends towards negative categorization and a great deal of ambiguity about direction. A typology suggests ways of discussing, with some degree of comparative understanding, what is meant by planting an appropriately styled church in a certain way in a particular cultural context. All church types may be equally valid but all not equally effective in every context. Lateral movement from one position to another is possible either towards a cultural relevancy or away from it. It is hoped that all types are in the process of transformation and meaningful spiritual growth.

Application of C1 to C6 to Thai Folk Buddhist Context

What follows is an expanded description of the six church types found on the C1 to C6 spectrum as it has been adapted for the context of popular Buddhism in Thailand. With further research, it is hoped that this scale will become a tool with application throughout the broader Buddhist world. In each description, leadership styles, meaning, and identification for the members, and engagement with the local culture are illustrated by examples and a brief evaluation of strengths and weaknesses.

C1: Intentional Transplant / Dominant Language Church

The C1 church type deliberately attempts to transplant forms and structures of Christianity from another culture (usually Western) to the folk Buddhist receptor culture using the dominant national language of the new host culture. This church is consciously, culturally alien and openly, aggressively anti-Buddhist and anti–local culture. If the dominant national language is also the insider language of the members, a church in this context would then be referred to as C2 (described below). C1 appeals to those who, for a variety of reasons, desire to identify with forms that use the dominant language and are primarily Western. C1 believers call themselves "Christians" who practice Christianity.

The leader of a C1 church may be a native of the target culture, generally trained in a central language Bible school, college, or seminary that has a Western-based curriculum. He or she will identify with Western communication methods, theologies, and organizational structures of Christianity and will be taught to incorporate them into the life of the church. There may be very little academic focus in the training of such a person to communication in "high-context cultures." At the same time, the understanding that God is already present and actively at work through the *missio Dei* in that location may be a new concept.

As previously mentioned, members of C1 churches have a variety of motives for identifying with foreign Christianity presented in the dominant national language. Those already marginalized by their society may see the possibility of greater personal advance by linking with a missionary or a foreign religion (finding a new patron). Others may seek status, cultural or career advancement, or genuine freedom from spiritual enslavement and may feel a strong desire to reject anything having to do with Buddhism and related cultural expressions.

Many who follow Christ in a C1 approach make significant personal sacrifices and are often cut off socially from their communities. They develop strong allegiances to forms and practices, even relationships, consciously alien to their original culture and religion. As a result, C1 churches have limited interaction with their local non-Christian communities. Some may invite their communities to a celebration at Christmas; however, the forms used will remain firmly outside of the local language and customs.

A subcategory of C1 are international churches that use English as the common idiom, even though they are located in such places as Bangkok, Jakarta, or Katmandu. This church type deliberately attempts to replicate Christian forms and styles as they exist in the West in order to reach expatriates located temporarily away from their home culture. It will not attract many local people who do not speak English.

Examples of C1: The First Gospel Church of Thailand (GCT) in Khon Kaen, in the center of northeast Thailand, is an example of a C1 church. Started by American missionaries in the 1930s, it uses the central Thai language and imports and employs well-publicized foreign structures and models known to be successful elsewhere. Although it is in the heart of the Lao-speaking northeast Thai region known as Isaan, GCT members almost visibly shed their northeastern Thai identities at the door. This is true throughout the breadth of Isaan and is also true of some churches in the *kammüang*-speaking churches of Thailand's northern region. Very few churches in Thailand employ anything other than the national language, in spite of the fact that over half of the Thai population speak a different mother tongue (Smalley 1994, 1).

Strengths Within C1, the separation from local culture is distinctly clear. The intentional use of foreign forms and outsider language are probably the most important distinctives of the church. This is what builds the cultural framework that makes the worship and the congregational experience appealing to the target group. C1 churches build a new identity that reinforces those separated from their host community. Some have established programs that help their new members through the initial painful periods when unbelieving family and friends inevitably reject them (Caleb Project 1988, 56).

Weaknesses Due to the large cultural chasm, social rejection is high. Those who get involved in a C1 church may be viewed with suspicion by family, or may be encouraged to get involved for ulterior motives. Locals who are not fluent in the dominant language may be hesitant to get involved. Sometimes C1 can contribute to feelings of ethnic inferiority by exclusively promoting a national identity when the majority of the members speak something different at home. Another weakness of C1 churches is that they attract social outcasts and misfits. These are brought in one by one but are not bridges into the cultural mainstream. Such individuals are willing to sacrifice whatever remains of their cultural and/or religious identification, because the former ways have already failed them (Keyes 1993, 271).

C2: Church Transplant Using Local Language

C2 is essentially the same as C1 except for the use of the local language and a subtle degree of mellowing of attitudes towards the local culture. Though insider language is used, religious vocabulary, ritual, structures, and forms would stress non-Buddhist, formal equivalency easily identified by C1 as distinctively "Christian." Few churches originate as C2; most were started as C1. However, over time, the radical conscious cultural and religious alienation wears down to where the ethos or the subculture of the church itself, although still overtly alien, becomes a degree more tolerant, at least towards local language usage. Leaders may come from popular Buddhist contexts or from Christian family backgrounds, but most would have been trained in forms familiar to the C1 approach. They would use C1 terminology referring to themselves, dependent upon their particular denominational ecclesiology. Though they may or may not be familiar with Western forms used in the church, they are willing to learn about them. When referring to themselves, C2 believers willingly call themselves "Christians" who practice Christianity. In spite of using the local language, the cultural separation between the surrounding popular Buddhist context and the C2 church is still distinct. Interaction with people in the local context is limited similarly to C1.

Examples of C2: It might be assumed that in a city like Bangkok, located in central Thailand where the heart language is central Thai, that most church members would be central Thai speakers, which would then make the churches C2. This was not the case. One survey indicated that of forty-seven Bangkok churches contacted, none had purely central Thai members; most were a mixture of Chinese-Thai and members from the north, the south, and the northeast regions of the country. Less than twenty percent of any church was made up of members originally from Bangkok or central Thailand where central Thai is spoken in the home (Caleb Project 1988, 53).

The Mahaporn church, born originally out of the Christian and Missionary Alliance's C1 English-language Evangelical Church on Sukhumvit Soi 10 in Bangkok, is one of the best examples of a C2 church. This congregation has given birth to several other Thai-language C2 congregations in the greater Bangkok area and has sent Thai church planters from the mother church to plant other C1 and C2 churches in other areas of Bangkok and other provinces in Thailand and has even sent Thai missionaries to other countries.

Strengths People are attracted to C2 for a wide variety of reasons. These may range from strong feelings of disillusionment with their Buddhist past to a strong desire for freedom from spiritual bondage in animistic practices. Some have experienced physical healing. For many of these people a definite sense of separation from their non-Christian past is critically important. Their new sense of loyalty is to Christ and his church, and they are eager to embrace this relationship. As in the case of C1, the sense of a Christian identity is clear-cut in C2 churches. Separation from local culture, while often painful, is distinctly clear. C2 eagerly identifies with the larger global Western church in form. Expatriate visitors can be deeply moved hearing their own songs sung in foreign languages. Uniformity is an important strength.

Weaknesses As in C1, C2 can result in cultural ostracism of members, little opportunity to interact freely with community and family members, as well as social (and sometimes physical) martyrdom. A C2 church can often feel as if it is on the defensive culturally and may develop a preservationist attitude (not unique to Thailand). If missionary leadership was involved in starting the church, the transition to local leadership can be difficult. Sometimes the initial forms that the missionaries introduced in order to get things started become sacred. As Paul Hiebert has said, "The scaffolding somehow got built into the structure itself." (Class lecture. Diversity is viewed with suspicion; preservation is key. Formal equivalence is important.

> Missionary Christianity planted within the Thai church a Western-style dualism deeply concerned with protecting Christian purity from any defilement by "heathen practices." The Thai church has especially emphasized refraining from participation in Buddhist-animist ritual and ceremony as a key way of protecting its purity, and one finds Thai Protestant Christians constantly worrying over the question of idolatrous behavior in situations in which they are faced with having to join in Buddhist rituals—such as funerals, opening exercises in schools, and community events. The general rule has been to take a hard-line approach, one that adheres to as strict a definition of the boundaries between Christianity and Buddhism as possible. (Swanson 2001, 14)

Forms used in C2 churches can be confusing initially to outsiders who are trying to understand what Christianity is all about. Thai believers tell numerous (often humorous) stories on themselves about their first encounters with Christianity; however, here is missionary observer Thomas Wisley's report on a church experience in northeast Thailand:

> The elder stood before his congregation directing the twenty-five or so men and women as they sang one of their favorite hymns, *Phralohit Phrayesu* (Nothing But the Blood of Jesus). On one side of the *sala* (open air chapel) a young new convert perched on the backless bench and looked quizzically at the open

hymn book in his hands. Obviously he was having a difficult time reading the words and following the music . . . Because of the addition of western musical notes to the indigenous Thai tonal pattern a strange new language had been created thus complicating even more this Thai attempt to worship God . . . The leader was using his hands to beat out the time directing the song as he had been taught to do in the Bible school. But instead of directing 4/4 time as the song was written, he was beating 3/4 pattern that did not match the timing of the song . . . I began to wonder whether Christianity in Thailand might be more western than it was Christian. (1984, 127–28)

C3: Local-language Churches Using Religiously Neutral Cultural Forms

C3 attempts to reduce the cultural chasm between the church and the surrounding popular Buddhist community. This is done by including into the life of the church local forms from which Buddhist or animistic elements have been filtered out in an attempt to retain only nonreligious cultural elements. Meeting facilities may be in Western-style churches, local buildings, or homes. Religiously neutral forms may include some local music (whenever appropriate); culturally neutral combinations of local and Western instruments; use of artifacts, time, space, artwork, architecture, furniture (or lack of); and local communication methods. Elements from popular Buddhism (where present) are filtered out so as to use purely nonreligious cultural forms as much as possible. The aim is to reduce foreignness of the gospel and the church by adapting to biblically permissible cultural forms. The members would come from a popular Buddhist context, and most would not be familiar with Christianity but would be learning about it.

Leaders may have come from Buddhist backgrounds or from Christian family backgrounds but most would have been trained in central Thai using forms familiar to the C1 approach. Forms of Bible teaching may be preaching or Bible discussion. They would use C1 terminology when referring to themselves, depending upon their particular denominational ecclesiology and church polity.

C3 church members would strongly identify with C1 and C2 Christianity. However, the issues of separation so dominant in the first generation may be somewhat softened in the succeeding generations. While identification with Christianity is strong, there is a willingness to consider what it means to integrate some Thai forms into the Christian walk and into the life of the church. Members and leaders may have a C1–2 background but find meaning in the filtered cultural forms from the context of the popular Buddhist community. C3 believers would still refer to themselves as "Christians."

Like C2, a C3 church is in process. It is distinguished from C1 or C2 in that it is beginning to attempt to consider ways in which it can interact with its local society while remaining loyal to its faith in Jesus Christ. It recognizes some of the barriers either of forms or attitudes inherent in their practice of Western Christianity and is beginning to contemplate ways in which these barriers can be addressed or removed without compromising Christian commitment. Unlike C1 and C2, C3 churches view cultural forms as potential points of connection with outsiders that need to be considered.

Examples of C3: A good example of a C3 church in the folk Buddhist world exists in the capital city of a neighboring country to Thailand. Here a well-established, Western-style church, started by missionaries nearly eighty years earlier, replaced the wooden pews with the familiar woven straw mats used in every home. Shoes are no longer worn within the church but are kept on racks outside. Other than this, the church has basically maintained its C2 approach, but in this one area it is attempting to transition into C3.

Another example of C3 is the Suwanduangrit Church described by Herbert R. Swanson, an expatriate member and employee of the Church of Christ in Thailand (CCT). This church is in the community of Ban Dok Daeng, located twenty kilometers east of Chiang Mai in northern Thailand. This church was originally started by American Presbyterian missionaries in 1880 using a C1 approach that gradually became C2. Over the years it developed into a fairly strong Christian minority located in its own segment of the village.

> Like other Thai Protestant churches, the Suwanduangrit Church
> has generally stood apart from the communal life of its village
> in spite of the facts that there were several inter-faith nuclear

families and that most of the Christians have Buddhist relatives. Christians took no part in *wat* (Buddhist temple) activities other than to help with cooking at temple festivities when called upon to do so. Christians would attend those festivals and other events, such as funerals, but strictly as visitors. In this atmosphere of mutual distrust, the church lived largely for itself and took no thought as to how it might act as a witness to the love of God in Christ or carry out peacemaking activities. Its neighbors, in any event, would have treated any form of community involvement with suspicion, based on their general perception of Christians as being soul winning "head hunters." (2002, 61)

When, in 1996, the local Buddhist temple built a new *phraviharn* (main ritual building in any Thai Buddhist *wat*), representatives from the temple committee contacted the church to find out how it would participate in the dedication festivities. "They made it clear that the usual policy of silence by the church was unacceptable to the larger community" (ibid., 62). The resulting crisis that faced the church caused the members to struggle with the reality of the cultural chasm between themselves and their community that had existed for over one hundred years.

In spite of the conflict that ensued, the church eventually followed the temple's suggestion and participated in the *wat* festivities by donating a *tonkuatan*, known as a money tree, which is a bamboo frame upon which currency and other small items are hung. These money trees are then paraded through the streets and into the temple with loud music, drums and gongs, cheering, and "well-oiled" dancing. Although this is a very typical sight in much of Thailand, "what was new was the Christians, straggling along at the back—but *in* the procession" (ibid., 7). This was seen as a major breakthrough by the community (ibid., 75).

While this one-time event may seem insignificant, it set in motion a new relationship between the Christians and their Buddhist community that was not forgotten. Five years later when the Suwanduangrit Church was close to completing its new multipurpose hall, members of the temple committee asked if they could donate a money tree to the church and sparked a second processional celebration. This time the church invited a Christian music group that contextualizes local music in worship to provide the music, and during the procession of the money trees church members were seen dancing as well. "Being a Christian or with Christians, for once, was fun" (ibid., 68).

The final event recorded by Swanson in this ongoing transition occurred the following year, 2001, when the Buddhist temple was going to dedicate its own multipurpose building. At this point the church not only donated a money tree but also set up a booth at the temple festival, brought their own drums and gongs, and were seen as part of the community. It was agreed by the members and "even the leading elder of the 'separatist' group (that) the ceremony was 'really' only a traditional Thai one and not essentially religious" (ibid., 72). Through this process they were able to engage in a "redefinition of religious boundaries, a key issue for Thai local theology" (ibid.).

Strengths When Christians borrow and incorporate popular forms from the local culture, it can facilitate greater dialogue with the surrounding community members. It indicates a church that is struggling to theologize locally for itself, which, although sometimes a painful process, can promote deep spiritual growth. C3 indicates a church in transition desiring to become more culturally relevant with its local community.

Weaknesses Not all secular forms, even if they are not strictly religious, can be assumed to be value-neutral. The so-called filtering process assumes a distinction between culture and religion that is not a reality for most of the Buddhist world. C3 downplays the reality that religiously neutrally forms may carry strong cultural values that need to be addressed biblically. Some Buddhist, and even animistic, forms contain biblical truth and therefore may not necessarily require elimination (example: five major precepts of Buddhism). Because C3 attempts to transition from a completely outsider perspective to an integration with local perspectives, it will be attacked by C1 and C2 as compromising and yet still viewed as Western by those in C4 or C5. Buddhists may resent the attempt to "filter out" elements of their practices. Additionally, in the process of "filtering," the question remains as to what is then substituted for the removed element. Unless it is initiated and accomplished internally, the transition in C3 from a Western orientation in form or attitude towards a new substitute can be imposed with paternalistic fervor equal to that of the original culturally alienating approach.

I strongly suspect that the "three selfs" are really projections of our American value systems into the idealization of the church, that they are in their very nature Western concepts based upon Western ideas of individualism and power. By focusing them on other people we may at times have been making it impossible for a truly indigenous pattern to develop. We have been Westernizing with all our talk about indigenizing. (Smalley 1958, 51–55)

C4: Local-language Christ-centered Communities Using Cultural and Biblically Permissible Forms from Popular Buddhism

C4 adds to C3 biblically permissible forms from popular Buddhism that the members find acceptable and meaningful. C4 communities are comprised almost entirely of believers from popular Buddhist backgrounds who may recognize C1–3 forms as representing the same Christianity of which they are a part, but find biblically permissible local forms most meaningful. Western cultural forms as found in C1 and C2 are avoided. Meetings are not held in Western-style church buildings but generally in homes, shops, or public meeting areas. C4 communities are comprised almost entirely of believers from Buddhist backgrounds who know little of Western forms of Christianity and are not learning about them or adopting them.

Leadership for C4 movements should ideally be those who have not been so removed from their original context of popular Buddhism as to be unable to relate naturally to it. Believers raised within popular Buddhism, trained in a C1 approach and later attempting to minister in C4 work, have rarely been successful. Personal internal conflict within the individual quickly surfaces, and degrees of being disingenuous become obvious to all. Equipping leaders for a C4 approach is a challenging new direction that most Bible schools, colleges, and seminaries in the Buddhist context have yet to fully resolve.

Members of C4 are hesitant to use Christian terminology when such terms might build a barrier between themselves and those of their social context. They recognize areas of conflict between their Buddhist background and their faith in Christ and try to bring new meaning to forms that may not have been familiar but can be learned as functional substitutes. Their identification would be as followers of Jesus but still also part of the Buddhist community, engaging in some cultural forms that do not conflict with Scripture. C4 believers might identify themselves as "followers of Jesus" or "children of God" (or similar terms), and avoid the term "Christian" because of its Western association. C4 believers, though highly integrated, are usually not seen as Buddhist by the surrounding popular Buddhist community.

Examples of C4: An example of one church that successfully transitioned to using biblically permissible cultural forms is the CCT church in Sri Vilai district in the Sakorn Nakorn province of northeast Thailand. Originally a C1 missionary plant, the church, under new missionary leadership, began to incorporate the *wai* (palms together) during prayer, using rice for Communion, using local music and dance in worship, and sometimes even saying "*Satoo*" (Pali for "So be it") at the end of prayer as is also used in Buddhist prayers. The Catholic Church in Thailand has moved towards a C4 approach as well.

> Indigenization of the Catholic Church has entailed adapting the Christian message to the local cultures, including to existing religious traditions insofar as this is possible without compromising fundamental Christian dogmas. In Thailand the church has adopted many Thai Buddhist terms for Christian concepts and has adapted Buddhist temple architecture for Catholic churches. (Keyes 1993, 273)

Strengths The cultural chasm between C4 and the community is significantly reduced from C3. The biblical distinctives of Jesus followers are more clearly identifiable than in C5 (see below). When appropriating local customs for use in the Christ-centered community, the church will address issues of spiritual power that are deeply significant in the popular religious context. C4 is an attempt at a dynamically equivalent church using local forms that communicate as much as possible. If the first generation is planted this way, many of the mistakes of C1 and C2 can be avoided. If successful, the worshiping community will be able to manage the local ministry and carry on outreach within the confines of its own resources and giftedness. Overhead costs for a church structure are not necessary, and leadership can be voluntary.

Weaknesses C4 will be under pressure to conform with the already established C1 and C2 churches. C1 and C2 groups may view C4 as outside acceptable limits and question their practices and/or leadership qualifications. In some cases the national government may insist upon a certain Western orientation and restrict movement by Christian groups beyond C3. Because of the emphasis on dynamic equivalency, outsiders will notice and there may be negative reactions. "Indigenization of the Catholic Church in Thailand prompted a reaction by some conservative Buddhists who perceived a threat from a Christianity that was no longer clearly 'foreign'" (ibid.). If clear communication is not established from the beginning, the results can actually be damaging.

> It appears that at least one difficulty in the overall communication of Christian meanings in this situation had to do with the alleged failure of Roman Catholics to observe the appropriate beginning levels of communication before going to a more advanced level that required greater degrees of confidence. The Roman Catholics assumed that the community would feel more comfortable with indigenous architectural roof design. This may have been true for the Christians in the community. Due to a lack of trust at the preliminary level a total breakdown in the community image took place. (Wisley 1984, 170–71)

C5: Christ-centered Communities of Buddhist Followers of Jesus

C5 believers remain socially within the context of popular Buddhism. Aspects of popular Buddhism that are incompatible with the Bible are rejected or reinterpreted if possible. This would include issues related to idolatry, merit making, reincarnation, and others. C5 members celebrate their new life in Christ in ways that are familiar and meaningful to them, including location and forms of gatherings, communication styles, organizational structures, and methods of leadership and discipleship. Meetings are not held in Western-style church buildings but generally in homes, shops, or public meeting areas. C5 believer communities are comprised entirely of believers who come from folk Buddhist backgrounds, know little about Western forms of Christianity, and are not learning about them or adopting them.

An image that many might feel would describe C5 leadership in a Buddhist context would be a man with a shaven head, wearing something that approximates a Buddhist robe. In most of the Buddhist world, the impersonation of a Buddhist priest is a crime punishable by law. More importantly, however, is the emic understanding of the function of the Buddhist priesthood. Is there an equivalent position within the church that could serve as a functional substitute?

Further research into the insiders' perspective on the role of the monks in modern Thai Buddhist society is needed. An in-depth study of the role of Buddhist priests in popular Buddhist contexts is beyond the scope of this chapter. Tambiah summarizes the role thus:

The role of the monk in a village is primarily a ritual one; one we have already seen that in order to perform his parish and monastic role he needs only to acquire a certain amount of literacy in the sacred Tham and secular languages and to memorize a body of oft-used chants. (1970, 138)

The ritual roles of monks can therefore be summarized briefly as:

1. a means to making merit in times of crisis (funerals, *daak baht*, novitiates)
2. a source of Buddhist teaching
3. a source of animistic power
4. a moralizing force in society

Can a Christian leader of a C5 Christ-centered community fulfill this ritual role? Without wearing a robe, many secular leaders already do. The understanding that a dynamically equivalent church leader in C5 must look like a Buddhist monk is a false formal equivalency. The function must have priority over the form. C5 leaders do not necessarily have academic training, but their status in the community is one that must be earned rather than achieved through formal Bible training or the earning of degrees.

Members of C5 groups would not use the terms "Christian" or "Christianity" to describe themselves. Their identification would primarily be as Buddhist followers of Jesus. They would not claim to be accepting, following, or practicing Christianity but following Jesus Christ. C5 believers claim primary allegiance to the one true God and are viewed as Buddhists who have Jesus by the Buddhist community. They refer to themselves as "children of God" or a similar name that would not build barriers between them and their communities.

C5 groups desire to engage closely with their people. They understand that there are certain aspects of popular Buddhism that are incompatible with following Jesus. However, they try to use culture as a bridge to reaching out, rather than focusing on the issues that separate. Community members in popular Buddhist contexts may view C5 believers as not being true Buddhists because they do not seek means of making merit or appeasing spirits as other Buddhists do. Participation by C5 believers in some Buddhist and animist functions varies from person to person and group to group. C5 believers do, however, participate in some of the popular Buddhist functions in the name of Jesus.

Examples of C5: A group known as the Church of the Grace of God, found in northeast Thailand, Chiang Mai, and Bangkok, Thailand, would, by most definitions, fit the description of C5. They meet in homes or other neutral meeting areas, some with merely a sign that states, "The Meeting Location of the Worshiping Community of (Village Name)." They employ local musical forms, song, dance, and instruments. When they celebrate Communion they use the local staff of life (rice) to represent the body of Christ. Some members of the community have participated in giving food to monks in the name of Jesus. Others participate in a variety of community festivals. The group has developed a number of its own ceremonial practices that are functional substitutes to those found within folk Buddhism including Christian funerals, weddings, house dedications, baby dedications, and a number of others (Institute for Sustainable Development 1993). Many of these ceremonies, for those in the northeast, involve the use of string tying, a long tradition in the Lao culture that comes from animistic practices but is redefined to visualize the invisible concept of the love of Christ. Careful explanation is given beforehand that the strings have no magical power. For those who participate, this signifies a new understanding of the power found in relationship with Jesus Christ. Many have stated it is the first time they feel they could follow Jesus and still remain a Thai. Other examples of C5 are found in some villages in Det Udom district of Ubol Ratchatani, Thailand, as well as in neighboring Buddhist countries.

Strengths C5 is attractive to rural folk Buddhists. Gatherings that celebrate Christmas and Easter can attract many of the village communities. Communication of meaning is high; participation is high; local ownership, due to local leadership, is high. C5 focuses on transformation, not separation. Issues of spiritual power are clearly discussed and biblically addressed, and relevant rituals are incorporated into the life of the community.

Weaknesses C1–2 groups may view C5 as unfaithful, syncretistic, or pagan. Opportunities to enrich one another between typologies through dialogue and interaction become difficult because of any number of reasons including mutual misunderstandings, fear, jealousy, or name-calling. This may result in C5 churches moving towards isolationism or, even worse, a superior attitude that views other typologies as less than effective. According to Massey, one weakness of C5 is to

accuse brothers down the spectrum of obstructing the flow of the gospel with a culturally insensitive, extractionist approach. Pride can easily develop in those who are early adopters of God's unpredictable ways, as if they are on the cutting edge of a movement of God due to some personal ability of their own. Many fall into a trap of believing the approach God has called them to is the approach for everyone. (1999, 191)

Another potential weakness is that meaning of forms can revert to the original definitions and thereby reinforce a movement away from Christ towards syncretism.

C6: Secret Groups of Underground Believers

C6 describes persecuted believers who, due to fear, isolation, threat of extreme government repression, or social restriction, cannot or do not confess their faith in Christ openly. When C6 believers worship, it is in secret meetings and they may use any form from C1 to C5. C6 is not actually a typology, but it is a real situation of which all believers need to be made aware. God desires his people to witness and to have regular fellowship. Nonetheless, C6 believers are part of the family of Christ. Though God may call some to a life of suffering, imprisonment, or martyrdom, he may be pleased to have some worship him in secret, at least for a time. C6 believers would privately claim Christ as their Lord but would be perceived as Buddhists by their popular Buddhist community and would identify themselves as Buddhists.

Leaders for C6 communities can be of many types. Some are former leaders from other types of approaches (from C1 to C5) that have gone underground and avoided detection. Others are gifted lay people. Leadership structures are sometimes intentionally ill-defined. C6 believers, depending upon a variety of factors, may use any forms available to them ranging from C1 to C5. The C6 believer would identify himself or herself as a Buddhist like those in the surrounding community.

Due to intimately personal situations, the goal of C6 believers is to appear as one of the crowd as much as possible. There is no desire to confront the culture or engage it in the sense of a traditional witness for Christ. At the same time, these brothers and sisters do bear a silent witness for Christ, with occasional verbal opportunities as well.

Examples of C6: C6 believers, while not evident in Thailand at present, probably exist in some form in every Buddhist country. Few Thai Christians seem aware of the fact that there are documented cases of their spiritual brothers and sisters imprisoned only a few kilometers away in the neighboring countries of the Peoples' Democratic Republic of Laos, Myanmar, Vietnam, and farther away, Sri Lanka, due primarily to religious persecution. Christian Aid Mission reports:

> Christians in Laos are facing cruel forms of physical and psychological abuse as authorities appear to be working to wipe out Christianity in the country. A confidential source said

last week that since the country's new religious laws came into effect in July, Lao authorities are using new forms of persecution against churches in Laos. These methods are called "forced labour" and "community vocal shame." In the forced labour penalty, Christians are taken to a remote area to perform hard labour without pay for an extended period. They are told if they deny Christ, they will be returned to their home village and never taken away again. "Community vocal shame" involves putting believers on display before a large crowd of people in a village. Then, one by one, the villagers shout shameful words of abuse at the believers. (2002)

The whole continuum for the context of Thai popular Buddhism would look like this:

C1	C2	C3
Intentional transplant church using dominant national language, consciously alien to local culture and religion	Intentional transplant church using local language, overtly alien to local culture and religion	Local-language church, overtly alien, but able to incorporate religiously neutral cultural forms
C4	**C5**	**C6**
Local-language Christ-centered community using cultural, biblically permissible, folk Buddhist forms	Christ-centered community of Buddhist followers of Jesus	Secret groups of underground believers

Figure 6: C1 to C6 spectrum adapted for context of popular Buddhism (With acknowledgment to John and Anna Travis)

Missiological Considerations

Viewing C1–C6 in Many Dimensions

Critics of the C1 to C6 spectrum have been quick to note that the spectrum primarily evaluates behavioral forms and virtually ignores the deeper cognitive (knowledge) and affective (feelings) domains (Viggo Søgaard, personal correspondence, November 11, 2002; Marten Visser, personal correspondence, November 3, 2002). All three are essential parts of a complete study of worldview (Hiebert 1985, 45). The accusation is valid since this is the major function of such a tool. For those cultures, such as the animistic, where forms are the means by which people perceive and apply significance to content, the focus on forms is important. Just as communication is culturally oriented, so also all theological and biblical understanding comes wrapped in cultural forms of expression. However, there is a need to look beyond behavioral forms and address the question of meaning at another level. Even critically contextualized, dynamically equivalent, biblically transformed churches can become nominal or, even worse, revert to previous allegiances. On the other hand, a strict separatistic approach that relies solely upon transplanted forms does not guarantee an avoidance of syncretism either. The C1 to C5 spectrum can be viewed (see Fig. 7) as a horizontal axis ranging from C1, transplanted outsider expressions, to C5, transformed local expressions. Across this horizontal line must be overlaid a vertical axis that measures meaning and nominality. On this resulting grid, it is possible to plot the position of any of the C1 to C5 types of church planting in regards to both form and function. This is one evaluative model that begins to address the behavioral, affective, and cognitive realms, and may provide a more rounded picture of the particular church type. Note that examples of C1–5 are shown above the horizontal axis indicating movement towards deeper meaning as well as below the line towards nominalism. Any model can go any direction, but it is direction that is most important. Since C6 can be anywhere on the typology spectrum, it is not shown.

In all approaches, from C1 to C6, it is possible for a believer to find significant spiritual meaning and pursue continued spiritual growth towards Christ. It is also possible for syncretism to thrive at every level.

No particular paradigm sets the standard for the church, though one has tended to dominate. Given the complex nature of the Buddhist world, and the vast creativity of God, it is time to begin to consider types such as C4 and C5 and recognize these are also valid ways in which Buddhists are coming to Christ.

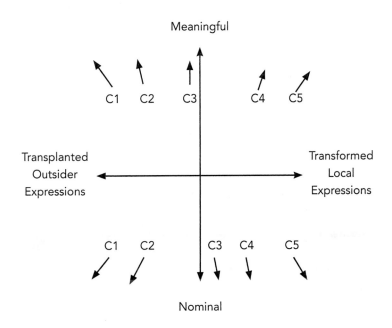

Figure 7: Grid for viewing direction of C1 to C5

A Need for Diversity

As previously stated, most missionaries and church planters in the Buddhist context focus primarily on elite Buddhism or high religion. In spite of thousands of Christian groups already present, I would venture to say that most approaches used in the Buddhist world today are not yet diverse enough to allow the gospel to reach members of the popular Buddhist mainstream in ways to which they can appropriately respond. Davis writes about Asia:

[Churches]should be *first* dynamically equivalent and *second* culturally appropriate (if that is possible without compromise). This means that there will not be some sort of predictable structures for all cultures. Various decision making procedures, types of leadership (plural!), methods of discipline, ways of worship will all be different, determined by the cultural matrix. There will be no doubt that on occasions a new church will have to break out from traditional forms and structures. (1998, 260–261,)

The Role of Background

Evaluating the C1 to C6 scale for Muslims, Massey raises the issue of the importance of the background of those working in a C5 type of ministry.

Every C5 worker I know sees a huge difference between someone from a Christian background taking a C5 identity and someone from a Muslim background becoming a C5 believer. In fact, one pro-C5 team I know has a country-wide policy disallowing anyone from a Christian background from becoming C5; their identity can go no further than C4. If someone from a Christian background goes around calling himself a Muslim, all they'll do (according to popular C5 opinion) is either look like a total phony, or mislead Muslims into thinking they converted to Islam. (1999, 196)

Many significant differences exist between the Muslim and Buddhist contexts, but there are significant similarities regarding the role of the background of those who minister effectively within a C5 context. Most Buddhists who come to Christ in a C1-2 church are taught to separate from all things animistic and Buddhist. The resulting social disruption is well documented (Chaochareonrhat 1998, 8; Keyes 1993, 259–83; Komin 1991, 10; Phrommedda and Wechkama 2001, 76). The high social cost paid by these believers includes leaving their former religious identity and establishing another entirely new one. It is unrealistic to expect persons who have experienced this pain to have any desire or ability to move to a C4 or C5 type of ministry without feeling as if they are compromising their faith. For them, this is partaking of meat offered to idols (1 Corinthians 8) and they should not. They should stay in a C1 or C2 ministry where God can use them.

Very few examples of intentional C4 or C5 ministry exist within the context of popular Buddhism. However, in those cases where these approaches have been used, it is evident by the worldview exhibited that those best involved in the front-line leadership of these ministries come from this background and have never left it. This would include missionaries, both local and expatriate. It has been extremely difficult for those trained in a C1–2 approach to transition beyond C3. Based on personal interactions, I observe that some of the most gifted and well-educated staff involved in the C5 movement described above continually struggle internally with C1 training methods that they had previously received. Some had to resign because it became obvious that their heart did not resonate with a C5 methodology and everyone could tell. One gifted Asian Christian leader, raised in the folk Buddhist culture but trained in a C1 context, told me, "I feel closest to God when I pray in English." A woman such as herself would never feel comfortable nor could she come across with any degree of genuineness in a C5 type of work.

The Role of Missionaries beyond C3

Many missionaries would like to see their ministry go as far as C4, but their national leadership is unwilling. In this regard, missionaries can be both an extreme help and a potential hindrance. The presence of a foreigner in almost any Christian work in Asia will often lead to deference to the missionary—particularly if that person is paying the salaries! Missionaries who have built up a level of trust from leadership within the local context can continue to provide motivation and encouragement to those on the front lines to remain engaged with the cultural issues of the society at hand. There are few resources that encourage churches in C1 to C2 to move in the direction of C3 or farther, but with spiritual sensitivity, and equal dialogue together to avoid paternalism, missionaries can enable movement even across the broad spectrum of mission strategies

Beyond Uniformity

Among Christian missionaries, there has been a widespread buying into the Asian cultural value that harmony equals consensus. Unity in Christ does not mean that we all look and act the same but rather that we are all headed towards Jesus Christ. Why aren't we practicing that now?

> If Christ is for all men, then evangelists must run the risk of being misunderstood, of misunderstanding elements in the gospel themselves, of losing out on the transposition of parts of the message so long as they bear witness to him. Christians are called to live dangerously . . . It would be good to be able to feel confident that the Churches of our own day were succeeding half as well, and were displaying anything like the same courage, singleness of aim, Christcentredness and adaptability as those men and women of the first Christian century. (Green 1970, 142–43)

References

Barker, Kenneth, ed. 1995. *The NIV Study Bible.* Grand Rapids: Zondervan.

Bharati, Dayanand. 2001. *Living water and Indian bowl: An analysis of Christian failings in communicating Christ to Hindus, with suggestions towards improvement.* Delhi: Indian Society for Promoting Christian Knowledge.

Caleb Project. 1988. *Reaching the peoples of Bangkok.* Littleton, CO: Caleb Project.

Chaochareonrhat, Sinchai. 1998. Khristachon bon witii *Thai* [*Christians on the Thai path*]. Bangkok: Baptist Christian Education Thailand.

Christian Aid Mission. 2002. Persecution of Christians in Laos. Newsletter, October 3.

Davis, John R. 1998. *Poles apart: Contextualizing the gospel in Asia.* Bangalore, India: Asia Theological Association.

Green, Michael. 1970. *Evangelism in the early church.* Grand Rapids: Eerdmans.

Gustafson, James W. 1983. The historical development of the Center for Church Planting and Church Growth in Northeast Thailand. Paper presented at the World Relief Phase III workshop, Udon Thani, Thailand, February 14 – March 4.

Hard, Theodore. 1989. Does animism die in the city? *Urban Mission* 6 (January): 45–56.

Heckman, Bruce. 1988. Arab Christian reactions to contextualization in the Middle East. Unpublished manuscript, Fuller Theological Seminary, Pasadena. Typewritten.

Heinze, Ruth-Inge. 1992. The relationship between folk and elite religions: The case of Thailand. In *The realm of the sacred: Verbal symbolism and ritual structures*, ed. Sitakant Mahapatra, 13–30. Calcutta: Oxford University Press.

Hiebert, Paul G. 1985. *Anthropological insights for missionaries*. Grand Rapids: Baker Book House.

Institute for Sustainable Development. 1993. Kho phrakamphi somrap phitii dtang dtang leh rabiep kanprakob phitii [*Scriptures for use in various ceremonies and order of ceremonies*]. Udon Thani, Thailand: ISD Printing.

Keyes, Charles. F. 1993. Why the Thai are not Christians: Buddhist and Christian conversion in Thailand. In *Conversion to Christianity: Historical and anthropological perspectives on a great transformation*, ed. Robert W. Hefner, 259–84. Berkeley: University of California Press.

Komin, Suntaree. 1991. *Psychology of the Thai people: Values and behavioral patterns*. Bangkok: National Institute of Development Administration.

Kraft, Charles H. 1996. *Anthropology for Christian witness*. Maryknoll, NY: Orbis Books.

Massey, Joshua. 1999. His ways are not our ways. *Evangelical Missions Quarterly* 35, no. 2: 188–97.

Mejudhon, Nanthachai. 2000. Sharing Christ with Thai people. Seminar presented at the Isaan Congress, Khon Kaen, Thailand, October 18. Trans. Paul H. de Neui. Unpublished translation. Typewritten.

Phrommedda, Tongpan, and Banpote Wechkama. 2001. Voices from Asia: Communicating contextualization through story. Trans. Paul H. de Neui. Unpublished manuscript, Fuller Theological Seminary, Pasadena, December.

Roxburgh, Alan J. 2002. Shaping the journey: Reforming the church in North America. Missiological Lectures, Fuller Theological Seminary, Pasadena, November 13–14.

Smalley, William A. 1958. Cultural implications of an indigenous church. *Practical Anthropology* 5, no. 2: 51–65.

———. 1994. *Linguistic diversity and national unity: Language ecology in Thailand*. Chicago: University of Chicago Press.

Smith, Alexander G. 1982. *Siamese gold: A history of church growth in Thailand; An Interpretive Analysis 1816–1982*. Bangkok: Kanok Bannasan (OMF Publishers).

Swanson, Herbert R. 2002. Dancing to the temple, dancing in the church: Reflections on Thai local theology. *Journal of Theologies and Cultures in Asia* 1 (February): 59–78.

Tambiah, Stanley J. 1970. *Buddhism and the spirit cults in North-east Thailand*. Cambridge: Cambridge University Press.

Thomas, Norman E. 1998. *Classic texts in mission and world Christianity*. Maryknoll, NY: Orbis Books.

Tippett, Alan R. 1973. *Verdict theology in missionary theory*. Pasadena: William Carey Library.

Travis, John. 1998. The C1 to C6 spectrum. *Evangelical Missions Quarterly* 34, no. 4: 407–8.

Van Rheenen, Gailyn. 2002. Evangelizing folk religionists. *Missiological Reflections* 23 (March 12). http://www.missiology.org (accessed March 12, 2002).

Walls, Andrew. 2000. *The missionary movement in Christian history: Studies in the transmission of faith*. Maryknoll, NY: Orbis Books.

Wisley, Thomas N. 1984. Dynamic biblical Christianity in the Buddhist/Marxist context: Northeast Thailand. Unpublished manuscript.

INDEX

A

Abraham, 188–89
  Abrahamic religions, 8
Africa, 161
All Japan Funeral Directors Co-
  Operation (AJFDCO), 150
Allen, Roland, 100
Ambalantota, 4
America(n). See United States of
  America.
American Brethren, 122
ancestor, 36, 86, 110, 123, 129, 148,
  188
  ancestral
    cult, 95
    issues, 110
    path, 89
    spirits, 97, 123, 148
    tablets, 96
animism, 36, 95, 188, 191
apocalypse, 49
Arndt, William, 104
Asbury Theological Seminary, 167,
  181
  E. Stanley Jones School of World
    Mission and Evangelism, 167,
    181
ASEAN, 118
Asia, 51, 118, 211, 213
  Asian
    countries, 23
    cultural value, 214
    leader, 213
    missionaries, 122
Asian Christian Service, 121
Assemblies of God, 4, 86, 122
awicha, 78, 83

B

baab, 77, 81
baht, 205
bana, 5, 7, 15
Bangkok, 133, 175–76, 194, 196, 206
baptism, 25, 27
Bible, 14–15, 23, 25–26, 68–69, 79,
  81, 84, 89, 96, 100, 103, 107–08,
  133, 145, 153, 161, 163, 183, 189,
  204–05
  Good News, 63, 65–69, 71–74, 78,
    83, 120, 145
  passage, 9
  school, 193, 198, 202
  Scripture, 26, 36, 50, 52, 54, 70,
    83–84, 100, 103, 105, 107–09,
    130, 133, 135, 174, 178–79, 182,
    188–89, 203
  study, 13, 25–26, 28
Blanford, Carl E., 167
bodhi-puja, 6
Bradley, Dr. Dan Beach, 168
Buddha, 5–7, 12, 14–15, 36, 96–98,
  106, 124, 151, 172–73

Buddhism, 3–4, 6, 8, 10–11, 13, 31–32, 35–40, 53, 71, 77–79, 83, 87, 96–97, 106–07, 109, 123, 144, 168–69, 171–73, 185, 187–88, 192–94, 197–98, 201–02, 204, 206, 209, 211, 213
Buddhist
  background, 3, 7, 10, 14, 17–18, 57, 71, 198, 202, 205
  folk, 89–90, 95–96, 108, 110, 171, 187, 193, 199, 205–07, 209, 213
  inquirer, 3–4
  leaders, 3, 205
  monk, 7, 15–16, 18, 37, 98, 121, 130, 132, 144, 173, 188, 205
  newcomer, 5, 11–18
  practices, 4, 13, 17, 87
  Sinhala, 3, 6, 9, 14, 16–17
  teaching, 5, 37, 205
  temple, 4–7, 10–11, 13–16, 18, 31–32, 35–40, 53, 56–58, 96–97, 107, 110, 130, 144, 146, 149, 151–52, 154, 156, 158–59, 191, 200–01, 203
  tradition, 3, 11, 36, 38, 40, 89, 154
  visitor, 3, 7, 13–14, 16
  worship, 5–6, 10, 12–13, 17–18, 53
    patterns of, 5
bun, 80–81
Burma
  Burmese, 37, 79, 107–08

C

C1 to C6 spectrum, 192–99, 201–13
Cambodia, 119
Campus Crusade for Christ, 122
Canada, 22
Chiang Mai, 122, 199, 206
China, 57, 118
  Chinese, 36, 122, 196
Christendom, 37, 39, 52, 58
Christian and Missionary Alliance (C&MA), 121–22, 196
Christian Mission in Many Lands, 121
Christianity, 3–4, 8, 14, 17, 21, 23–26, 28, 31–32, 35, 38–40, 50, 54, 64, 67, 78, 85–86, 98, 100, 108, 122–23, 125,

132, 134, 137, 143, 145, 167–68, 171, 178, 182, 187–88, 190–91, 193–94, 196–99, 202, 204–06, 208
chua, 81–82
church
  house, 21, 23–26, 28, 57–58
    megachurch, 22, 24
    urban, 58
  local, 24, 31, 64, 71, 93, 95, 100, 124, 133–34, 169
  new breed of, 21, 28
  plant, 21, 27, 31, 51, 58, 63–64, 90, 100, 122, 167, 192, 196–97, 210–11
chya, 104–05
Colombo, 4
colonial
  oppression, 3
  past, 126
  rule, 119
communication, 66–67, 69, 87, 93–95, 98–99, 101–04, 109–13, 120, 122, 125–27, 132, 135–39, 164, 184, 193–94, 198, 204, 207, 210
  intercultural, 66
  model, 123
  process, 69
  strategies, 117
  theory, 69
communion, 5, 43, 75, 108, 110, 126, 203, 206
communism, 38
community, 8, 17–18, 31, 34, 36–42, 44, 46, 48, 55–59, 69–72, 88–89, 93–95, 98, 100–01, 110–11, 113, 121, 125, 130, 144, 146, 155, 175, 192, 195, 197, 199–201, 203–09
  Christ-centered, 93–95, 110, 113, 155, 192, 203–05, 209
Conn, Harvie, 23
Contesse, Gabriel, 121
contextualization, 21–24, 57, 63, 65–66, 70, 72, 74, 89, 94, 98–99, 101–02, 108, 111–13, 124, 126–27, 131, 146, 167
Cooke, Joseph, 76, 78–79, 83
Corinth, 50–51, 74
cosmology, 106–07
cross-cultural

communication, 184
missionaries, 187–88
workers, 64–66, 90
cult, 38
ancestral. *See* ancestor.
divinities, 69
culture, 12, 23–24, 34, 37, 40, 57–59,
64, 74, 76, 87, 93–94, 98–103, 108,
110–11, 120, 127, 131, 134, 145–48,
153–54, 169, 171–72, 175, 181, 191,
193–96, 201, 203, 206, 208–10, 212
cultus, 31, 41, 46, 48

D
dagoba, 5–6
Danka, 144, 149, 151, 156, 158
David, 46, 49
Davis, John, 57, 67, 211
dayaka, 7
de Leria, Jean, 121
demon, 80, 96–97, 106–07, 161, 181
demonic, 35
elements, 87
powers, 35, 97
world, 100
worship, 13
devale, 5–7, 11
Dhammananda, K. Sri, 107
dharma, 7, 83, 98, 103, 188
diversity, 24, 35, 187–88, 197, 211
Douglas, Mary, 127
doy phrakhun, 79
doysadang jaikatanyuu, 82
dualism, 53, 197
dukkha, 83

E
East Asia, 38
Eastern, 101, 190
ecclesiology, 32, 40, 47–48, 54, 56,
58–59, 195, 198
economic, 35, 117–20, 126, 171, 181
education, 97, 99, 119, 122, 130,
170–72
Egypt, 41
Egyptian gods, 189
Eight-fold Path, 181, 188
ethne, 111–12

Europe, 22, 64, 118
evangelical, 3–4, 7–18, 42, 164
evangelism, 22–23, 26–28, 68–71, 85,
91, 102, 175, 187
context–sensitive, 63, 68, 71
environment that facilitates
effective evangelism, figure, 72

F
Five Precepts of Buddhism, 6, 188,
201
Flemming, Dean, 74
Four Noble Truths, 181, 188
Foursquare Gospel, 4
France, 161
French, 119, 122, 144
freedom, 8, 56, 107, 131–32, 192, 194,
196
Fuller Theological Seminary
School of World Mission (School of
Intercultural Studies), 39
funeral, 80, 110, 144, 146, 149–54,
156–60, 162–65, 197, 200, 205–06
cost of, 151–52
for nonbelievers, 154–56, 158,
163–64
funerary culture, 143, 149, 151,
153, 155, 165
graves, 144, 148, 151–52, 157
involving suicide, 159
secularization of, 153
system, 147–48
Furuya, Yasuo, 22

G
Galle, 4
Gellner, David, 34
German, 22, 109, 179
Gilliland, Dean S., 24
glossolalia, 8–9
Greek, 45, 54, 84, 104, 189–90
Grunlan, Stephen A., 181
Gusawadi, Brasert, 77

H
Hambantota, 4, 13
Hanwella, 4
Heckman, Bruce, 192

Hellenistic, 69
Hiebert, Paul, 138, 175, 197
Hindu, 36, 88, 125–26, 134, 183
Hinduism, 171–73
Hmong, 121–22, 125
hospitality, 120, 133–34
    welcome, 8, 12–13, 17, 151
Hughes, Philip H., 168

I

identification, 193, 195, 199, 203, 206
identity, 17, 34, 44, 57, 59, 86, 93, 97,
    101, 123–26, 131, 170–73, 175, 187,
    195–96, 212
idolatry, 33, 87, 109, 204
imago Dei, 50, 58
India, 134
indigenous, 75, 93–94, 98–100, 102–03,
    111, 198, 202, 204
    church, 32, 65, 94, 99, 101, 110–11,
        167, 175
    leadership, 3
Indochinese, 31
insider movements, 87
Isaan, 194
Islam, 38, 171, 212
Israel, 41–43, 45–46, 50, 56, 109, 190
    Israelite, 41, 189

J

jaikatanyuu, 82
Jakarta, 194
jamnon, 82
Japan, 21–26, 28, 38, 96, 143, 147,
    149–50, 152–53, 155–56, 165
    Japanese, 21–26, 36, 143–51, 153–59,
        163–65
Japanese Agricultural Cooperatives
    (JA), 150
Jerusalem, 42, 46, 48–50, 53–54, 59
Jew, 22, 42, 48, 189
Jewish, 42–45, 48, 50, 56, 189–91
Judaism, 43, 49–50, 189
Judson, Adoniram, 100

K

kapuwa, 7
karma, 77, 79–85, 97, 106–07, 129–30

Keller, Timothy, 70
khaochii, 126
kingdom of God, 53, 59, 68, 80, 95,
    98, 112–13, 131–32
koinonia, 50
Komin, Suntaree, 171
    model, 170–71
Korea, 22, 122
    Korean, 101
Kowae, Wirachai, 86
Kraft, Charles, 126–27
kwamrawt, 79
kyrios, 69

L

Lao, 117–39, 194, 206, 208–09
    worldview themes table, 129
Lao Evangelical Church (LEC), 122,
    124
Lao People's Democratic Republic
    (PDR), 117–19, 121, 123, 126, 128
Latin, 52
lingua franca, 58
liturgy, 5, 17
local church. *See* church.
luamsai, 81

M

Mahayana, 95, 97, 107
Malachi, 41–42
Marx, Karl, 35
Massey, Joshua, 207, 212
Matara, 4
materialism, 182
mawbhai, 82
Mayers, Marvin K., 181
McGavran Donald, 93
McLuhan, Marshall, 101
Mejudhon, Nantachai and Ubolwan,
    133–135, 175
Mennonite Brethren, 122
Mennonite Central Committee
    (MCC), 121
Methodist, 122
metta, 79
ministry, 42–44, 51, 55, 58, 65, 80, 95,
    113, 134, 167, 184, 203, 212–13
    pastoral, 23
    youth, 123

missiology, 35, 57, 145
Mission Aviation Fellowship (MAF), 121
missionary, 31, 37–39, 42, 56, 83,
    119–21, 123, 130–31, 168, 194,
    196–97, 203, 213
missions, 147, 191
  history of, 124
  oversea, 100
monastic
  orders, 36
  role, 205
  way, 59
mot kwamchua, 82
mot sattha, 82
Mount Sinai, 41
Muangthai Church, 167–68, 175–76,
    178, 180, 184
multicultural, 17, 101
multiethnic, 17
Muslim, 88, 125, 171, 189, 192, 212
Myanmar, 37, 107, 208

N
Namo tassa, 6
naos, 49
Nepal, 38, 58
Nevius, John, 100
New Age, 27
New Testament, 21, 23–24, 40, 55, 74,
    104, 184
Nida, Eugene, 168
nikaya, 5
nirvana, 106–09
Nokotsu, 154–59
Nokotsudo, 154, 156–58
non-Western. *See* Western.
North America, 64, 128
Nyunt, Peter, 108–09

O
Old Testament, 40–41, 55, 184
oppression, 35, 44
orphan, 176, 183
Overseas Missionary Fellowship
    (OMF), 83, 121–22

P
Pali, 6, 9, 16

Party for Freedom in Burial Rights,
    147
Passover, 54
paternalism, 201, 213
Paul, 22, 24, 40, 42, 45, 47–48, 50–51,
    53, 56, 73–74, 81–82, 99, 101, 189
Pentecost, 51
Pentecostal, 111
Petchsongkram, Wan, 77–78
Philippines, 123
phrakhun, 79, 82
phu, 78
pinkama, 5–6
Polyani, 70
Pope Gregory I, 191
poverty, 118–20
preaching, 5, 7, 12, 14–16, 26, 90, 102,
    178–79, 198
priesthood, 35, 48, 55–57, 123, 205
Protestant, 10, 57, 64, 121–25, 137,
    197, 199

R
RAC Network, 21
relational model, 167
religion, 4, 7–8, 14, 17, 31–40, 44,
    49–50, 54–56, 64, 67, 85–88, 95–97,
    123, 126, 130, 153–54, 158–59,
    167–69, 171–74, 178, 181, 184–85,
    187–88, 191, 194, 201, 209, 211
Rivers, William, 102
Roffe, G. Edward, 121
Roman Catholic, 10, 22, 37, 57,
    121–23, 126, 203–04
Roman Empire, 42–43
rural, 33–34, 58, 96, 106, 119, 153,
    187, 207

S
sadhu, 6, 14
Samaritan, 43, 53, 175
sangha, 7, 36, 40, 53, 96, 98
sanghika, 16
sangob, 83
Sanhedrin, 45
sasana farang, 64
Satan, 80, 138
  devil, 191

sattha, 81–82
Schramm, Wilbur, 102
Seamand, J. T., 181
SEANET, 71, 83, 100, 110
Septuagint, 69
Seventh Day Adventist Church, 122
sex, 106
   sexual abuse, 35
shamanism, 95, 111
Sharp, Lauriston, 170, 174
Shinto, 95, 143–44, 146, 153, 155, 158–59
Shintoism, 144
Siam, 168–69
sil, 5, 76
sila, 98
singsaksittanlaituasakonlok, 78
skene, 49
Smalley, William, 120
Smith Alex, 79
Snyder, Howard, 55, 57
Solomon, 41
South Korea, 8, 38
Southeast Asia, 37, 117–19, 168, 188
Southern Baptist, 121
spirits, 36, 95, 97–98, 102, 107, 109–10, 123–24, 129, 148, 188, 206
   evil, 80
   of the dead, 148
Sri Lanka, 3–6, 8, 17, 208
   Sri Lankan, 18
Srisuriyothai, Phranang, 79
Stephen, 40, 45–47, 56
Stott, John, 46
sutras, 36, 96
Swiss Mission Evangelique, 122

T
talenta, 14
tangka, 97, 106
tanha, 77–78, 84–85
Taoism, 95
temple
   architecture, 34, 203
   Buddhist, *See* Buddhist.
   ethos, 31–33, 35–40, 54–57
      contrast of, figure, 40
   structure, 34–35

systems, 34–36, 41–43, 45, 47–48, 51, 56–57, 158
Thailand, 38, 57, 63, 65–66, 73, 102, 104, 118, 121, 133, 167–69, 171, 175, 185, 187, 193–94, 196–200, 203–04, 206–08
Thai, 63–68, 73, 76–87, 90, 96, 102, 104–05, 108, 111, 167–80, 182–85, 187–88, 193–94, 196–201, 203, 205, 207–09
theology, 22, 47, 53, 98, 127, 178, 201
Theravada, 36, 67, 71, 95, 169
thuk, 83
Tibet
   Tibetan folk, 95, 106
Tippett Alan, 94–95, 191
tourism, 118
Travis, John, 192
Tripitaka, 96
tujarit, 77
typology, 192, 208, 210

U
United States of America, 161
   American, 101, 194, 202
urban, 187, 191

V
van den Toren, Benno, 70
van Gennep, Arnold, 144
Vientiane, 119, 122–25
Vietnam, 110, 118, 123, 208
   Vietnamese, 110, 121–22
village, 4, 37, 110, 122, 128, 132–33, 137, 149, 199, 205, 207, 209
violence, 8, 44

W
waiwanhjai, 81
Walls, Andrew, 39, 69
Weerasingha, Tissa, 78
Western, 3, 23, 57–58, 78, 83, 90–91, 98–102, 119, 121, 123–26, 144, 149, 167, 175, 193, 196–99, 201–05
   non–Western, 57
Whiteman, Darrell, 181
Willy, Maurice, 121
Wink, Walter, 44, 47, 49

Winter, Ralph, 39
witness, 9, 23, 52, 54, 56, 73, 75,
    82–83, 87, 90, 93, 105, 117, 120,
    122–23, 125–27, 130–39, 167, 169,
    175, 179–85, 187, 200, 208, 214
    context-sensitive, 66, 68, 70, 76, 90
World Vision, 121
World War II, 122, 152
worldview, 3–4, 67–71, 73–74, 76, 83,
    88–89, 91, 97, 103, 105, 109, 117,
    127, 129–30, 132, 170–72, 180, 182,
    210, 213
worship, 3–5, 7–13, 15–17, 24, 38, 46,
    53–54, 58, 94, 100–01, 110, 112,
    133, 163, 176–80, 185, 191, 195,
    198, 200, 208, 212
    Buddhist. *See* Buddhist.
Wright, N. T., 42

Z
Zahniser, A. H. Mathias, 169, 175

SCRIPTURE INDEX

Genesis 31:19, 189
Exodus 12:12,17, 189
Exodus 20:3, 189
Exodus 25-27, 46
Deuteronomy 17:14–20, 46
Joshua 1:3, 53
Joshua 24:2–3, 188
Ruth 1:15–18, 142
1 Samuel 8:5–9, 41, 46
2 Samuel 7:4–11, 41
2 Kings 5:15–19, 189
2 Kings 21:4, 7, 47
2 Chronicles 2:6, 41
2 Chronicles 6:18, 41
2 Chronicles 7:20, 42
2 Chronicles 33:7, 47
Ecclesiastes 12:7, 107
Isaiah 60, 49
Hosea 6:6, 47
Amos 5:21–24, 189
Amos 9:6, 107
Malachi 1:11, 41
Matthew 6:14–15
Matthew 9:13
Matthew 9:36, 175
Matthew 12:6, 50
Matthew 12:7, 45, 47
Matthew 13:19, 68
Matthew 16:16–17, 68
Matthew 18:18, 20, 55
Matthew 21, 45

Matthew 23:9–10, 55
Matthew 23:38, 51
Matthew 26:61, 45
Matthew 27:40, 45
Matthew 27:51, 45, 51
Matthew 28:18-20, 94
Mark 6:34, 175
Mark 11, 45
Mark 11:17, 45, 50
Mark 11:17b, 44
Mark 13:2, 45, 51
Mark 14:58, 45
Mark 15:38, 47, 51
Luke 2:49, 50
Luke 5, 66, 71
Luke 10:19, 138
Luke 19, 45
Luke 21:5–6, 45
Luke 23:45, 51
Luke 24:51, 107
John 1:14, 51, 54
John 2, 45
John 2:16, 50
John 2:18–22, 50
John 2:19, 45
John 4, 52
John 6:38, 107
John 9:39, 26
John 10:18, 79
John 10:30, 51
John 12:21, 54

John 13:35, 18, 58
John 14:1-3, 107
John 14:9, 51
John 17, 99
Acts 6:13-14
Acts 7:47-48, 47
Acts 9, 51
Acts 11:26, 189
Acts 17:16-23, 189
Acts 21:28, 45
Acts 24:6, 45, 47
Acts 26:18, 101
Acts 26:28, 189
Romans 1:16, 42
Romans 6, 25, 82
Romans 8:38-39, 161
Romans 12:1, 55
Romans 14:8, 161-62
1 Corinthians 1:22-23, 68
1 Corinthians 1:27, 25
1 Corinthians 3:16-17, 51
1 Corinthians 3:17, 50
1 Corinthians 6:19-20, 47, 51
1 Corinthians 7:14, 55
1 Corinthians 9:19-21, 22
1 Corinthians 9:19-23, 189
1 Corinthians 10:14-22, 87
1 Corinthians 12, 51
1 Corinthians 12-14, 55
1 Corinthians 15:1-11, 74
2 Corinthians 6:14-17, 99
2 Corinthians 6:16, 51
2 Corinthians 8:19, 55
Galatians 6:7-8, 84
Ephesians 2:5, 81
Ephesians 2:21, 51
Ephesians 6:2-3, 135
Philippians 2:17, 55
Colossians 1:19, 50
Colossians 2:9, 50
Colossians 2:13, 81
1 Thessalonians 1:9, 68
1 Timothy 2:5, 26
1 Timothy 3:1, 55
Titus 2:11-14, 62
Hebrews 6-9, 48
Hebrews 10:19-22, 55
Hebrews 13:10-16, 49, 55

1 Peter 2:5, 47, 55
1 Peter 2:9-10, 2, 53, 55
1 Peter 4:16, 189
1 John 1:1, 54
1 John 4:12, 54, 58
1 John 4:17, 54
Revelation 3:20, 90
Revelation 7:9, 190
Revelation 21, 49, 107
Revelation 21:2-3, 49
Revelation 21:22-23, 49
Revelation 22, 49, 107